The Making of
The Alnwick Garden

The Making of
The Alnwick Garden

Ian August *with foreword by* The Duchess of Northumberland

PAVILION

First published in the United Kingdom in 2006 by Pavilion

151 Freston Road

London, W10 6TH

An imprint of Anova Book Company Ltd

Publisher: Kate Oldfield

Senior Editor: Lizzy Gray

Copy-editor: Wendy Toole

Designer: Lotte Oldfield

Indexer: Patricia Hymans

ISBN 1 86205 715 x

A CIP catalogue record for this book is available from the British Library.

10 9 8 7 6 5 4 3 2 1

Reproduction by Anorax Imaging Ltd, England

Printed and bound by WKT Printing Co Ltd China

www.anovabooks.com

CONTENTS

FOREWORD

THE DUCHESS OF NORTHUMBERLAND

I well remember my early visits to the garden. I would walk our dogs through row upon row of Christmas trees, treading gingerly over fallen brickwork and skirting round piles of stone that had been dumped for safe keeping. Even in such a state of dereliction the garden was magical. It had beautiful bones, and because its beauty was so apparent, it was particularly tragic that it was unappreciated.

Ten years have passed since those early days and The Alnwick Garden has sprung up. The transformation is unbelievable. I assembled a team of experts in their fields who would be prepared to listen to the clear vision I had for the garden, and they have created a place of great beauty and innovative technology that is appreciated by hundreds of thousands of visitors annually. A garden creation on this scale had not been undertaken in the UK for over a century, so a record of the project and its development was of the utmost importance. However, it is the human element that really makes the story. The project attracted fierce criticism from a wide variety of groups and individuals, many of whom had no basis for their vocal, expensive and lengthy arguments. I dug in my heels and believed that one day people would understand what I was trying to achieve. The only person who didn't need convincing was Ian August.

Ian August was the Estates Clerk of the Works for Northumberland Estates, my husband's family estates. He was appointed as project director for the Garden when I made the decision to proceed. I realized very soon after my conceptual thoughts had become a clear vision that Ian fully understood what I was trying to achieve, and his support for me throughout the project has remained a stabilizing factor. Ian is the only person who could tell the accurate story of the monumental struggle we faced in building The Alnwick Garden. We worked closely together, meeting most days for hours on end. I would source experts and discuss those

ABOVE: The Duchess of Northumberland behind one of the water displays in the Serpent Garden.

selections with Ian, who would arrange to bring them to Alnwick, and together we would conduct initial interviews.

Ian is an artist. He appreciated beauty when he saw it after forty years as Clerk of the Works, and he also had the benefit of years of experience of working with people and buildings. I could never have seen the project through to this stage without Ian's involvement. His skills of tact and diplomacy are second to none. He tactfully told me when to back down from strong opinions I was clinging to, and sat on emails that I had fired off in a fury for twenty-four hours, 'in case you want to reconsider, Jane!' And he was right: I usually did want to reconsider. He kept a team of designers together and they are now his friends. It is not an exaggeration to say that The Alnwick Garden would not have been built without him. He is admired and respected by all who know him, and I consider myself fortunate to have spent so many years in the company of such a great man.

The Making of The Alnwick Garden describes the history of the Garden from its inception in 1750 through to the present day. It tells the story of my travels throughout England and Europe to try to get the right team of architects and designers who would work together. It covers the prolonged design period when Jacques Wirtz had been selected as the principal designer, and the search for other specialists, such as water sculptors, engineers, water technologists, lighting specialists, treehouse designers and architects, and the battles we faced along the way.

To view The Alnwick Garden as we view other gardens in the UK is a mistake. I built the Garden to be used as a venue day and night by different groups within our community. We have a great team of managers who work up programmes for the arts, education, older people, children and drugs advisory groups through our Poison Garden. I don't think that my critics will really understand what I'm doing until they watch 150 elderly people tea-dancing or speed-dating in the Pavilion on a cold November afternoon. To me, the Garden is at its best when it is full. I like to see families picnicking on the grass, children running in and out of the water features getting soaked. I like to watch the enjoyment the older visitors get from seeing the children playing in the water. I like to see people using the Garden and claiming ownership of it. An elderly man came up to me several years ago and said, 'I want to thank you for this garden. I'm unemployed and I used to sit on a bench in Alnwick and just watch the cars, but now I can sit here instead. But I want you to know it's not yours any more, it's mine.' And that was the best thing anyone had said to me.

Ian has produced an exciting and enlightening story of the journey that he and I have travelled together during the past ten years, interwoven with memories of the trials and tribulations, the dark days when I almost gave up, positive times, funny experiences and the exhilaration when milestones were successfully achieved. To date, the success of The Alnwick Garden has been phenomenal, better than I could ever have hoped for, and I believe that *The Making of the Alnwick Garden* is an accurate and important record of that success. It offers the reader a behind-the-scenes insight into the making of a truly unique garden, which some day could become one of the finest contemporary gardens in the world.

TIMELINE

1996 March	The Duchess of Northumberland decides to create The Alnwick Garden
1997/1998	Garden designers Wirtz International are commissioned
2000 March	Construction work begins on site
2001 October	The Garden is opened to the public as construction of Phase 1 continues
2002 January	BBC2 programme *The Challenge* covers the Grand Cascade build and water engineering
2002 September	Phase 1 is officially opened by HRH The Prince of Wales, consisting of: **The Grand Cascade; The Rose Garden; The Ornamental Garden; The Woodland Walk**
2003 January	BBC1 programme *Charlie and the Duchess* goes on air to show filming of the construction of Phase 1
2003 April	The Alnwick Garden Trust is formalized as an independent charity
2003 November	Construction begins on The Treehouse
2003 November	Work begins on the three themed gardens: **The Poison Garden; The Serpent Garden; The Labyrinth**
2003 (financial year)	Over 530,000 visitors come to the Garden in 2003, making it the third most visited paid-for garden attraction in the UK
	In 2002, an independent economic study estimated the Garden would only attract up to 230,000 visitors in this period
2004 April	It is anticipated that, when complete in 2008, the Garden will give up to £150 million back to the region over ten years in economic benefits
2004 June	The Garden launches gift scheme to raise funds for 20,000 plants and trees
2004 November	Home Office approval is granted to The Alnwick Garden Trust to grow cannabis and coca (cocaine) plants for educational purposes
2004 (financial year)	435,000 visitors come to the Garden
2005 January	The Treehouse and larger Car Park open
2005 February & March	**The Poison Garden, Labyrinth** and **Serpent Garden** open
2006 January	The Duchess of Northumberland is awarded Communicator of the Year, North East by the Chartered Institute of Public Relations
2006 January	The Alnwick Garden submits its bid for Living Landmarks Lottery funding to help complete the Garden
2006 April	Routeway project starts in The Alnwick Garden to help get long-term unemployed back into work
2006 April	**The Pavilion and Visitor Centre**, designed by Sir Michael Hopkins, opens on 4th April 2006
2006–2008	Forthcoming developments to finish the Garden:
	The Central Garden, The Spiral Garden, The Quiet Garden, The Pavilion Garden, The Garden for the Senses, The Cherry Orchard, Grotto and Pond, The Water Tower

PROLOGUE

I am drawn to the archway leading into the Garden, as I have been on many occasions in the past ten years, and I find myself standing on the Pavilion Terrace looking at the Grand Cascade, enjoying the sound and visual effect of the water display. This view brings home to me just how much has happened during those ten years, since that eventful day in March 1996 when this story began.

Today from this vantage point I see an ever developing pattern of evergreen and deciduous hedges that both link and form the various gardens, and the topiary features that are home to original water sculptures; I smell the perfumes wafting on that same breeze from the Rose Garden, while ivy-covered tunnels lead the visitor into the world of poisonous plants. All of this is a long way from the sad, neglected garden that I first viewed through that archway.

As I look around, people of all ages are having a good time, and I realize that the vision the Duchess had in 1996 to develop a garden for the community has been achieved. I feel a great deal of satisfaction and a certain amount of pride in the part I have played in supporting the Duchess throughout this challenge.

I have always had an excellent working relationship with the Duchess, and I like to think that, over the past ten years in particular, we have become firm friends through the trials and tribulations that this project has put our way. My total support for her and her vision has never been in doubt, and through my long-term commitment to the Percy family, I was in the privileged position to become the appropriate person to write the story of The Alnwick Garden.

I hope the book will afford the reader an interesting insight into the continuing development of a wonderful garden and its influences on those involved and the community in general, while at the same time telling the underlying story of the Duchess's total commitment to her vision. I hope that through its pages it will bring back happy memories for those who already know The Alnwick Garden well, and for those still to discover its charms a taster of what lies in store.

CHAPTER 1

'IAN, I'VE HAD AN IDEA ...'

Northumberland is border country, unspoilt and beautiful, with empty horizons stretching north to Scotland and a coastline of coarse-grassed dunes standing high above long miles of deserted white sands. The soft rolling hills and gentle wooded landscape come as a surprise to the first-time visitor, especially given the county's turbulent history as an isolated outpost, the gateway north and south over which Romans, Saxons, Vikings, Celts, Scots and English have battled for supremacy over the centuries. The long years of fighting have left Northumberland with a landscape dominated by fortified medieval castles and ruined priories, and its people a fierce pride in the North-East's legacy of independence and strength.

Five miles inland from the dramatic delights of the Heritage coastline sits Alnwick town, small and bustling, nestling into a quiet curve beside the banks of the River Aln as if in ignorance or defiance of the county's tempestuous past. The streets of the medieval town are narrow and quaint, a single lane passing through Hotspur Tower nowadays making the weekly market – a rural tradition for over 800 years – a bedlam of traffic queues and voluble drivers. Above the quiet streets of the town stand the medieval walls and fortified towers of Alnwick Castle, the ancient seat of the Dukes of Northumberland and the second largest inhabited castle in Britain, today instantly recognisable as the setting for Hogwarts School in the first two Harry Potter films. Since 1309, through times of war and peace, the Percy family, dynastic lords and feudal masters of the agriculture and economy of the surrounding areas and wider patrons of arts and culture, has made its home at Alnwick Castle.

Over the river from the Castle you can see the undulating, wooded parklands fashioned by Lancelot 'Capability' Brown in the eighteenth century under the patronage of the 1st Duke of Northumberland. But between the Brown parkland

LEFT: Ian August stands by the Italianate gates
in the Ornamental Garden.

RIGHT: The Duchess's View.
Looking to the west, Alnwick Castle
and the Capability Brown landscape
can be seen.

and Alnwick town lies a more modern horticultural wonder, a testament to the determination of Jane, the 12TH Duchess of Northumberland. This twelve-acre walled area, nestled into the ancient Percy lands bordered by the Castle and Bondgate Without, is now home to The Alnwick Garden. Today, more than 600,000 people a year visit the site but when this story begins, on 7 March 1996, it was a derelict ruin empty of both inspiration and visitors, the unhappy remnant of a glorious garden that had once supplied an ambitious range of culinary produce, from peas to pineapples, for those who lived and worked in the Castle.

7 March, I remember well, was an ordinary morning. As Clerk of The Works for Northumberland Estates, I was in my office in the Clock Tower, the outer bailey of Alnwick Castle, when the telephone rang, inviting me to step into the head agent's office. There, upright on a hard-backed chair, sat Jane, the 12TH Duchess of Northumberland, with the Duke's agent Rory Wilson. After we'd exchanged greetings, the Duchess came straight to the point. 'Ian,' she said, 'I've had an idea...'

I'd hear this phrase many times over the next few years, always as the prelude to some fantastic leap of imagination, but this was the first and I looked at her enquiringly. The Duchess laughed and said, 'I think I have to show you what I mean.'

She led the way out of the Castle, through the Lion Tower and into Barneyside, an area leading down to the river and the Percy family's private gardens. On our left was the rolling lushness of the Brown landscape; on our right, a small copse of trees through which we made our way towards a curved gateway in an old sandstone wall, almost hidden behind a thick covering of creepers.

The Duchess pushed open the gate, which squeaked with rebellion, the noise rebounding into the heavy silence beyond. We walked through the gate into the old twelve-acre walled garden, overgrown and neglected. Picking our way over the dilapidated terrace, the remains of a glass conservatory knocked down nearly a century before, we stood at the bottom of a hill flanked by two ruined hothouses, self-seeded trees sprouting through their brickwork and made impenetrable by brambles and ivy. Looking up the slope, I could see a sad and empty bow-fronted pond, bordered by the tired remnants of two lime tree avenues on each side.

'Let's go to the top,' the Duchess said, guiding the way past the pond through an area of thick laurels and spruce trees that led, with beautiful symmetry, to three stone arches in a warm, sandstone wall. The rusted old gates between the arches were hanging off their hinges but you could see how beautiful they must once have been. Behind them was a small walled kitchen garden planted with larch trees, and in the corner was a potholed, moss-covered tennis court that had long since seen better days.

Pausing at the top I looked down at the long, axial views of the enclosed garden, as I had done many times before in the forty years I'd worked for Northumberland Estates. From this vantage point, the garden's disarray and neglect contrasted sadly with the majesty of the smooth, beautifully manicured 'Capability' Brown parkland beyond. To the left were the dramatic towers and turreted walls of Alnwick Castle, internationally renowned as the location for the Harry Potter films *The Philosopher's Stone* and *The Chamber of Secrets*. 'Just look at this magical garden,' said Jane. 'It's got unbelievable bones. It's waiting for someone to bring it back to life.'

Standing there that day with the Duchess, it was if I was seeing the potential of the site for the first time. I'd always loved coming here, especially in the early morning or late afternoon when the light bounced off the warm red brick and sandstone walls and you could feel the good times of ages past, when this had been a busy working garden providing food and a place of beauty and respite for earlier generations. Now it was derelict and overgrown, part of it laid to hardcore, but an otherworldly magic still lingered.

'I've been walking round looking and trying to get a feel for the garden,' said the Duchess. 'I think it should be filled with people, I see it as a theatre, an incredible venue: the open site at the base opening up above along these gorgeous bones so people get a sense of drama and excitement. A huge public garden of classic symmetry and astonishing beauty...'

RIGHT: *Circa* 1996. A view from the summit point looking north towards the ornamental pond and the conservatory terrace. Today this would be equivalent to being at the top of The Grand Cascade and looking down towards the Pavilion and Visitor Centre.

LEFT: Aerial view of the Garden taken in 1996. This picture reveals the 'bones' of the Garden and the central 'spine' that became The Grand Cascade. The Poison Garden was built on the left and the Bamboo, Rose and Serpent Gardens on the right. Alnwick town can be seen top right.

RIGHT: A water colour impression of The Grand Cascade. This was produced by Jacques and Peter Wirtz in 1997.

It was an extraordinary moment, standing at the top of the hill, listening to the Duchess's inspiring words, suddenly realizing this site was indeed a canvas of the highest quality.

'It's an unbelievable place and we can do something wonderful here,' she was saying. 'I think we can make this an extraordinary success. I'd like a garden where children can run around and touch things, no rules, with water everywhere – using the latest technology to make it move in the most exciting way. I've got a clear vision of how the Garden could be, but I can't do it by myself. Ian, I need your support – will you help me achieve this?'

I didn't need to think about my answer for a second. 'I'd be delighted, Duchess,' I said.

The significance of this split-second impulse didn't hit home immediately. I was fifty-five, and four years away from retiring from my job as Estates Clerk of the Works, where I was responsible for maintenance and development works on one of the largest ducal agricultural estates in the country. Perhaps this wasn't the best time in life to be taking on an ambitious new venture. But if I'm honest, my driving instinct then, as always, was to give the Duchess my fullest support and to take care of her as best I could. I've worked for the Dukes of Northumberland all my life, and over the years my ever-deepening loyalty to the Percy family has become an integral part of who I am. It's become my history, spanning five decades of my life, since as a young lad I looked after Dowager Duchess Helen, the widow of the 9TH Duke Henry, who died fighting in the Second World War. I worked under the 10TH Duke for thirty-three years and watched his children, including Jane's husband Ralph, grow up. And of course, I've known Jane and Ralph's children almost since the day they were born. It was true to say I'd give the new Duke and Duchess my wholehearted and ungrudging backing in any venture they wanted to pursue. But to come to the end of my working days on a huge and innovative new project seemed like a joy in life offered to few people.

And so the adventure started. I became Project Director of The Alnwick Garden, fitting the work in around my full-time job as Estates Clerk of the Works. Having worked on the Estates so long, I knew the lie of the land: this was a place run on traditional, even old-fashioned lines, and there would be many people playing devil's advocate, putting obstacles in the Duchess's way. I made it a point of honour that, whatever the circumstances, I would always be positive and totally supportive of her ideas. She needed someone who was wholly, uncritically on her side in the inevitable battles to come.

At first, Jane and I talked every day, jotting down ideas and sketches. In her head, she saw the finished project: she wanted lights and water, a garden that appealed to children and the elderly, not just to the horticultural élite who love borders full of obscure plants with long Latin names discovered in China by someone's great uncle. She wanted a garden for everyone, following in the tradition set by the 4th Duke of Northumberland, who had opened this twelve-acre walled site to the local people. She wanted a pleasure garden of spectacle and awe, with fountains and action, stimulating for children of all ages and affordable for families. And, finally, it had to be great day and night, throughout every season of the year, in fog, rain, snow or mist. That, in our unpredictable North-East climate, was a very tall order indeed.

I don't think Jane's husband, Ralph, the 12th Duke, had any idea what he was letting himself in for. When he'd suggested Jane renovate the walled garden, he probably thought she'd plant some roses and a few bags of bulbs, and be happy pottering around taking cuttings like a latter-day Constance Spry. But quite quickly, his tranquil vision was shattered. The Duchess and I drew up some rough budgets suggesting that the garden as we saw it was going to cost about £1 million. 'OK,' said Jane cheerfully. 'Let's go and see what Ralph says.'

In the conference room, Ralph and his right-hand man, the Estates' Head Agent, Rory Wilson, listened with mounting astonishment as the Duchess outlined her ambitious vision, and I remember much sucking of teeth and many concerned glances. But their jaws hit the table when Jane told them the price tag. 'To do something good with the garden,' she explained, 'would probably cost around £1 million.'

Three weeks later, that estimate had leapt to £3 million; after two months' detailed research we were up to £5 million, and everyone was worried where the Duchess was heading. The words 'loose cannon' were never spoken, but there was a sense in the Estates' office – run as a tight financial ship by Rory – that things were getting out of hand and the Duchess needed to be kept on a tighter leash. Rory was first and foremost the Duke's man, running Northumberland Estates in a traditional, almost feudal manner, and his driving focus was to protect ducal interests. Although technically I reported to Rory as my immediate superior, as the Duchess's main spokesman and supporter, all my sympathies were with her.

Rory Wilson is a great manager but he does tend towards plain speaking at difficult moments. One day when Jane was enthusing about bringing visitors in and creating a public resource for the North-East, he replied in a cool put-down that Northumberland Estates was not in the business of running visitor attractions. In a way he was right: the Castle opened for six months of the year, but the mainstay of the Estates was agriculture, not tourism, and no one working here had ever conceived of an ambitious visitor project like this before. But Jane was infuriated by his lack of spirit and adventure. She hurried down to my office, seething inside. 'Rory doesn't know what's going to hit him,' she muttered crossly to me, 'because I'm coming from a totally different angle and I'm going to create the mother of all attractions!'

Creative enthusiasm and vision like the Duchess's need to be harnessed before real progress can be made, and it was clear to me that we needed to take notes from inspiring people who'd already achieved what we were setting out to do. One day at lunch, the Cornwall-based explorer Robin Hanbury-Tenison told the Duchess about Tim Smit, who'd masterminded the restoration of a big garden project in Cornwall. The Lost Gardens of Heligan had just opened to the public, but Tim Smit was far from being the household name he is today, and neither the Duchess nor I had heard of him. Jane contacted him personally and invited him to Alnwick. Accepting the offer, Tim wrote:

The British disease of worshipping the past and making restoration no more than history in aspic is a recipe for misery. How much better that [a new garden] bears the stamp of your own personality and while perhaps celebrating aspects of the past also presents glimpses of an exciting future! I know that at Heligan it felt almost heretical to recognise that many designs of the past actually were ugly, misconceived, uncomfortable or unfriendly ... but the moment one breaks the shackles of tradition for tradition's sake, you feel a huge weight lift from your shoulders.

I picked Tim up from Newcastle airport – he hates flying, and I got the impression he'd come north against his better judgement, fearing (as he admitted once we got to know him better) that the Duchess was going to be one of those grand lady gardeners he had a phobia about. In the car, he looked down at his open-necked shirt, jeans and orange Tuff boots, and said, 'Christ, am I properly dressed to meet a Duchess?'

'I think you're all right,' I said, amused. It was clear he thought he was coming to see a stately lady in a tea dress and pearls. Everyone gets a surprise the first time they meet the Duchess: she's usually dressed in baggy combat trousers and a T-shirt, is as friendly as can be and asks everyone to call her Jane. The only time I ever address her as 'Your Grace' is in company when it's important to me, not her, that I don't presume upon her friendship.

The Duchess, Tim and I had a rip-roaring lunch together in the Castle, at which much wine was drunk and many cigarettes smoked. It was getting dark when we went out to the Garden – a good five minutes' walk – and Tim ran straight up to the top of the hill, just as the Duchess and I had done a few months before. 'Isn't this great!' the Duchess said, turning to me. 'Someone who's full of energy, who doesn't mince his words and who's interested in what we're doing.'

We got to the top, and I waited for a comment like: 'This is crap ...' But Tim turned to us, sighed profoundly and said: 'God, this garden is so fucking sexy ...'. The Duchess suddenly seemed to find her feet more interesting than the vista in front of us. I tried to pass the moment off and, wholly ignoring Tim's comment, started burbling on about the beauty of the site. 'You can see here, Tim,' I said, 'we've removed the laurels to show the nineteenth-century banks, and in the distance there's the "Capability" Brown landscape ...'

But Tim wasn't going to let it drop. 'Have either of you heard a word I've said?' he asked. He looked at our abashed, surprised faces in some amusement, then cranked up the volume and proclaimed: 'For this garden to work, you have to want to bring a woman here and make love to her in every single corner ...'

I could feel myself going red – this wasn't the sort of conversation the Duchess and I had in everyday discourse – and shot her an anguished, apologetic look. Meanwhile, there was no stopping Tim. 'Yes, do it, of course do it,' he was continuing, 'but do it differently. Let's not see another boring restoration ...'

Tim's language was rich, but I was mentally applauding his bravura style. He's got charisma and passion, and you knew he'd bust a gut to see a great idea through to the end. Just the Duchess's kind of person. 'Brilliant,' she told me later, 'Here's a man who's thinking exactly the way I'm thinking ... and who believes it *can* be done!'

Tim Smit was the single biggest catalyst in the development of The Alnwick Garden. He'd seen the potential of the site and was daring us to be different; not to slip into the 'Victorian' mode of gardening, full of frilly borders and nostalgic charm. Nice is easy, he seemed to be saying, but achieving greatness is a bigger challenge, and he promised to offer us all the help he could, becoming the Duchess's most important early mentor.

PATRONAGE

Yes, we would take up the gauntlet and dare to be different, as the Percy family had done with courage ever since Harry 'Hotspur' in the fourteenth century. Now all we needed was a patron, someone to bring gravitas and cultural authenticity to the project. One weekend, the Duke and Duchess were invited to Sandringham, the Queen's Norfolk home, for a shoot that the Prince of Wales was also attending. His Royal Highness is renowned for his wide-ranging interests in architecture, the countryside and environmental issues, and it suddenly struck us that he would be the best patron we could possibly have. 'I'm going to show him our plans and ask him to help,' said Jane.

The Duchess and the Prince of Wales had only met casually before and it's an indication of Jane's persuasive skills that he agreed to become patron of the Garden on the spot. 'What a leap of faith,' Jane said when she got back. 'I'm not sure I would have done the same in his position.' She thought perhaps he agreed because the Garden is in a rural location that needed an economic boost.

I think he did it because, like so many others, he was bowled over by the Duchess's keenness to create a garden that would help people lead fuller, richer, more satisfying lives. She's so positive and committed to her ideal that you can't help but get caught up in it. Her enthusiasm was the engine of the project: we had no money or proper designs to show people; all we had was a concept in her head. We were selling an idea, and if she faltered we were lost.

Once the Duchess and I were taking some oil executives round the derelict garden, trying to excite them to invest in the project. She was standing talking about her plans for a big cascade plunging down the hill, a glorious torrent of water the likes of which had never been seen before, when she suddenly seemed to falter. I thought she was tired and quickly ushered everyone back to the Castle. On the way, she said, 'I don't know what's wrong with me. I just can't be bothered. At this moment I don't care whether this cascade's built or not.'

The next day she came out in a profusion of nasty red spots and was diagnosed with chicken pox. The funniest thing was her relief at discovering she was 'properly' ill. Her lack of spirit, frightening at the time, was just a temporary blip.

The Duchess and I gave several informal talks about the future Garden to people on the Estates and in the town. There was a moment during the second talk when I got carried away and started improvising, enthusing about how we were going to develop the Garden into something great of which the North-East could be proud.

'That was a fantastic moment, Ian,' said the Duchess as we left. She told me that as I talked she had felt my own commitment to the project, and sensed my belief in what we were trying to do. Perhaps this was the first moment she truly understood that she was not on her own.

That day I had a vision of the future too. Running through my head was a picture of Jane a hundred years hence, just one in a line of historically important Duchesses of Northumberland who'd put an innovative mark on The Alnwick Garden. Jane's influence, I saw, was of massive significance, as far-reaching as that of Elizabeth, the 1st Duchess, who commissioned 'Capability' Brown to create the exquisite rolling parklands we delight in today. In scale and importance, the new garden would rival any horticultural development that had gone before. Jane's vision, it suddenly struck me, had the presence and majesty to inspire and delight contemporary thought just as Elizabeth's had done 250 years before.

CHAPTER 2

THE VIEW FROM THE GROUND

When I first met Jane in 1979, she was known to all as Jane Richard. Ralph brought her to Alnwick Castle a few weeks before their wedding to introduce her to the staff. She was twenty-one and obviously apprehensive about taking on a new role as Lady Percy, but despite her initial shyness I remember thinking how lovely and friendly she was. She had a natural charm and could get on with anybody and everybody – which was to be a very useful attribute in The Alnwick Garden.

For the first seven years of their marriage, she and Ralph lived in West Sussex, in a house near Petworth. I knew the county well, having been born at the opposite end in a little village called Sharpthorne, near East Grinstead. My mother and younger sister, Pauline, lived in the area, and though I've resided in Northumberland for more than fifty years I think of Sussex as my second home.

When I was eight, my life changed in a big way. Our family moved to London to follow my father's work as a stud groom with the dray horses at Watney's Brewery in Victoria. Being transported from a quiet rural environment to the centre of a bombed and devastated London in 1948 was traumatic – not least learning to get on with tough, war-weary Londoners, so different from the country folk I knew – but it was also full of novelty and excitement. We lived on Palace Street, just two minutes from Buckingham Palace and Victoria Station, surrounded by the grandest royal buildings in the capital. The day after we arrived, the youngsters next door dragged my sister and me off to St James's Park to watch the Changing of the Guard and stare through the gates of Buckingham Palace to try to catch sight of King George VI or Queen Elizabeth. We didn't, of course, but this most royal part of the city seemed exhilaratingly close to the centre of power throughout the ages. You felt the weight of history in every crack in the paving stones beneath your feet, and I learned a love of tradition that made my future role working for a great aristocratic family seem a natural progression.

THE DUCHESS'S EARLY YEARS

In building a garden, a person's early influences and passions are hugely relevant: the references and oblique connections made with a child's eye seep into the unconscious and bubble under for years before emerging in the earliest plans. Jane was born and brought up in Edinburgh and the Scottish Borders, the second of the four children of Angela and John Richard, a stockbroker. Her family owned Kailzie, a rural estate in Peeblesshire with gardens that Angela, a good gardener and horticulturalist, opened to the public in the early 1970s – and so the idea of sharing a garden was always a natural part of Jane's upbringing. As a child, whenever she wanted to talk to her mother, she'd find her in the garden and have to help with whatever job she was doing: digging, pruning or pushing a wheelbarrow.

Every Friday afternoon during term-time, her family decamped to Kailzie for the weekend – except Jane, who for five years from the age of eight often remained in Edinburgh to practise figure skating, her passion. When the door closed behind the rest of the family, most of the nannies would shrug off their shoes and switch on the television. The Duchess remembers one in particular who would even send her out for fish and chips. She led a different life from her sisters and brother, who were driven out to their country home to ride and mess around. She became self-disciplined and independent from a young age.

She wanted to be a championship skater, and every school morning got up at 5.30 a.m. to practise at Murrayfield ice rink. When her instructor turned on the rink lights, hundreds of rats would scurry from beneath the warm radiators where they'd been scavenging. It was far from glamorous, but it gave her a core of steel.

At twelve, her parents gave her an ultimatum: go to Canada for professional training, or forget skating and go to boarding school. She chose boarding school, realizing she wasn't extrovert enough to make it as a championship skater. So off she went to Cobham Hall boarding school in Kent, happy not to have to get up at the crack of dawn every morning. She says that nothing since, not even working ten-hour days to get The Alnwick Garden off the ground, has been as tough as that early, self-imposed regime.

A JOB WITH NORTHUMBERLAND ESTATES

By the time I was eleven, my family had moved from London to Northumberland, to live in Newton-on-the-Moor, five miles south of Alnwick. I went to school there, then to a private college in Morpeth, nineteen miles away. Times were hard, and when I saw an advertisement in the local paper for a junior's job in Northumberland Estates clerk of the works department, I applied. I got the junior's job for the princely sum of £1.10s a week, and started working for the Duke of Northumberland. It was 1955, and I was just fifteen.

There wasn't a great deal for an industrious lad to do, and by lunchtime I'd be sitting twiddling my thumbs. One day the architect in the drawing office said to me, 'Do you want something to do? Why don't you have a go at drawing.' I was like a duck taking to water. I found the creative discipline of technical drawing very satisfying. I blossomed, and a couple of days a week went to college in Newcastle to study for the Higher National Certificate in Building and to sit the first stage of the Institute of Clerks of Works exams. The rest of the time I learned the trade in the office.

By 1969, I'd met and married my wife, Ann, a teacher. That year, the incumbent Estates Clerk of the Works was due to retire. I remember badgering the agent, the Duke's right-hand man who ran the Estates and had the major say in any new appointments, for weeks until he caved in and gave me the position. The Estates Clerk of the Works is a big job, running a team of fifty and looking after a budget of several million pounds a year – and I was still only twenty-nine, the youngest man in the country to hold such a position. It was a great honour.

Northumberland Estates is not as big as some aristocratic estates but it is one of the most diverse, with 120,000 acres of land, 171 tenant farms and 700 houses and cottages, plus the Castle. I was responsible for the design, repairs and maintenance of all the property, and the job was certainly varied. When the local authorities introduced mains sewerage in the 1970s we started a major programme of modernization, building bathrooms and upgrading the kitchens in all the Estates cottages. We designed groundbreaking new portal-framed agricultural buildings, with controlled atmospheres to prevent animals from getting pneumonia. We looked after the ducal family's residences, converting a wonderful farmstead for Dowager Duchess Elizabeth, the current Duke's mother.

My job entailed working closely with the Duke, at that time Hugh, the 10TH Duke, Ralph's father. He was the longest-serving Duke in Alnwick's history and over the thirty years I worked for him he became like a second father to me. He was a real countryman and agriculturalist, kind and gentlemanly, and we had a good rapport. Regularly on a Saturday evening, there'd be a knock on my door and the Duke would be standing there. 'August,' he'd say, 'have you a minute? There are a few things I'd like to go through with you.' He'd come in and sit down in a chair near the fire. 'Would you like a whisky, Your Grace?' I'd ask. 'That would be ideal,' he'd say, and for about an hour and a half we'd drink and talk about Estates matters.

He was never someone who'd give direct orders. Instead, he'd comment, 'I was driving down such and such a road and thought it would be nice to see a view to such and such.' I would have to determine, 'Is he telling me to do that, or just commenting that in an ideal world ...?' Then he'd finish his drink and say, 'Well, time for dinner,' and get up and go home to the Castle. Afterwards, I'd sit with a piece of paper and write down everything we'd discussed until I could figure out exactly what he wanted. That's the way we worked. It was informal and personal, and made me feel an important part of his wider 'family' on the Estates.

The Duchess always says my job taught me to be diplomatic, and it's true. Northumberland Estates is broken into fourteen smaller units, so it was always a balancing act with the budgets. I could tell one farmer we could get his roof repaired within a couple of weeks, while his neighbour half a mile down the road, who was in a different estate, with its budget already spent, might have to wait until the following year. I learned that tact, kindness and diplomacy were the best ways to navigate these tricky waters and keep people happy.

In 1988 the 10TH Duke died. I was bereft. His eldest son, Harry, became the 11TH Duke, but he preferred metropolitan life and spent most of his time at Syon House in London. Ralph (Harry's younger brother) and Jane had meanwhile moved to Northumberland with their children. Ralph, who'd trained in land management after reading history at Oxford, would work on the Estates and in return they would live in Chatton Park, a lovely seven-bedroomed Georgian house in the Cheviots sixteen miles north of Alnwick. I was briefed to organize whatever he and his family needed to turn this into a home, and as a result I got to know Jane, then Lady Ralph Percy, very well.

Our relationship was still formal – she called me Mr August and I called her Lady Ralph – but I was growing to understand what she liked, and to appreciate her energy and style. Whenever I popped by, we'd sit and have a cup of tea in the kitchen and chat about the world. She always had quirky, interesting ideas – for example, she loves taxidermy and surprises visitors by placing stuffed dogs strategically on chairs and sofas around the house – and made Chatton Park into an interesting family home. By this time she had two young children, but she and Ralph still did the chores around the house, cleaning, cooking and washing. After their third child, Melissa, came along, she employed a nanny but always joked that she'd got it wrong: she'd hear laughter echoing down the stairs – the nanny was playing with the children, while she was clearing up in the kitchen.

THE DUCHESS'S FIRST GARDEN

Jane had always been a keen practical gardener and decided to re-do the garden at Chatton Park. In the early 1980s, she'd attended a three-week garden design course with the influential garden designer John Brookes at Denman's garden outside Chichester. She disliked drawing up designs on paper so the Chatton Park concept was all in her head. I remember her laying out incredible lengths of hosepipe in the shape of beds, then digging and planting them out. It was a cottage garden design, with curvy flower beds and roses and shrubs spilling out over the paths. Even then she took delight in ignoring the advice of horticultural experts. She'd

RIGHT: An Alexander Creswell painting of Alnwick Castle, which was drawn during the construction of the Garden. Creswell has included a distant tower crane working within the Garden in the left of the painting.

blithely divide perennials and transplant shrubs in the middle of the growing season, saying to me, 'Don't look so worried, Ian – everything will grow again.' It always did.

A few years later, she decided she'd got Chatton Park garden wrong, and redesigned it with square and rectangular beds that mirrored the Georgian lines of the house. She wasn't keen to tell Ralph, so dug up as much as she could, then asked me to organize a digger to do the heavy work while she and the family were away on a skiing trip. Our timing was slightly awry and the digger arrived just as the family were about to set off in the car. Ralph caught sight of it, turned to Jane and simply said: 'I won't ask.' Off they went to the airport without another word being spoken. They returned two weeks later to a garden churned up like a mid-winter 1970s football pitch. It took a few months, but this time Jane got the garden just right. The linear, box-edged beds were softened by the planting. Roses, shrubs and perennials were underplanted with great displays of hostas and white 'Triumphator' tulips. Her main interest even then was to create a garden that looked good at all times of the year. The structure and bones of the garden and the architecture of the planting were what mattered if it was to look beautiful.

As a couple, Ralph and Jane's one abiding principle has been to create a normal family life for their children. When they were Lord and Lady Percy, they organized their life as they wanted and lived away from public gaze. But on 31 October 1995, Harry, the 11TH Duke, passed away at the premature age of forty-two, and everything changed.

Harry had been depressed for many years, but it came as an appalling shock when he was found dead at Syon House, after taking an accidental overdose of amphetamines. Ralph, just three years younger than Harry, never expected to inherit the dukedom. In fact, Jane always reassured her children that Harry would live to a ripe old age and have a brood of ankle-biters running round him in his fifties and sixties. But none of this came to pass, and on Harry's death the title passed to Ralph. With no warning or preparation, Jane found herself the 12TH Duchess of Northumberland.

CHAPTER 3

POCKET DYNAMITE

The next few months were dramatic. The new Duchess didn't so much bring a fresh breeze into the Castle as a raging gale. Along with most Estates employees, I was thrilled at the possibilities: here we had a new Duke, a countryman in the mould of his father, a new Duchess, a vibrant young lady with great and progressive ideas, and their four children – we hadn't had children at Alnwick for over thirty years! – coming to live in the Castle. During the seven years of Harry's dukedom, Alnwick had been neglected and was like a museum, dark, soulless and stuffy, the private rooms shabby mausoleums to the memory of previous incumbents, and the corridors laid with curling, grey lino.

It was no surprise that the Duchess was reluctant to leave the family home at Chatton Park and move into the Castle. She remembers her first night there with Ralph, eating dinner cooked by the Castle chef in the gloomy and imposing dining room. 'Dinner' was a hard, dried-up chop she couldn't cut into never mind swallow. She didn't want to worry Ralph who was happy to be back in his childhood home, but he noticed that she was miserable. At Chatton, which they'd left that morning, they'd have been eating a bowl of garlic prawns with salad, made by Jane herself. Ralph said, 'I promise you we won't live like this. We'll make changes and you can turn this into a home. We can make it work the way we want.'

Being suddenly thrust into the limelight as a duchess didn't suit Jane. Everyone said how lucky she was but she felt exactly the opposite. She loved her old life in the comfort of Chatton Park, with her close family around her, where she could behave as she wanted. In the Castle, there was little privacy, solace or comfort: everything she did was observed, often disapprovingly, by retainers who'd worked there for years. At Chatton, Jane and Ralph had established their own familiar, everyday routines but now they couldn't even sit down to a relaxed home-cooked meal together. It was a concern. I remember Jane's mother, Angela, coming to my office in late 1995. Publicly Angela was putting a proud face on events but privately she was worried. Jane perched on the fireplace fender while Angela said: 'Ian, you do realize what Jane is going to be faced with in her new role. She needs help and I'm asking you to give her your support whatever happens.'

'I promise I'll do everything I can to help and support her.' I replied. Even before the Garden project started, my every instinct was to protect the Duchess and help negotiate any difficulties she might encounter.

While Harry had been ill, a lot of people had been given free rein around the Castle, and the new Duke and Duchess needed to stamp their authority as quickly as they could. Some members of Ralph's family told Jane she was going to have an awful time ahead; she was going to have to be really tough with family and retainers, and shouldn't expect to be popular or to make any friends. At the time Jane thought this was ridiculous, and couldn't imagine what they were talking about. She found out soon enough.

A TEST OF CHARACTER

The first hurdle was a dispute with the auction house, Sotheby's. A sale of furniture and artefacts had been organized for May 1996 to raise a £5 million endowment fund for the restoration and maintenance of the Estates' chattels. Ralph had asked Jane to make sure everything ran smoothly with the sale. It was her first job as Duchess, and she was determined to do it properly. She came to it knowing nothing about furniture or the family collection, so asked furniture expert Robert Kime – who designed the interiors at Highgrove and later Clarence House for HRH the Prince of Wales – to give her independent advice. Robert Kime told her to withdraw 90 per cent of the items marked for sale. Why sell potentially very valuable furniture in a bad state of repair, he reasoned, as future generations would never be able to afford to buy it back? Keep it, and in time it could be restored to its former glory. Robert Kime came up to Alnwick every couple of weeks to go through the stock of marked furniture, saying, 'Withdraw this, pull this out, don't give them this, give them that ...'

So Jane began to withdraw furniture from the sale. The tricky thing was that Ralph's older sister, Lady Victoria, had organized the sale and was understandably angry when Jane took items out of the auction. Victoria had grown up in the Castle and been in charge of the chattels for seven years while Harry was Duke. Moreover, she was the family's representative with Sotheby's, and now here was the new Duchess coming in and overruling decisions she had made. Victoria rang Jane up asking why she was withdrawing that piece or pulling out this one, and told her bluntly that she was ruining the sale. But Jane was determined to follow Robert Kime's advice, not only because she was paying him highly for it, but because she genuinely thought it was in the best long-term interests of Northumberland Estates.

It was a period of great stress, and it was Jane's first test of character as Duchess. At the time, we were also planning a redesign of the Castle to make it welcoming and homely for the children, plus a refurbishment of the staff quarters, all of which added to the mayhem. Jane and I would wander around the dark corridors, working out various living and bedroom configurations, and eventually picked out the area we thought would work best for the family's private rooms. This was the old 'death wing', a set of rooms where in the old days people had been laid out or quarantined when they had infectious diseases. The atmosphere was dark and gloomy, the furniture black and grim, with rotting mattresses and stained carpets, and in one cupboard we even found an old urn of forgotten ashes. It seemed a monumental task to make this into a warm family home, but Jane and I set to the task with gusto. We were helped by John Waddell and Ian Tate, long-time employees of Northumberland Estates, who knew how difficult things were going to be for Jane because they'd watched many previous dukes and duchesses come and go.

Pretty soon, I began to feel the pressure of work too. I'd been feeling rather unwell, and was sent to a heart specialist in Newcastle. I was diagnosed with angina and put on medication that I hoped would clear things up and give me back my usual reserves of energy and enthusiasm.

In February 1996 the Duke went to South America on a fishing trip, leaving Jane in charge of Alnwick. He was in Patagonia when someone from Sotheby's tracked him down on his mobile phone with the alarming news that his wife was ruining the sale by withdrawing everything, and that he was going to be the poor relation in the country house stakes. To his enormous credit, Ralph replied that he'd asked Jane to look after the sale, it was her job, she'd taken advice, and if she was doing what she thought was right, he respected that. It was a huge vote of faith and support.

Despite the Duke's wholehearted endorsement, back home things weren't much easier for the Duchess. A few weeks before the sale, Robert Kime saw two horrible purple-and-white painted beds being loaded on to the lorry and told Jane she'd have to withdraw them. The Duchess replied that she couldn't: the catalogues were printed, and everything was ready. The beds were valued at £1,500, and she felt that at this stage they should just let them go. Kime told her that if she didn't withdraw the beds, he'd bid up to £5,000 each for them because he thought they were possibly really good. Jane looked at the beds and thought, 'These old bits of wood?' But she trusted Kime and had the strength of character not to consider the inevitable outcry from Sotheby's in her final decision to withdraw them.

In the event, she and Kime were vindicated. These 'old bits of wood' turned out to be the earliest examples of Robert Adam beds in England, and have since been restored and valued at around a quarter of a million pounds.

The Sotheby's episode caused a rift between the new Duchess and some members of Ralph's family that was only exacerbated by a dispute about their old clothes. Like many children who leave their family home, the Duke's brothers and sisters had left wardrobes full of their belongings behind, plus there were rooms full of clothes belonging to Harry, the 11TH Duke, and Hugh, the 10TH Duke, who had died seven years before. When Jane and the family moved in, there was not a single empty cupboard, wardrobe or chest of drawers in the Castle in which they could put their own belongings.

There was no tactful way of dealing with the problem. The Duchess realized that if the Castle was going to be her family's home, she had to clear out the cupboards. It would make her unpopular, but it couldn't be helped. She contacted her mother-in-law, the Dowager Duchess Elizabeth, who wanted to let the children choose which of the 10TH and 11TH Dukes' clothes they would like to keep. So Hugh's and Harry's clothes were piled on the beds, to allow the family to take what they wanted. Jane also asked Ralph's brother and sisters to come and collect their remaining belongings. But nobody did. She asked again; still no response. So after a few months, the Duchess piled their clothes into black bin liners and sent them to their respective homes. Lady Caroline's filled eighty bags, which took two minibus journeys down to Syon House, where she lived.

Later, Ralph's mother said to Jane, 'Goodness, that was pretty hard, what you did to Caroline. I'd have been furious if someone did that to me.' The Duchess remembers thinking, 'Well, actually, exactly the same thing is about to happen to you!' and despatched the 10TH Duke's clothes to Dowager Duchess Elizabeth's house forthwith. It should be said that Jane adores her mother-in-law and they are good friends.

James, Ralph's younger brother, later told the Duchess that receiving his old clothes in this way was the most hurtful thing that ever happened to him. Jane sympathized, but said it was better that she and not Ralph had done the awful deed. 'I had to do it,' she said to me one day when we were inspecting the building work in her children's new bedrooms. 'I know it's upset everyone, but if Alnwick is to become our home it had to happen. And it had to be me that did it, because it couldn't be Ralph.'

It was a lonely and difficult task, especially today when most families divide their assets equally between siblings and no one is favoured on the grounds of birth order or gender. But it's important to recognize that big heritage estates like the Duchy of Northumberland only hold together when by birthright one sibling, usually the oldest surviving male, looks after the whole inheritance for future generations. Primogeniture is painful, but it ensures the survival of the estate and in the long run that is more important than the individual sensibilities of anyone concerned.

Watching the new Duchess go through these traumatic personal events, two things struck me. She wasn't frightened to do the right thing, even when it was unpleasant and would make her unpopular. And she was like a powerhouse of energy, racing through the old establishment and shaking everything up. Chris Gough, our first head gardener, always called the Duchess 'pocket dynamite', and that's exactly the quality she brought to the Castle and Garden. She was a dynamo of pure energy, and the rest of the world beware.

CHAPTER 4

WHO DOES SHE THINK SHE IS?

From this moment on we turned our attention onto the Garden. Tim Smit's whirlwind visit in May 1996 gave us a huge burst of energy, and we knew now that our ideas weren't mad or impossible to achieve. The site had the bones upon which to create a great, new and different pleasure garden for the public. Any half-baked idea of doing a restoration was shelved. The Millennium was coming up and we were looking to the future, not the past. We weren't going to faithfully rebuild the eighteenth-century garden, or turn ourselves hostage to the restoration lobby by making a modern-day pastiche of the Italianate parterres, oblong ponds, sunken gardens and conservatories built by the 4TH Duke. Instead, we were going to create something that acknowledged the structure and influence of the past but harnessed the very best of modern design and technology. The Alnwick Garden was going to make people sit up and take notice.

Even before Tim's visit, we'd been meeting English designers and the Duchess had been canvassing opinion from anyone who knew anything about gardens and design. Friends, relatives, neighbours, anyone she came into contact with, were asked whom they thought were the best British gardeners. The Duchess didn't only want names, she wanted specifics: what was X good at, what was Y's weakness, did W really go twice over budget in that garden, and would Z be willing to compromise and work with others in a team?

She scoured gardening books and magazines, and when she decided someone sounded promising, she'd come to me saying, 'Ian, can you find out more about so and so, then let's see if we can get them up here.' For me this was a delightful way to operate. As a keen amateur gardener, who toiled weekly in my own one-and-a-half acres, I was coming into contact with people I'd read about with interest for years, and got a real buzz from the encounters.

Rosemary Verey was the first designer to arrive at Alnwick, in March 1996. Everyone had mentioned her name, and she had a reputation as a phenomenal plantswoman. She'd redesigned the garden of Barnsley House, her husband's family home in Gloucestershire, to critical acclaim and in the process turned it into a very popular visitor attraction – exactly what we hoped to do at Alnwick. She wasn't a businesswoman, but the garden had become a successful business, and that was reassuring and inspirational. That year she showed my wife and me around the garden at Barnsley House, full of dramatic plantings such as the wonderful laburnum allée underplanted with purple alliums and hostas, and traditional potager and box-edged knot gardens.

She was by now in her late seventies and rather frail, but completely charming, enthusiastic and open-minded. During lunch in the Castle, she talked about using different designers for different parts of the Garden. She suggested a long list of names including Anthony Archer-Wills and Beth Chatto for a water garden, Xa Tollemache for roses, Penelope Hobhouse for perennial borders, and Jane Fearnley-Whittingstall for a scented garden.

After lunch, Jane and I took Rosemary Verey over to the Garden itself. She wasn't able to walk very well, and certainly couldn't make it up the steep, slippery banksides, so we drove her to the top of the hill. She saw the site's potential but it was apparent to the Duchess and me that she was too frail to be able to take on a major role herself, though she helped in other ways over the next year, giving advice and support.

Anyway, the Duchess wasn't convinced that Rosemary Verey's traditional approach would work at Alnwick. She had been influential in re-establishing English country gardening style, the fashion for romantic, blazing borders full of colourful herbaceous plants that had evolved from the designs of Gertrude Jekyll and Vita Sackville-West decades before. Whenever you see those big, beautiful but labour-intensive borders, you're immediately transported back to Edwardian times, when fleets of gardeners spent summers deadheading and staking plants in country houses across the land. But we were nearly in the twenty-first century, and the Duchess didn't want a genteel reworking of an old-fashioned theme.

This was 1996, a year before the gardening world was revolutionized by Alan Titchmarsh, Charlie Dimmock and the *Ground Force* movement. Looking back now, it's difficult to appreciate just how élitest garden design was at that time. It was hard to find a designer interested in creating a modern garden for the general public. The designers we heard about, who seemed to get all the plum private jobs, were undoubtedly talented with plants but they created gardens full of Edwardian flower borders and traditional focal points and vistas. Most of them had never been involved with public projects, never mind one on the scale of The Alnwick Garden. They were building gardens as quiet and secluded private spaces, whereas the Duchess saw Alnwick as a ball of fire, a vibrant public arena with lots of activities and hundreds of children racing around. As Rosemary Verey said of one of these grand lady designers: 'Well, she will certainly make you a very pretty little rose garden, dear.' But that wasn't what the Duchess wanted.

The irony to me was that the Duchess was also a lady of a certain social class with a background in amateur gardening. But her gut feeling was that at Alnwick, it wasn't good enough to produce the same pretty borders that could be seen at National Trust houses up and down the country. Her decision to create something different and accessible was to get her into serious trouble, not just with English Heritage and other pressure groups such as the Garden History Society, but also within her own social circle. She annoyed people because she was prepared to stick her neck out to get the Garden built and do things duchesses were not 'supposed' to do, such as ask people for money, talk to the newspapers, and spurn the advice of posh gardening 'experts' who wanted a hand in the project.

There's no doubt in my mind that because the Duchess alienated these grand, English designers at the very beginning, she and the Garden became the focus of their distaste. The common refrain we heard was: 'Who does she think she is?'

LEFT: During a trip to Italy the Duchess visited Villa Lante near Viterbo. The combination of water and topiary structure inspired her.

Quite often, the Duchess got phone calls from friends saying, 'I was at dinner with so-and-so last night, and Jane, you must watch your back. She launched into a tirade about you and Alnwick. She hates what you're doing. She really has the knife out.'

She often felt, when she looked around the room at a dinner party, 'Three-quarters of you have it in for me.' She always thought her worst critics were from her own social set. They saw a garden built by a Duchess as a private fiefdom rather than a popular venue to be enjoyed by the general public, whereas the Duchess's view has always been that something beautiful should not be the preserve of just one family.

THE SEARCH BEGINS

But all that was a battle for the future. Now the pressure was on to find designers who could come up with something bold and original. One of the Duchess's most enthusiastic helpers at that time was her good friend Lord Lambton, then in his seventies. For a few days every spring, the Duchess and Duke visited him at Villa Cetinale, his home near Siena in Tuscany. Lord Lambton had restored the baroque gardens of the seventeenth-century villa and was extraordinarily knowledgeable about garden design and designers. The Duchess always says that it was thanks to Tony Lambton's influence that she developed an eye for what worked in a garden.

In spring 1996, Lord Lambton and the Duchess visited several spectacular gardens including Villa Lante and Villa d'Este, with 'poor, long-suffering Ralph', as Jane called him, driving them around the countryside. The Duchess was most interested by the water displays and how the layout of public gardens worked – whether visitors were enchanted or bored as they moved around the various attractions and vistas. She was fascinated by specific details: the depth of drop on a water staircase, the pressure through a nozzle, whether a water spout was made of verdigris or copper. She came back exclaiming about the beauty of some specific feature and would ask me to research exactly how it worked.

Along with Tim Smit, Tony Lambton became an advisory 'Director' of The Alnwick Garden in July. That summer he suggested many potential designers to Jane, including the British landscape architect Geoffrey Jellicoe who, at ninety, was 'getting on a bit', as even Lord Lambton admitted. Another recommendation was an Italian couple, Guido Ferrara and Guiliana Campioni Ferrara, eminent landscape architects from Florence. Lord Lambton wrote to the Duchess:

> The Italian and his wife came over to lunch last week. He is obviously talented but what I've come to realise is that in Italy, landscape gardeners depend nowadays more on official proprietors than landed ones. In other words, municipal gardening is their bread and butter. I can only think of one private Italian who has made a garden in Italy in the last 20 years.

We were keen to meet anyone recommended by Lord Lambton, and invited the Ferraras to Alnwick. We put them up in the Castle, and it was obvious from their comments of surprise and delight at the opulent surroundings – the Titians, Canalettos and Van Dycks, the Meissen china collection, the Louis XIV furniture – that they hadn't realized the scale of the project. Alarmed, the Duchess took me to one side. She asked me to explain diplomatically that this was a public project, and we didn't have money to burn.

Although by now we were focused on creating a self-funding and self-supporting public venture, many people still assumed the Garden was for the use of the Percy family alone. Perhaps it was hard for them to believe Jane could want to create a Garden for the people, or that public money could be forthcoming for a project with a duchess at the helm. Perception, even then, was our biggest hurdle.

Before the Ferraras' arrival, The Duchess and I had already done some preliminary sketches of how we saw the Garden and we gave these to the couple, along with some aerial photos. I remember feeling a little disappointed as we showed them round the site: this was our first experience with potential designers but the couple didn't volunteer many thoughts or ideas. To be fair, perhaps they didn't realize the scope of the Duchess's vision. They promised to work up some concepts, however, and send them to us.

When their presentation came back five days later we were astonished: their two sheets seemed hardly different from our own original sketches. When the Ferraras' bill arrived, we were even more amazed: in the dazzlingly high figures of Italian currency, it sounded very expensive. In pounds sterling the amount was less frightening but still more than we'd anticipated for two sketches we probably wouldn't use. In the future, we'd get used to paying designers for proposals, but at that time the process was new to us. So I wrote back, querying the professional fees, and asking for them to be reduced. To our relief, they duly were.

This episode gave us our first indication that inviting designers to stay in the Castle might cause more problems than it solved. But at the time we had no alternative: the Garden itself was an overgrown wilderness and we had no office space, not even a Portakabin, in which to entertain visitors. We had to use the Castle for meetings and overnight stays as a way of minimizing costs. I was still working full time as Estates Clerk of the Works, and everything the Duchess and I did regarding the Garden was unpaid. All the seed money we spent, which came from Northumberland Estates, went on designers' fees and expenses, and we needed to keep these costs within the bounds of reason.

After our experience with the Italian designers, we decided to go back to basics. The Duchess wanted to get a proper design down on paper, to try to formalize her ideas and provide a starting point for debate and discussion. Landscape architect Dominic Cole of Land Use Consultants was drawing up a ten-year management plan for Northumberland Estates on the 'Capability' Brown landscape, restoring the trees that had blown down and rotted away over the centuries. Dominic was a quiet, confident person with very good ideas. He was a member of the Garden History Society, later to become its chairman, and his main interest was heritage work – he'd supervised Tim Smit's restoration of the Lost Gardens of Heligan and the restoration of the 'Capability' Brown landscapes at Stowe. As he was on site, the Duchess asked him to produce some designs for the Garden. We were thinking he might plan the layout, while Anthony Archer-Wills, an expert on water garden technology whom Rosemary Verey rated highly, designed the water features. Other experts in lighting, planting and productive gardens would be invited in later because we realized that one designer couldn't possibly be an expert in every area we needed.

Dominic Cole showed his design to the Duchess and me at a private meeting in the Castle. It was a formal, Italianate interpretation that retained and updated the historic element of the 4TH Duke's garden. After a few minutes' chat, the Duchess asked Dominic to talk her through some details. 'What's happening with that line of beech hedges?' she asked. 'It looks a bit square, as if a bus could be slotted into every space. It doesn't look quite beautiful enough to me. Also, we talked about a rose garden, but there's not one in your plan.'

Dominic, perhaps shaken by her criticism, said she couldn't possibly put a rose garden there. He didn't seem to notice it, but I saw the Duchess stiffen. She felt that Dominic was being very patronizing – an 'expert' telling a client that her ideas about the garden weren't going to be incorporated in 'his' plan. She instantly decided: 'Big mistake, Dominic. You've just blown this £3 million job.' To her it was black and white: if someone didn't listen to her, they were out.

In the end, I thought that Dominic Cole's design for The Alnwick Garden, though well presented and professionally devised, didn't have the 'Wow!' factor the Duchess was looking for. Although Dominic was still involved, drawing up plans for the car park and attending design meetings, in her eyes he was no longer in the running for the big job – the design of the Garden itself. He went on to work on the landscape architecture and outside planting at the Eden Project, about which the Duchess has some reservations, so it's probably best they parted.

In April 1996, I'd been despatched to hear Anthony Archer-Wills talk at a two-day symposium on water gardens at York University. The Duchess thought we should invite him to Alnwick to see the site. At our first meeting, he drew up a sketch for a grotto, which the Duchess thought was perfect, so she asked him to create some designs for the Grand Cascade water feature.

At the beginning of the project, the Duchess was very free-thinking about the Cascade. As she explained to Archer-Wills, it could be a series of formal pools with fantastic, memorable fountains or a wild, informal torrent raging down the hillside over huge boulders. But whatever was decided, the Duchess emphasized, it had to be a new and different way of moving water down a slope.

I set off to photograph rocks and boulders at Northumberland Estates' Hulne Park, which we thought could be used in the 'wild' design – but in the end Archer-Wills didn't go for this option. Instead, at a meeting at Syon House, he presented his plan for a formal water cascade. It didn't fire up the Duchess: she said it reminded her of the cascade at Chatsworth, the Duke and Duchess of Devonshire's gardens in Derbyshire, where a dramatic water staircase of twenty-four steps plunges down a 200-yard slope. 'What's the point of difference?' Jane asked. 'Why would anyone come to Alnwick to see something they can already see beautifully done at Chatsworth?'

In response, Archer-Wills said to her that, with the greatest respect, he was the water designer; he knew what was needed, so would she please leave it to him. The effect was instantaneous: the Duchess looked over as if to say, 'Here we go again.' At that moment I knew: Archer-Wills was out of the project. I later had to write informing him we no longer required his services, which I did as respectfully and sympathetically as I could.

Looking back, I can see that many of our early difficulties with designers often arose because many of them couldn't understand the scope and passion of the Duchess's vision. To realize her dream she needed the expertise of a first-class design team but she was never prepared to give anyone free rein to do what they liked, no matter how brilliant they might be. Her style is always friendly and informal and perhaps that blinded people to the fact that she is as tenacious now as she was as a ten-year-old skater. Underestimating her always had the same result, and in the year to come I got very good at writing that 'thanks-but-no-thanks' letter.

Our search for designers soon moved back to Europe. One of the Duchess's friends, Angelika, Dowager Countess Cawdor, had restored the Tibetan Garden at Cawdor Castle in Inverness-shire with her late husband, Hugh, the 6TH Earl and 24TH Thane of Cawdor, in the 1980s. The Czech-born Dowager Countess was extremely knowledgeable about European garden design and said that if the Duchess couldn't find someone to fulfil the brief in Britain, she should look to the Continent, where exciting things were happening in design circles.

Lady Angelika knew many eminent French, Belgian and Spanish designers, and invited the Duchess and Duke to Paris for a 'beauty parade' to meet some of them. The Duchess's plan was to show the designers aerial photographs of the site, brief them on her ideas for developing it as a public pleasure garden, and sound out their interest in the job.

The first meeting was with Louis Benech, a *paysagiste* or landscaper, widely considered to be one of France's best plantsmen, who had helped restore the Tuileries garden in Paris. The Duchess, Duke, Lady Angelika, Louis Benech and his partner, shoe designer Christian Louboutin, had dinner together. The Duchess was impressed by his work and asked him to visit Alnwick to see the site.

The next day was lunch at the Hotel Duc de Saint Simon with Belgian designer Jacques Wirtz and his son, Peter. This was a defining moment in the history of The Alnwick Garden. Jacques Wirtz was then seventy-three years old, and a legend in landscape design. His most famous work was the Carrousel Garden in the Tuileries, which he'd redesigned, along with the gardens of the the presidential residence, the Elysée Palace, at the request of François Mitterand, then French President. His pedigree was impeccable: as well as his corporate and public projects, such as Belgium's BMW headquarters and the campus at Antwerp University, he'd designed private gardens for many wealthy clients including Catherine Deneuve and the financier Edmond Safra. He's often called the modern-day Le Nôtre after the great seventeenth-century French designer André Le Nôtre, who created the gardens at Vaux-le-Vicomte for finance minister Nicolas Fouquet and Versailles for Louis XIV, over 300 years earlier.

ABOVE, CLOCKWISE FROM TOP LEFT: Jacques and Peter Wirtz standing by the old conservatory in the Garden, 1997; Jacques Wirtz; Tim Smit, an early advisor to the Garden; and, left to right, Louis Benech, The Duchess of Northumberland, Peter Wirtz, Tadao Ando and Jacques Wirtz.

What impressed the Duchess at that first meeting was not just the experience the Wirtzes could bring to the job, but their professional, dedicated approach. Father and son were both charming, with an air of quiet, cultured authority. The Duchess told me later that she could immediately see Jacques Wirtz was a true artist – a genius, she thought. 'They are such intelligent, artistic people,' she enthused. 'Polite, friendly, charming and very interested in the job.' Perhaps naively, this surprised her. In theory, every designer should want the job – after all, this was a big, high-profile contract – but in reality the Duchess thought she'd be lucky to get an internationally acclaimed designer to come to Northumberland, which was still considered a cultural backwater.

The Wirtzes' view of gardens and gardening impressed Jane hugely. Their aim is to create 'green architecture' in which the underlying structure of a garden ensures it looks beautiful all year round, regardless of the season. The Wirtzes never rely on flowers or borders to give impact, instead creating a restrained, geometric elegance to which is added mystery, mood and surprises at every turn. The Duchess knew instantly that Jacques and Peter Wirtz would be perfect for the job. Although they had an international clientele stretching from Japan to the US, the Wirtzes had never designed a garden in Britain before. But that didn't worry the Duchess. She was glad to be out of the claustrophobic world of English garden design. 'It's such a joy,' she said with relief when she returned, 'to meet really charming people who aren't interested in slagging off other designers. The Wirtzes were friendly, open and listened, really listened, to what I wanted to do.'

During the rest of the week she met other designers, including the renowned landscape architect Pascal Cribier, who had restored the Tuileries with Louis Benech. But, unlike Benech, he was unwilling to work alongside the Wirtzes or other designers, and the Duchess decided not to involve him further.

The Wirtzes and Louis Benech visited Alnwick Castle on separate occasions during March 1997, to see the site and draw up preliminary plans. At this stage, the Duchess was leaning towards using the Wirtzes as the main designers, with Benech doing specific areas of planting and Dominic Cole co-ordinating planning and heritage. But it was still up for grabs: if Benech came up with a master plan that swept the Duchess off her feet, she would go with him.

The Wirtzes and Benech presented their final designs to the Duchess and me at a meeting on 18 April 1997, in the drawing room at Syon House. We knew this was going to be a momentous occasion and my son Simon, a documentary producer, recorded the events for us on film. Since that day we have recorded on film everything we have done at Alnwick, and now have hundreds of hours of footage for our records.

Looking back, it was a very amusing day. The Wirtzes gave their presentation first, every inch the consummate professionals. Peter opened his large portfolio, and pulled out their master plan, beautifully drawn and coloured. It was an exquisite piece of work, imaginative and of great character. He placed it on a large footstool in front of us, and the Duchess and I kneeled, poring over it, while Peter explained the concept and talked us through the details of each area.

The central axis or 'spine' was a three-tiered Cascade with a Lower Basin, flanked with topiary hornbeam hedges that would grow twenty feet or more in height. The hedges provided the green architecture, organizing the space and giving shape and substance – laying flesh on the axial bones of the hard landscaping. At the top of the mound was a walled Ornamental Garden. Peter imagined it 'a hidden paradise' laid out in a repeating square design packed with colourful perennials, divided by rills, paths and fountains, and given an upward perspective with tall, pleached crab apples. That was the quiet area of the Garden, where people could sit and reflect and a pleasant reward after the steep climb up the Cascade. Below in the Lower Garden was a series of repeating squares, a theme that could establish mood in various separate garden rooms, as required.

After his presentation, we sat stunned for a moment. The plans were so clear and Peter's narrative so persuasive that we were able to envisage the whole panorama. The Duchess adored the Wirtzes' design – it had almost everything she wanted, and was in tune with the character of the historic garden and sensitive to

ABOVE: The Duchess and I visited private gardens in Belguim that had been designed by Jacques Wirtz. Walking around these elegant spaces, with their clear lines and use of 'green architecture', influenced the Duchess in her decision to appoint the Wirtzes.

the 'Capability' Brown landscape. Her only reservations were that the area of the Lower Garden wasn't exciting enough – she wanted to see more energy there, perhaps flowing curves and swirls rather than static squares – and that the water features in the Ornamental Garden had to be made fascinating for children.

When the Wirtzes finished, the Duchess turned to Louis Benech, who had been sitting quietly throughout, and asked him to give his presentation. Louis started by saying that, of course, he didn't have a drawing office the size of the Wirtzes', so we'd have to bear with him. He brought out some basic A3 and A4 drawings, showing where he'd put the Cascade, sculptures and planting areas. He talked through his ideas for a few minutes, then paused and looked at us expectantly.

At first I thought the Duchess was going to giggle. I could tell she wasn't particularly impressed, but she composed herself and said: 'Louis, today is a big day. We're talking about spending millions on the Garden, and I find it difficult to consider your proposals based on the sketches you have presented here.'

Louis said we had to trust him, he was a great designer and plantsman and would make the garden beautiful. But the Duchess couldn't see why she should give a multi-million-pound commission to someone who hadn't got the detailed groundwork necessary to convince her he was right for the job.

Benech was genuinely upset. He thought the Duchess was making a huge mistake. Again he said she had to trust him, to ask around: he had a great reputation, he would do a fantastic job, she had to put her faith in him. But of course she couldn't; this was to be a public project and had to be publicly accountable, costed down to the last penny.

In the end there was no contest: the Wirtzes were in a class of their own. The meeting ended, and they went off to redesign the Lower Garden area, as the Duchess had suggested. The plan they brought back to Alnwick a while later was majestic. In the Lower Garden, everything was now sinuous, organic curves, with many different garden areas – the Serpent, Rose and Poison Gardens, the Quiet Garden, the Garden for the Senses – each offering their own private atmosphere and surprises. Visible from everywhere in the Garden was a tall, topiary spiral – clipped hornbeams on trunks – which Peter described as being like a 'swinging movement in the air of a green festoon', adding to the drama and distinctiveness.

The updated design was visionary and sympathetic to the site, and incorporated all the Duchess's hopes and creative ideas. That 1997 plan is the heart of the Garden: we made a model of it, and have followed it almost exactly since.

One day, I remember discussing the model with the Duchess. I'd been feeling tired for a while, and had found it a struggle that day to climb the stairs up to the first floor. The model was on a stool between us, and the Duchess's spaniel, Pod, was leaning its head against my knee. I wasn't feeling right, and told Jane she would have to excuse me, as I felt faint and needed some fresh air. Ann, my wife, immediately drove me down to the heart specialist in Newcastle. The specialist said I was incredibly lucky to be alive: apparently I could have had a heart attack at any moment. The medication I was on for angina had slowed my heart so much that my pulse was down to twenty-five beats per minute, and an artery was silting up badly. I needed an angioplasty to clear the artery, and my medication was changed.

Any health scare is a shock, but this one didn't just frighten Ann and me: the Duchess also told me it was a moment of awakening for her, because she realized that she might not be able to continue with the Garden. She said afterwards, only half-joking, that if I'd been seriously ill she'd have been 'scuppered'. I was the only person she could trust to help her do this job.

It would be a good few years before anyone else shared our hopes and dreams for the Garden, and at that stage we felt it was us two against the world. That isolation was compounded by the fact that the Duchess had many other commitments – as well as her duties as Duchess, her youngest child, Max, was still only seven and, without a nanny, she relied on me to do the research and groundwork for the Garden. I, meanwhile, was still fully employed as Estates Clerk of the Works. It was lucky that after a few weeks I was back to normal, and (touch wood) have never had another episode since.

LEFT: The pivotal meeting on 18 April 1997 at Syon House, London. The design created by Jacques and Peter Wirtz can be seen laid out on the table. From left to right:Peter Wirtz, The Duchess of Northumberland, Ian August, Louis Benech (back to camera), Dominic Cole and Jacques Wirtz.

ABOVE LEFT: The original design by the Wirtzes. The Duchess asked for the square features on the bottom left and right corners to be changed to incorporate a smoother flow in the garden. The revised, approved plan can be seen on the right.

RIGHT: The final plan. Here the Serpent, Rose and Poison Gardens and Labyrinth are all more sinuous. The Pergola is opened at the top, extending the vista all the way from the Ornamental Garden through to the Pavilion.

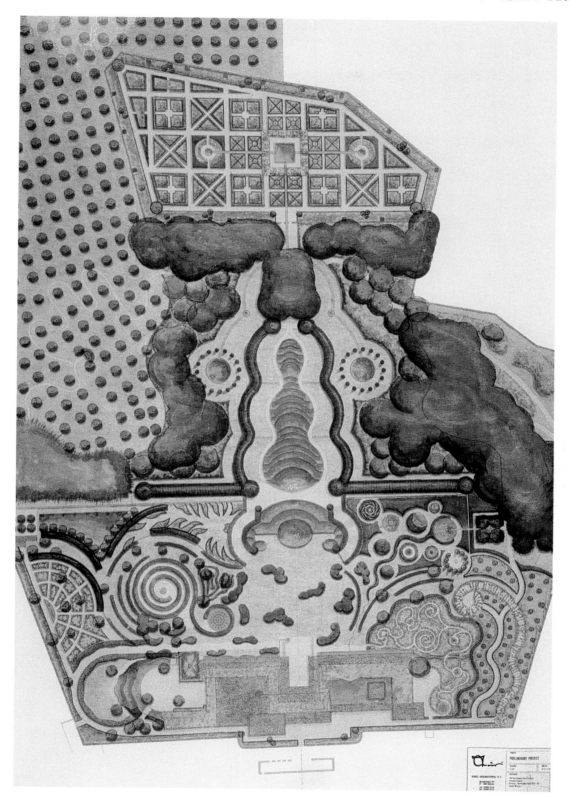

A little while later, Peter Wirtz told us he budgeted that the Garden and Pavilion would cost around £10 million to £12 million to build. I was alarmed at this figure because just a few weeks earlier Rory Wilson, the agent, had written to me saying: 'I have agreed the garden position as approximately £4 million total cost – this is the bottom line which we must achieve.' I was trying to imagine how flexible Rory's concept of 'approximately' might be, but knew it wouldn't stretch to £10 million. The Duchess, however, wasn't worried – in fact she saw £10 million as a realistic figure, even if it was higher than anticipated. She reckoned she could see from the Wirtzes' plan where every penny was going to be spent.

In May, a press release went out:

DUCHESS OF NORTHUMBERLAND TO LAUNCH GARDEN PROJECT

The Duchess of Northumberland is to launch the creation of a garden at Alnwick Castle, which promises to be one of the most exciting garden projects seen in Europe this century.

Her plan is to transform a derelict 12-acre walled garden set in 27 acres that was originally planted over 250 years ago. The Prince of Wales, who is patron of the scheme, has expressed his enthusiasm for the project saying: 'In seeking to recapture the lost world of this great garden, and sharing it with others, the present Duchess of Northumberland is taking up once more the innovative ideas so brilliantly demonstrated in previous generations. The proposed designs will not simply recreate the past, but also provide for a variety of educational and botanical uses needed in the century to come.'

Though the garden will reflect the history of Alnwick and the gardening inheritance of previous Dukes, the Duchess is working with leading continental garden designers such as Jacques and Peter Wirtz from Belgium and Louis Benech from France in her search for a final plan ....

The effect was immediate. Every newspaper in the land wanted to interview the Duchess about her choice of designer. In the Press reports that followed, there was more criticism than praise: a sign of things to come. Why we were using Belgian and French instead of English design talent? Surely a Duchess should support her own countrymen, not hire fancy foreigners? I remember the Duchess saying to me, 'It's remarkable. Why does everyone in this country respect the same dull British designers when others can do it ten times better?' She's never let what's written about her in the papers sway her from her vision, nor has she ever regretted her choice of designers. Then, as now, she was prepared to take the flak if it meant she had the best designers for the job. I had to admire her strength of mind. But as she has always said, in the end, these petty rows and misunderstandings will be forgotten and the Garden will stand or fall on its own merits.

My conviction that the Wirtzes were perfect for the job grew as I got to know them better over the next few weeks. They had a great respect for history and the past. Peter and I would often stroll around the Garden together, and he would always mention the beauty of the 'Capability' Brown landscape and his awareness of 'the master at his shoulder'. 'Everything we do has to fit in with him,' he said. Brown got his nickname from his habit of wandering round assessing the 'capabilities' of a site. I thought, on that day, Peter was following in his footsteps in more ways than one.

Wirtz International was our main designer, but the Duchess wanted to bring other people with specific expertise into the mix. She believed no single designer could be expert in every area from layout to the latest high-tech lighting, and thought bringing in people with other skills and talents could only improve the quality of the Garden. Despite the events at Syon House, Louis Benech was still keen to get involved. The Duchess admired his planting work and thought he might design some special areas. A few weeks later she was staying in a hotel in Italy on a visit to see the Padua poison garden, when she bumped into Louis Benech. It was obvious he was still upset by his rejection, and he asked her to reconsider her decision to hire the Wirtzes. She wasn't prepared to do that, but she did invite him to several meetings at Alnwick so he could stay in touch with the design team and to pave the way for his planting plan at a later stage.

By September, however, it was clear that, in the first phase of the Garden at least, the Wirtzes' expertise was going to be more than enough. I wrote to Louis regretfully, saying we wouldn't need his help at this time. He sent back a sweet but disappointed letter. 'As such is life,' he concluded, 'I am sincerely pleased for Jacques and Peter. It shall be a very exciting project for both you and them, and a great success I am sure.' Privately, perhaps, he felt a little differently: in a phone conversation soon after, he bluntly told the Duchess he was not inclined to put 'curtains on the Wirtzes' house'.

Finding a garden designer had been problematic enough, but finding an architect for the Pavilion was to prove even more challenging. I'd been trained in technical drawing as a youngster, and in 1996 drew up plans for a Queen Anne-style Pavilion, influenced by the Great Conservatory at Syon House. This was to give an idea of the scale and layout of the building we required: how large the cafés, shops and toilet area needed to be to accommodate the visitors we anticipated.

Once the Wirtzes had drawn up their Garden plan, we quickly realized that a contemporary building would be an exciting counterpoint to their classical framework. The Duchess had no idea whom to approach for a modern project as ambitious as this, so asked around to find who was thought the best architect to work with water and gardens. She always saw the garden as theatre, with the Pavilion providing the perfect vantage point from which to watch the spectacle of water and light at play. She imagined the building floating on a lake, with stepping stones into the Garden and water bubbling all around so people felt they were an integral part of the display. Who on earth could create such a wonderful concept? The name that kept cropping up was that of Japanese architect Tadao Ando.

Neither Jane nor I had heard of Tadao Ando, which was perhaps not surprising as he is based in Osaka, Japan, and had never built anything in Britain. Still, people in the know kept telling the Duchess he was the best and that she'd never get someone so eminent to come to Northumberland just to design a Pavilion. Then in spring 1997, in a strange quirk of fate, the Duchess picked up a newspaper and saw a paragraph mentioning Ando's name. He had just been awarded the Royal

Institute of British Architects' prestigious Royal Gold Medal, and was coming to London in June to pick up the award. I got his address and fax number in Osaka through the Japanese Embassy, and wrote asking if he would like to visit the Garden after picking up his RIBA medal. Yes, came back the speedy answer, and we fixed the date of 4 and 5 June. This was falling into place very nicely, we thought. Even better, the Wirtzes were genuinely excited at the prospect of collaborating with Tadao Ando: they told us he was legendary, and thought very highly of his work.

Ando was coming in less than a month, yet we still knew very little about his architectural style. In retrospect, it sounds daft of us not to have done our homework before inviting an internationally famous architect to visit the site. But in our defence, it was difficult to find much in English about his work – he was an architect's architect, revered by those in the business, but hardly a household name. Anyway, the Duchess was always keen to remain open to others' creative input. She thought the way to achieve excellence was to explain her vision, then allow each creative individual to be inspired by the site. She also needed to meet potential designers to see whether they were in tune with her personally. The experiences with Dominic Cole and Anthony Archer-Wills had made us realize that the chemistry between the Duchess and the designers was as important as the integrity and beauty of their plans.

Tadao Ando arrived with more than a bit of mystique around him. First, he didn't speak English so came with a translator, as well as his wife. I'd been swotting up on Japanese etiquette: I knew that behaviour acceptable to us can be regarded as an insult to the Japanese, and didn't want to sour our relationship with a careless comment or discourtesy. On the advice of Brian Hardy, the structural engineer working on our behalf through Fairhurst & Partners in Newcastle, I had a crash course in Japanese social niceties with Anne Regglesworth, the wife of a director of Nissan UK, who had lived in Japan and who hosted events for visiting Nissan contractors when they came to the North-East. Over a traditional Japanese lunch, she told me never to sit your guests with their backs to the door in case an enemy enters and attacks them. (I mentally revised our seating plan: the Duchess always sat next to the door. I hoped she wouldn't mind moving to the other side of the table beside Tadao, to protect his back if not hers.) Secondly, we weren't to blow our noses, grin widely – though a genteel smile was acceptable – stand with our hands in our pockets, or stare. We had to present our business cards in a formal manner, and read his slowly and with deference, leaving it on the table in front of us rather than putting it away. We weren't to give him spicy, hot food, and definitely not English beef, as Japanese people were highly concerned about BSE: perhaps salmon and potatoes, I wrote in my diary, would fit the bill. Finally, we weren't to crowd him with our ideas or conversation: in Japan, silence is highly regarded as time for reflection, and long gaps in a conversation are to be welcomed, not filled with idle chatter.

When I first met Ando, my immediate thought was, 'Uh oh, this man is going to be very hard to read.' He was serene and impassive, and although it was immediately apparent he was more westernized than we'd expected, lunch in the Castle's private dining room was difficult. The Duchess, Jacques and Peter Wirtz, Rory and I engaged in stilted conversation with the Andos via the translator, with lots of stiff smiles and nodding. After lunch, the Duchess and I took Ando to the Garden, walking up to the top of the hill with the wonderful panorama of the Castle and the 'Capability' Brown landscape spread out below us. The Duchess said to the translator: 'Can you tell Mr Ando that we will leave him here for a couple of hours. But afterwards, would he like to come back to the Castle for a cup of tea and talk about what he's seen?' The translator turned to Ando, and there was a lot of fast chat in Japanese. He turned back to Jane and, with a small bow, said: 'Mr Ando has decided that he would like this commission. He cannot believe the opportunity of designing a contemporary pavilion with a medieval castle in the distance surrounded by "Capability" Brown parklands. He would like to go back and talk about it now.' We were astonished by Ando's instant decisiveness, but were also mentally punching the air in jubilation.

Back in the Castle, we all listened while Ando started talking about his ideas.

'Right,' he announced via his translator and without any preamble, 'I want to design this whole garden myself. In my opinion, there is no great garden designer alive today' – this sitting next to Jacques Wirtz – 'and no great garden has been built in the last hundred years. My way of thinking initially is that we might have a stainless steel cascade with a big building at the end, but I emphasize that I would like to design everything myself, including the garden.'

We sat, stunned. The insult to the Wirtzes was worse for being so casually delivered, but Ando seemed oblivious. A deep silence fell in the room as we assimilated the subtext of his words. This was tricky. The Duchess had already appointed the Wirtzes and now Ando, one of the most distinguished architects in the world, was trying to oust them from the project. I felt distressed on the Wirtzes' behalf, but they showed nothing but polite enthusiasm for Ando's input.

The afternoon ended in pleasantries, and Ando flew back to Japan. The Duchess and I were uncertain what to do next: having Ando on board was more than we'd hoped for, but the path ahead looked rocky. As Jane wrote to Lord Lambton:

> It is fantastic news. Tadao Ando has agreed to design the Conservatory but only if he can do the water works too as he did not like the Wirtzes' plans. He felt they were too classical and boring and announced that in front of them, which went down like a lead balloon.

Meanwhile, the meeting at the Castle had not gone unnoticed by the Press, who leapt on the story that RIBA Gold Award winner Tadao Ando had been appointed architect for The Alnwick Garden. It was only at this late stage that the Duchess finally got a chance to look at a monograph of Ando's architectural work. The buildings he created were beautiful, soaring, spiritual spaces made of minimalist concrete and glass, but her immediate thought was, 'My goodness, this is not what I'm after at all.' She didn't want a Pavilion that intimidated or overawed, and she didn't want the Garden to be seen as an exercise in architecture: she wanted somewhere that local people would feel comfortable, where children could wander around playing while their parents had a cup of tea. It had to be beautiful, but it

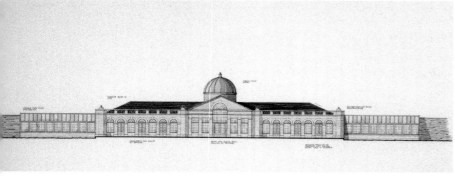

PAVILION – SOUTH ELEVATION

LEFT: top, The remains of the last conservatory terrace before work started, 1996; middle, Ian August's design for the Pavilion, 1996; bottom, Paul Robbrecht's design, the contested tower feature can be seen on the far left.

also had to be welcoming and accessible. Tadao Ando's minimalist concrete structures were places of quiet and contemplation, whereas the Duchess was interested in creating a buzzing, theatrical forum for the community. For the first time, she said: 'Ian, I've really done it now. How on earth do we get out of this one?' She soon found a clever way, through which everyone could save face.

A couple of weeks later, one of Ando's assistants arrived from Osaka to do some initial drawings. The Duchess said to her, 'Look, I've sourced some incredible mussel shells from the North-East – would you ask Mr Ando if he'd mind if I stuck these shells over the outside of his building? I love the idea that the mussels will reflect on sunny days, and mirror the water around, making a link between the coast, five miles away, and the Garden.' For good measure, she added: 'I'd also like to stick on some oyster shells, which I'm sure he'll agree will look wonderful shining by moonlight ...' Given the uncluttered lines and delicate purity of Ando's facades, she hoped this approach would make him think twice.

Sure enough, his assistant hotfooted it back to Japan and a fax arrived within hours. It confirmed that Ando had been rethinking the project. He felt that the distances between Alnwick and Osaka were just too great, and sent his deepest apologies, but thought it would be better for us to use another architect.

Ando's work is impressive and imaginative, but his style was not right for our purposes. It's lucky we all recognized that before it was too late. But his resignation meant we were back to square one.

When big ideas go awry retrenchment often follows, and our reflex reaction was to look closer to home. We asked local architects Faulkner Brown, who had a reputation for innovative, high-quality work, to get involved, but sadly the Wirtzes didn't like their plans. They felt the Pavilion looked like an airport terminal or train station, an empty meeting point rather than a dynamic interactive space. So the Duchess suggested that the Wirtzes find an architect they'd be happy working alongside. That way, we would have a design team that respected one another's work, which would benefit the overall concept of the Garden.

Peter Wirtz came back a while later with the name of Paul Robbrecht, a Belgian friend in his mid-forties. In October, Robbrecht came over to meet the Duchess and to see the Garden for the first time. He's a delightful man with an impressive professional portfolio: his company, Robbrecht en Daem, has designed an astonishing range of buildings, including a biotechnological farm in Astene, the Bacob Bank in Kerksken and, more recently, the Concert Hall in Bruges.

He produced a very beautiful design, which fulfilled most of the Duchess's criteria and was in complete harmony with the Wirtzes' plan for the Garden. The long, low-lying building gave a nod to classical antiquity, with elegant colonnades and open forum spaces within rectilinear boundaries. It had ample covered space where people could sit and watch the water, and keep dry if the weather were bad. The Duchess liked the design apart from one element: a tall, square Observation Tower, which she bluntly said seemed to her like a 'vast crematorium chimney'. Robbrecht and the Wirtzes disagreed: to them, the Tower was the essential vertical counterpoint that kept the Garden and Pavilion in balance. The eye would sweep from the height of the 'green festoon' of the topiary spiral, to the Tower and across to the summit of the hill in a neat, containing triangle. It brought an artistic integrity to the whole, and was not something on which they would compromise.

From the two-dimensional paper plans, it was hard to assess the impact of the Tower. The Duchess often says she can't 'read' a building until she has a three-dimensional representation of it in front of her, so we built a scale model of the Garden and Pavilion, which looked wonderful – apart from, the Duchess still thought, the Tower. I tried to persuade her that the building would look good once planting was in place, especially since Robbrecht had designed the roof as a garden, and its lush greenery would blend into the whole.

Months went by, and in order to get planning permission we submitted the Robbrecht Pavilion along with the Wirtzes' Garden to English Heritage and the local planning authorities for approval. They thought the Pavilion was too big, because it filled the space between the perimeter wall and the old Peach Houses, and they also found objections to the Tower. They wanted the Tower to be built of stone, with mullion windows, in keeping with vernacular architecture. Robbrecht thought this would result in a 'pastiche' – pronounced in a tone of voice that left no doubt he thought it the most pedestrian, unimaginative idea ever.

Still, the pressure was on to lose the Tower, not least because we were over budget and needed to save money. In January 1998, we'd estimated £10 million to £12 million for Phase 1 of the Garden and Pavilion. By March 1998, that figure had leapt to nearly £14 million, and we had to prune costs. One obvious saving – at least to the Duchess – was to get rid of the Tower. But despite these arguments, Peter Wirtz was still on Robbrecht's side. In October 1998, in one of his charming, lyrical letters to Duchess, he championed the Tower again:

> We just learn that Mr Gee [planning officer of Alnwick District Council] wishes again Paul [Robbrecht] to turn the Tower into a banal solid structure with windows. Although I appreciate enormously Mr Gee's enthusiastic support, I think here he misses the point, that [it] takes us to a higher artistic level. The appeal of Paul's mullion tower is just the salt on our hot potato! It's the major element that takes up the level of the entire pavilion to a piece of art, worthy of the environment, what we all need. Remember our old discussions at Ando's time: this has to be a prime piece of architecture that people will come to look at. Banality is not fitting in our picture, it cannot be compromised or we will all look weak ...Think about the lightness and elegance of the Pavilion, the soft light glowing of the Tower at night time with the water moving at its feet, it just makes you dream.

Despite Peter Wirtz's support, and under persuasion and much protest, Robbrecht revised his plans. A little while later, I sent a memo to the Duchess outlining progress: 'At very short notice over an annual Belgian holiday, Paul Robbrecht duly prepared a new drawing showing the Pavilion with a vernacular Tower.'

Suffice to say that, after many more revisions, Robbrecht's Pavilion was eventually passed by the planners. It wasn't due to be built until Phase 2 of the Garden, so we put it on the back burner and forgot, temporarily, all about it.

CHAPTER 5

THE LOVE OF A GOOD MAN

A couple of years ago, the Bishop of Winchester, the Right Reverend Michael Scott-Joynt, came to Alnwick with a group of other prelates. The Duchess and I gave a presentation and showed them round the Garden. Afterwards, the Duchess asked the Bishop what he'd thought about the Garden but instead of answering directly, he said he thought she must have a very strong marriage for her husband to have so much faith in her. The Duchess was surprised by his unexpected answer, and thought it was exceptional for a visitor to look deeper into the motives and emotions behind the story. 'There aren't many comments that surprise me after ten years doing the Garden,' she said later, still pleased by the compliment. 'He's the only man ever to have voiced such a thought and he's right. Without Ralph's confidence in me, the Garden wouldn't have been built.'

The Bishop immediately saw that building the Garden has been an enormous test of the strength of Jane and Ralph's trust and commitment, and their marriage had to be extraordinary to withstand the pressures. A project this big and ambitious demands enormous reserves of time, thinking, research and planning. It needs hands-on management and a watchdog – in this case the Duchess – to keep standards high at all times. But there's a human cost. Ralph suddenly found his wife eating, sleeping and drinking the Garden. It became obsessive: whenever the Duchess and I passed each other in the corridor we would stop and discuss it. When we attended the same Estates function we'd end up huddled together trying to sort out some problem, until the Duke would come over to us and quietly hiss, 'Would you two stop talking about the Garden!' The Garden had become Jane's passion, and that took its toll on everyone around.

The Duke jovially nicknamed Jane 'Shrub' in honour of her dedication to the Garden, but he was dismayed that at every social gathering, Estates meeting or

ABOVE: The Duke wearing the jumper Jane made for him.
Clearly all the Garden talk was getting too much for him!

general discussion, the topic of 'the Garden' inevitably dominated. He'd go out for a quiet morning's fishing and come back for lunch, and all his guests would want to talk about would be the Garden. It drove him to distraction and, in the end, Jane decided humour was the only way forward. She had a jumper made for him with the words 'Please don't ask me about the bloody garden' written on the back, which to his credit he wore to dinner with guests that night. There's a photograph of him wearing it in a loo at Burncastle Lodge, where Ralph and Jane live during the summer months when the Castle is open to visitors.

To some extent my wife, Ann, also felt upset as the Garden started to hijack my life. I worked six and often seven days a week at the beginning, with early starts and late finishes. Weekends were not my own, and Ann used to get annoyed at the disruption to our lives. In the end, she decided if you can't beat them, join them. She was a keen gardener and became devoted to the cause, joining as the first 'Friend' a few years later and running the Volunteer force that helped keep the Garden afloat for many years and is still going strong today.

The Duchess always says that when Ralph gave her this derelict twelve acres he thought she'd re-landscape a bit, plant a few flowers and bulbs, and that would be it. He himself is uninterested in horticulture – he likes wild, open, country spaces and can't understand how anybody could be bored enough to spend a whole day looking around a tamed garden landscape – and thus he couldn't anticipate how involving Jane's vision would become. Looking back, that was the only time he underestimated the Duchess, and ever since he has supported her completely and wholly, even at times against the wishes of his personal advisers and legal representatives. He knew that once Jane set her mind to doing something it would get done, and donated over £8 million to the Garden because of that belief. What faith, indeed. On her side, I think that knowing she could trust him to support her whatever unpalatable decisions she had to take made her a better fighter for the cause. All of which makes me think the Bishop of Winchester was right: without the Duke and Duchess's strong marriage and faith in each other, this Garden would never have been built.

BEGINNINGS

Jane and Ralph met when they were sixteen and eighteen respectively, and people –
especially journalists who come to interview the Duchess looking for a heart-
warming angle – often comment on how romantic and fairy-tale their story is. A
shy, ordinary Edinburgh lass meets a stranger at a party, falls in love, and marries
him. Then – lo and behold! – he ends up a duke, she ends up a duchess, and they
both live happily ever after. Of course that interpretation of events drives Jane mad.
She says hers is a marriage like any other, with all the joys and problems of raising
four children, and that becoming Duchess of Northumberland was an out-of-the-
blue surprise which occurred only because of the premature death of Ralph's
much-loved older brother; and that in any long partnership there's an element of
luck in how each person develops along the way. If the latter point is true, then she
and Ralph can count themselves extremely lucky: from where I'm standing, their
marriage seems happier than ever, and the demands of their public positions have
strengthened their family unit as time has gone by.

They met when Jane was still at school, and Ralph was in his gap year between
Eton and Oxford. It was at the twenty-first birthday party of Ralph's cousin
Richard, Earl of Dalkeith, in Boughton House in Northamptonshire. Both were
shy teenagers, hanging round in a room full of big blocks of ice for the drinks.
For want of anything else to say, they started talking about the ice. But as neither
of them was good at social chit-chat, and Ralph was preoccupied with his father's
recent operation for stomach cancer, he suggested they go home, and dropped
Jane where she was staying near by. Richard's younger brother, John, who knew
them both and could see they were smitten, organized a dinner party in the
Borders, where they soon met again. That was over thirty years ago, and they have
been together ever since.

Their courtship was unusual. At school, Jane had 'educational' Fridays, when
about twenty girls in the upper year would get a train to London to visit an art
gallery for the day. In the best St Trinian's tradition, they sent one girl off to the
gallery to collect whatever information they needed to fool the teachers, while

the rest met their boyfriends at Victoria Station. Most Fridays, Ralph would take Jane to see the Rocky Horror Show – he, along with almost every other teenager in 1976, was obsessed with it, and Jane is still word-perfect in every song. After the show, they'd go to a crêperie on the Kings Road where they drank too much cider, before Jane caught the train back to school. Goodness knows why the teachers never twigged ...

While Ralph was up at Oxford, Jane did a year at Hartwell House in nearby Aylesbury, a 'house of citizenship' her mother had also attended, and the couple soon decided they wanted to marry. Jane's parents had just been through a divorce, and the experience had made her look for stability and security. Their parents thought they were too young, and tried to persuade them against it, but eventually relented. Ralph and Jane were married in 1979 in Traquair church in the Borders. Jane was just twenty-one.

At the time, Ralph was working for the land agent Cluttons in Arundel, and studying land management, via a correspondence course, at Reading University. They moved into the house near Petworth where they had their first two children, Katie and George. After a few years they moved up to Northumberland, where their two younger children, Melissa and Max, were born. All through, the family has been the most important thing in her life, and even now Jane says her favourite evening is not a glamorous ball or supper party, but a baked potato with Ralph in front of the telly watching a DVD.

They thrive on their differences, Jane being quick and impulsive, while Ralph is quiet and thoughtful. His attitude to the Garden was always: get on with it if you must, but please don't talk to me about it all the time. He had considerable pressures of his own as Duke, and was very concerned with updating the Estates to meet the challenges of the twenty-first century. Still, for someone whose priority was to avoid getting involved, he put in a good few hours at unpalatable fundraising events and other schemes that the Duchess and I hatched up.

One of the two big problems we faced in the early days was how to raise the money to build the Garden (the other being getting planning permission). By 1997 we knew we needed at least £10 million, and probably more. Neither Jane nor I had any fundraising experience, but we had a blithe optimism that somebody, somewhere would hand us the cash – we just had to go out and find them. As it was to be a public project, the Duchess thought the money would come from a mixture of public funding – grants or other aid – and commercial sponsors. We started asking people for advice about how to raise such a large sum but encountered a reaction we hadn't anticipated: people laughed in our faces. They said nobody would fund the Garden: a duchess can't apply for public money, and why would anyone in the private sector give money to the Northumberlands, who were perceived to be quite rich enough to build the Garden themselves? This missed the point entirely – that the Garden was a public project for the people of the North-East, not a private garden for the Duchess – but it proved a very long, hard battle to change people's minds.

At the time, Jane's great friend Matt Ridley, the scientific journalist and author, was involved in a bid to the Millennium Commission Fund to open the International Centre for Life in Newcastle, a 'genetic theme park' with a science park and university research facility. Jane was deeply shocked when Matt told her bluntly that she stood absolutely no chance of getting a penny of public funding. They were in a Chinese restaurant at the time, picking each other's brains, when Jane said to him, 'You're asking the Millennium Commission Fund for £30 million – why can't I do the same thing for the Garden?' Matt retorted, 'But you're a Duchess, and you can't get public money for a private idea,' knowing that the Millennium Commission didn't allow individuals to apply for funds. Jane came back chastened: when somebody like Matt Ridley tells you your mission is impossible, you have to listen.

Except, of course, she didn't. She decided that all nay-sayers were talking out of their hats and she wouldn't allow their opinions to sway her. In the early years, the Duchess was quite timid and always joked she wouldn't say boo to a goose, never mind demand money from a hard-nosed businessman. But I thought she started showing true grit from the very beginning. In fact, she'd ask anyone and do anything to get the Garden built, and her energy and drive didn't falter even when we faced huge disappointments.

Our plans weren't advanced enough at this stage to meet the deadline for Millennium Commission funding, which forced us to look elsewhere. Tim Smit told us he'd knocked on hundreds of doors to get the sixty or so sponsors who finally contributed a total of £3 million to rebuild Heligan. 'For God's sake,' he'd warned, 'don't go down that route.' He thought it was time-consuming and involved too many people with too many opinions in the process. We could see his point, but Jane thought it worth exploring every option. We wrote proposals for a shared sponsorship scheme with twenty 'principal sponsors' who would put in over £100,000 each, with other 'donors' giving from £20,000 to £100,000 and 'patrons' from £1,000 each. There'd be good benefits for the sponsors, and the Garden would be divided up into various self-contained sections to attract individuals. Under the 'Benefits to Sponsors' section of this document, the Duchess scrawled 'The chance to go down in history with an exclusive project!' – and this was pretty much our thinking at the time. We were so excited by the Garden, we couldn't see why everyone else wouldn't be as well. We were convinced that national and local businesses would be falling over themselves to support us.

To woo them, we decided to use our best asset – the Duchess, whose enthusiasm could convince anyone. We calculated that dinner or a stay at the Castle with the Duke and Duchess was not something people would turn down lightly. She and I drew up a list of business grandees who had interests in the region, wealthy people who had sponsored other gardens, as well as those we thought might be able to offer advice and help. The list was nothing if not wide-ranging, from HRH Sheikh Dr Sultan Bin Mohammed Al-Qasimi, Supreme Ruler of the State of Sharjah in the United Arab Emirates, to J. Paul Getty; from Sir Chippendale Keswick, then chairman of Hambros Bank, to Barry Gilmour, of the locally based International Maritime Group.

To anyone with professional experience of fundraising, this might seem a haphazard way of approaching big sponsors, who are used to glossy brochures and detailed business plans. All we had was a pack prepared by Cravens, our PR and advertising company from Newcastle, containing Dominic Cole's layout of the Garden, an inspirational letter of support from HRH the Prince of Wales and Jane's mission statement. We hoped that a site visit and the Duchess's visionary talk would fire people up, and their imaginations would do the rest.

How badly we miscalculated! One of the most important early sponsors we targeted was James Sherwood, the head of Sea Containers Ltd, which owned the franchise of GNER, the railway that serviced the North-East, as well as the Orient-Express Group and the Cipriani Hotel in Venice. We were sure he could be persuaded of the business benefits of sponsoring the Garden. If we attracted even 100,000 visitors a year, many of them would come by train: case made! The Duchess wrote to him in February 1997, inviting him and his wife to stay, and just for good measure corralled her friends Lord Lambton and Hubert de Givenchy to entreat him on Alnwick's behalf. Later that week, Jane sent a letter to Lord Lambton that showed the pent-up enthusiasm she was feeling:

> I had a very funny train journey from London last week when I thought I was sitting opposite James Sherwood. He was being treated with great deference by the staff, was aged 70-ish, and had a slight American accent. Anyway, we started talking and I was beside myself with excitement and was working out how I could start talking about the Garden and £5 million when he asked me to 'join him' for supper. So off I trotted. As we sat down in the buffet car he said: 'I'm so sorry, I haven't introduced myself ... I'm Lord X, a Labour peer.' I could hardly eat, I was so disappointed ...'

In March, the real James Sherwood responded, and he and his wife visited the Castle in May. We had dinner together, and although Shirley Sherwood was very enthusiastic about the Garden, the Duchess got the impression her husband thought this might be a grand lady's whim. In a thank-you letter written a week later after a trip to the south of France with Sir Jocelyn Stevens, Dame Vivien Duffield and others, James Sherwood offered some good business advice, but also a couple of blunt and unpalatable home truths. One in particular remained with us:

Without wishing to appear indelicate, one view expressed by those in the south of France was that 'the Northumberlands are rich as Croesus and should just pay for the garden out of petty cash' because there are so many other projects which are more needy. It is quite possible that this sort of thinking will make it difficult for you to source public or foundation funds.

And instead of the £1 million or so we'd been hoping for, he offered to sponsor a fountain in the Garden. There were some rich words spoken, although in reality we were glad of any contribution. As Jane wrote back to James Sherwood:

Your letter was extremely interesting and, indeed, has been reread many times while I absorb the contents; it has certainly given me much to think about ... The Garden project, I am determined, will eventuate and I realise in these formative stages the importance of seeking and taking advice is vital. Therefore I am most grateful to you for your honest directives ...

One of the predicators for success is an unwillingness to be knocked off course by setbacks. We decided to look on this meeting as a learning opportunity: it made us realize that nothing was going to come easy, and that only hard work and time would persuade people the Garden was a worthwhile cause that would bring jobs and regeneration to the area. I think, with hindsight, that Jane and I were so enthusiastic about the project it blinkered us to people's real opinions. By meeting businessmen like James Sherwood we got a more realistic take. His gritty, no-nonsense response warned us that raising funds for what was still a concept was going to be a horribly tough battle.

We were aiming to start building work in June 1998, so had no time to waste. As a fundraising tool, we asked KPMG to draw up a business plan to estimate revenue and visitor numbers. To make it clear the Northumberland family was not benefiting financially, we decided to make the Garden a charity, part of the Lovaine Trust that also runs the garden at Syon House. Our charitable status came through in autumn 1997 and now we could, hand on heart, assure sponsors this was not 'the Duchess's garden', but a resource for the general public to enjoy.

Meanwhile, we had other irons in the sponsorship fire. Agent Rory Wilson had contacts at Northumbrian Water, and in August we gave a presentation to the directors, hoping to build a good relationship – we knew we'd need their support when the water features were being planned and built. They later gave us an enhanced water supply at a generous discount, in effect a kind of backdoor sponsorship. Northern Electric were also more than generous. We asked them to run a new supply of electricity on to the site, and although we had to pay for the line, they gave us the design works for this high-voltage underground electric supply – worth around £5,000 – free. Both these donations were enormously valuable, giving us the service supplies we needed on site before building started.

It was around this time that the Garden started getting lots of Press coverage. Wirtz International had been announced as designers and Tadao Ando was mooted as architect, which seemed to outrage or delight various newspapers depending on their politics and world view. The irony was that every time an article appeared, the public would send in many, many letters of support, often enclosing generous cheques to help towards building costs. One kind person even sent a copy of Francis Bacon's essays containing 'Of Gardens' for Jane to read. It was evident that the British public were on our side financially and emotionally; it was their business leaders who couldn't find the resources to help. The Duchess was overwhelmed by the public's generosity, and personally replied to every letter. Of course we sent the cheques back – at this stage the future was uncertain – but we were warmed by people's extraordinary empathy and support and realized that the idea of the Garden had become popular across the nation. Knowing ordinary people were rooting for us kept our spirits high.

Lots of influential people were lobbying on our behalf; others were giving help and advice, for example about professional fundraisers. From time to time, Jane invited potential sponsors for dinner in the private dining room with Ralph, Rory and myself. None of these dinners raised a penny in the short term, and my abiding memory is of the long-suffering Duke chatting gamely to his neighbours and doing his duty to Jane and the Garden. Then when coffee arrived, he'd quietly slip away.

For him, the fundraising dinners were a chore he did out of duty, and out of devotion to Jane.

Just how much devotion is obvious from a couple of letters in the files. Lord Lambton – who could be mischievous – wrote to Ralph after reading Casanova's memoirs to tell him that the great lover had insulted an earlier Duke of Northumberland who'd beaten him to the attentions of a certain lady:

> I would like you to answer two questions. One, have you ever tried to swap Jane for another man's wife? Two, do you carry with you [as the earlier Percy did] a miniature of your mother, framed with magnificent diamonds to give to rivals who will further your amours? I only ask because the French claim old families go on repeating themselves …

Ralph's reply was equally humorous but shows the depth of his feeling:

> Casanova must have been a moderate fellow not to appreciate the qualities of a Percy … Anyway, Percy had his way and a successful military career to follow – whether either were the result of his innate charm, or his fortune, is another matter. Sadly, the latter has now dwindled, and the former has probably gone as well, so I had better hang on to my precious things – besides, I haven't found another man's wife to compare with mine …

Meanwhile, I was taking a two-pronged approach to fundraising: establishing contact with local companies whom we considered potential sponsors, as well as sounding out what public funding we might be in line for. It was crucial with the latter to be able to prove that the garden would create jobs – the KPMG report estimated we'd bring twenty-five new full-time jobs – provide educational benefits and increase tourism to the North-East. In the next couple of years, I was to send applications to the KickStart Fund (run by Northumbrian Water), Northumberland Strategic Partnership, National Windpower, NWET (the Northumbrian Water Environmental Trust) and the ERDF (European Regional Development Fund).

LEFT: The Grand Cascade in full display. Forty water jets are used to fire the vertical curves and a further eighty are required to create the horizontal arcs.

By this stage we'd spent two years fundraising and were getting desperate – we still hadn't raised a penny. Perhaps Tim Smit was right: a single sponsor would be easier than 200 small ones. I remember having a giggle one morning with Jane, reading out her horoscope for 'Taurus, the year ahead'. 'It seems,' she read with what we both hoped was brilliant foresight, 'you are able at last to head in the direction you want to go ... your vision and pioneering spirit will bring the applause you deserve ... On no account think small.' Jane, who normally wouldn't give a jot for such superstition, was particularly taken with the last line.

So we decided to think big, and started looking for a private individual or multinational company willing to put in the whole £10 million. What benefits could we offer for such a meaty investment? Ralph and Jane came up with a deal to offer Alnwick Castle and the use of the state rooms to a team of eight guns and partners for two days a year over a period of ten years, two days' annual grouse shooting in the Lammermuirs at Burncastle, plus the use of the Castle or Syon House once a year for entertainment. The Garden project was getting so much media attention that we had fifteen television companies on our tail. Rosemary Forgan and Frances Berrigan of Bamboo Productions and Cicada Films were commissioned by the BBC to consider making a six-part series about Alnwick along the lines of their 'Lost World of Heligan' programmes – so we calculated that the sponsor could get national television publicity if they wanted. Then there was the licensing, merchandising and other events ... We hoped this might be a tempting deal and fired off letters to numbers of well-known business leaders.

The Duchess also approached many wealthy individuals. In the summer of 1997 she'd had dinner with J. Paul Getty and now sent him a begging letter stressing the local community and charitable aspects of the Garden. He was not impressed. Jane, tongue in cheek, scrawled a letter to Lord Lambton:

> Mr Getty wrote to me saying that he didn't consider us to be in severe need of charity – which as you know, of course is really not true ... More seriously, it is unfair that so many people miss the point of what we're trying to do.

In February 1998 the Duchess and I held a big fundraising dinner in the state dining room at Alnwick Castle, to which we invited thirty-six business people from the North-East. The dining room is one of the grandest rooms in the Castle, designed to impress with its red walls and roaring fire, a wonderful ceiling carved in Brunswick pine, and pictures of the Duke's ancestors on the walls. Patrick Garner, the household controller who'd worked with the Duke of Marlborough in the days when footmen still wore white stockings and breeches, always set the table exquisitely with the ducal gold plate. I sat next to Margaret Ash of Barbour, the country clothing company, a charming lady and a wonderful supporter of the North-East, who would later give a very generous donation to the Garden. But that evening, no firm support was forthcoming. It was frustrating, but it was a situation we were getting used to.

Analysing the problem, we decided it was one of perception. The Canalettos on the wall and the opulence of the place made our job harder. We could almost see people thinking: 'Why on earth are they asking us for money? What they want is peanuts compared to what this place is worth.' Perhaps, with the Duke at dinner, it was also hard for people to dissociate his business running the Castle as a tourist venue from the charitable aims of the Garden. It was clear that although being a duchess opened doors – everybody wanted to visit the Castle and find out about the project – they slammed shut in her face pretty fast afterwards.

But Jane remained resolute: there was no alternative but to keep fighting. We widened the net and approached more commercial sponsors. Ralph Carr-Ellison, a friend of Ralph and Jane's, started pursuing Prince Jean Nassau of Luxembourg, Vice President of International Business for the water company, Suez Lyonnaise des Eaux, which owned the water treatment facilities at Northumbrian Water. As the water features at Alnwick were going to be the most spectacular in Britain, the local water company would surely like to get involved in some kind of sponsorship. But in March 1998, after much wooing, the blow fell: 'I do very much regret,' Prince Jean charmingly wrote, 'that this captivating project will not have the support of our group, our sponsorship committee having decided to concentrate its actions of support towards disabled children.' You can't argue with a cause like that. The only consolation, someone jokingly pointed out, was that in his letter the Prince mistakenly elevated Jane to 'HH', or royal status.

In desperation, the Duchess asked Jeremy Palmer-Tomkinson, Senior International Manager of IMG, part of Mark McCormack's International Marketing Group, to approach US companies such as Ralph Lauren whose profile fitted well with that of the Castle. We were very keen to have IMG on board but the Duchess got the impression they didn't think the public or private sector would support what was seen as one posh lady's personal agenda.

EUROPEAN FUNDING

It was a low point, but then we had some excellent news: the ERDF application I'd put in had been approved. The European Regional Development Fund were prepared to give us £300,000, provided we started building work within the year 2000. Eureka! This was the boost we so badly needed. A press release was prepared:

> Alnwick has won the lion's share of the current round of European Regional Development Fund grant awards. Out of a total ERDF tourism budget of £1.49 million for all of Northumberland, the Alnwick Castle Garden project and the Aln Valley Railway have secured £800,000 between them, £300,000 for the Garden and £500,000 for the railway. Garden Project Director Ian August stated: 'This is a further vote of confidence for the proposed scheme, which is being considered by the Planning Authority at present ... and is a remarkable achievement and a major boost to Alnwick. It is a reflection on how others perceive the importance of these projects both to Alnwick and to the county as a whole.'

Meanwhile, behind the scenes, the Duke offered the Garden over £3.5 million from the Lovaine Trust charity to get things moving. Agent Rory Wilson and the Duke's lawyers cautioned him against this donation. Building a public garden was new territory for Northumberland Estates and they were worried. By the very nature of their position as guardians of the ducal Estates, the agent and lawyers had to play devil's advocate and warn the Duke that unless substantial private funding was forthcoming. The garden might never be built. In that event, the charitable donation would be wasted in professional fees and other preliminaries. Knowing Rory's opinion – his earlier comment that we were not in the business of running visitor attractions was still ringing in our ears – we were overwhelmed by the Duke's generosity. This was a great act of faith on his part. If the Garden failed and the money was lost, there would be many questions to answer in the full glare of the public domain.

Accepting the money was something of an about-turn for us. From the very beginning, Jane had been determined not to ask the Duke for funding, but we were stuck: we had neither funds nor planning permission. Ralph's generous offer kick-started the project and gave us the seed money to pay designers and other consultants, as well as underwriting the costs of Phase 1 – building the Cascade, Pergolas, Ornamental Garden and lower areas – which were estimated at £5 million. Perhaps the Duke was getting tired of the relentless fight for fundraising. I know he felt it was undignified.

Meanwhile, Jane was getting tired of being thought of as an annoyance to Ralph. As always, there was lots of Press coverage about the Garden, since the Duchess's policy was to give interviews to raise its profile and encourage fundraising. But putting your head above the parapet and courting publicity is frowned upon by many of Ralph's wider family and friends. At every gathering or dinner party, people would come up to Ralph, raise their eyebrows and say pointedly in front of Jane: 'Poor you, Ralph, I can see you've got your hands full.' To someone of the Duchess's spirited personality, this was like a red rag to a bull. If she cared what people thought before, she pretty soon learnt not to give a damn. If people assumed the Garden was about Ralph indulging his duchess in some eighteenth-century parody of real life, then so be it – she'd prove them wrong in the long run. Interestingly enough, this still happens and Jane sits through dinners with friends waiting for one of them to say, 'Poor you, Ralph.'

Despite Ralph's generous offer and the ERDF money, we were still looking for our knight on a white charger to fill the funding gap, and by this stage, were clutching at straws. Jane approached Michael Eisner of Disney via Michael York, the venerable British actor who'd been filming at Alnwick with Whoopi Goldberg. The proposed fountains – spectaculars with shooting fire, light and ice – had been designed by Wet Design, the company that created the waterworks at the Disney parks: a fact we hoped might make Eisner want to support us. 'The designs are absolutely breathtaking,' wrote the Duchess to Pat York, Michael's photographer wife, 'and many of the features have never been seen in the world. There are fountains with fire, wind fountains, ice fountains to name a few.' Eisner didn't bite. I remember Jane saying, 'I can understand why it's hard for businessmen to think I'm credible. I have no track record, I've never done anything similar in the past, and this is still just a concept. Why should they support me?'

Our proposed costs kept rising, by now to around £15 million, our self-imposed building date of June 1998 had long since passed, and we had only raised the promise of £300,000 ourselves. The Wirtzes were almost as frustrated by the fundraising delays as we were. Jacques Wirtz was used to working for wealthy, cash-rich private clients and we realized he was genuinely worried that the Garden would never be built. On one visit, he walked over to a small but priceless painting on the Castle wall and asked why the Duchess didn't just take that down and sell it. This horrified Jane, partly because these paintings were in trust for future generations, but also because it seemed to indicate Jacques Wirtz didn't understand that the Garden was a public not a private one, designed to benefit the community. Once the Wirtzes realized the Duchess couldn't simply square the finances this way, they started lobbying people such as billionaire George Soros and Edmond Safra, the banker and former owner of American Express, on our behalf.

LAUNCHING THE WEBSITE

IMG's specialist multi-media arm, TWI Interactive, designed a website for The Alnwick Garden, which was launched at our first major press event on 4 February

1999 in the guest hall at the Castle. We presented the Wirtzes' designs, the Robbrecht Pavilion and the new website to national and local Press. We were hoping to reach out to a new audience of potential sponsors, and set up a closed area on the website for them to access – an entirely novel approach to fundraising. As our press release explained:

> To fund the gardens, the Duchess and consultants IMG are using the World Wide Web in their search for a sponsor for the £15 million scheme. This is the first time the Web has been used to help search for a company that wishes to be linked to such a prestigious project.

These few sentences provoked an outcry: 'Wealthy aristocrats appeal on internet for cash to do up their back garden – Now that's rich, Duchess' screamed the *Daily Express*; 'Duchess makes Internet appeal for £15 million garden' said *The Times*; and 'Great idea – but why shouldn't the Percys pick up the tab?' was the London *Evening Standard*'s take. The *Standard* asked why the Percy family weren't paying for the whole Garden, lock, stock and barrel. The piece concluded: 'The Percy family, who already have Kew Gardens to look at when they wake up at Syon House, will get Britain's other best garden to admire over breakfast at Alnwick.'

It was untrue and unfair. This was a very sensitive time in terms of fundraising – we were still battling with our 'perception' problem and didn't want to put off potential sponsors with any controversy. So imagine the Duchess's horror when, the very next week, she idly turned on the radio and heard a news bulletin: 'The Duke and Duchess of Northumberland are disinheriting their son George in court.'

'You'll never guess where I was when I heard the news,' she said to me next day. 'In the bath! Can you believe it!' The phones didn't stop ringing as journalists called for quotes and the news was plastered across newspaper pages and television screens around the world.

It's true the Duke and Duchess had been in court, but to delay their elder son George's inheritance until he was twenty-five, not to disinherit him. By the terms of an old will, created by the 7TH Duke in 1918, George was in line to receive a £1 million inheritance plus an annual income of £250,000 when he turned eighteen. This was not a cash pay-out, as the Press seemed to think, but part of an estate that George had to learn to manage, and the sum had to be ploughed back to pay salaries and maintenance, not used as pocket money. Still, the Duke and Duchess felt it was wrong in today's world for someone to inherit so much money at the age of eighteen. They wanted George, then a quiet, hardworking fourteen-year-old, to finish his schooling, go to university, get a job and make his way in the real world.

So the Duke and Duchess, unbeknownst to George and his siblings, had gone to the High Court to change the ruling of the will. They had asked for a private hearing, but the judge overruled them. As it happened, a Reuters' journalist was in the Press gallery, and the story quickly spread through the media. It was terrible timing: a few weeks before, the Marquess of Bristol – who'd inherited a large sum of money at the age of twenty-one – had died of organ failure after a life of chronic drug abuse. Perhaps as a result, the Press coverage applauded the Duke and Duchess for their foresight in protecting George from temptation. Even Jamie Blandford, heir of the Duke of Marlborough and a renowned ex-addict who had also inherited young, called their actions 'sage' in the pages of one newspaper.

Perhaps because of the fallout from these two Press controversies, our fundraising activities completely lost impetus. We needed to rethink. The Duchess decided that as no money was forthcoming from Britain we should focus our energies on the US. She got hold of Tara Olson of the New York PR firm Goodman Media International, who'd been recommended by the Wirtzes. Although not a professional fundraiser, she helped us get in touch with potential sponsors in the States. I contacted Gil Truedsson of GTA USA, a marketing consultant who came recommended by the husband of a friend of the Duchess's and businessman Joel McCleary, who was married to the niece of billionaire philanthropist Paul Mellon. Mike Archer of TWI contacted JP Morgan, Northern Rock, American Express, EMI, the Prudential, Proctor & Gamble and Glaxo Wellcome. Jeremy Palmer-Tomkinson of IMG was following up leads with businessmen Albert Frère and Hubert

Guerrand-Hermes. Grotto designer Belinda Eade was friends with Isabella Blow, then fashion editor of the *Sunday Times*, who contacted me to suggest that Swarovski Crystal might be interested in sponsoring the grotto. Things were picking up again.

In early summer, Joel McCleary came to visit Alnwick and asked Jane what were the ten most common reasons given for not backing the project. Jane wrote back:

> No 1: the family's wealth, art collection, houses, land.
> No 2: ditto
> No 3: ditto
> No 4: ditto
> No 5: ditto
> No 6: ditto
> This is our major stumbling block. However, it is superficial in that when Ian and I give our talks and presentations (over 40 to date) no one has ever commented negatively. It is only the British Press who say: 'How will they get this sponsored and why should they?' I think people understand the merits of the project but can't forget what they've read: e.g. 'George's Inheritance Law Case' …

I prepared two paragraphs that I hoped would answer Joel McCleary's question for potential funders:

> *Given the family's wealth, why are we looking for outside financial support?*
> The full cost will not be met by sponsorship. The Percy family have already spent three-quarters of a million pounds developing the project to its present stage and have committed a further £3 million towards the development. In addition, the forty acres of private grounds adjoining Alnwick Castle will be opened on a permanent basis to the general public.
> The Gardens will be run by a charitable trust and the Percy family will not benefit financially from this investment. The income derived from opening to the public will be reinvested in the gardens for general upkeep and maintenance, together with continual development.

Meanwhile, the US advisers sent us their fee structures, which were based on monthly retainers plus expenses. We considered them exorbitant! Our other fundraisers had deferred a percentage payment on results, and we simply didn't have the money to pay up front, with no results guaranteed. Tara Olson dropped out and Gil Truedsson resubmitted his fees. It was frustrating because we'd spent months wooing these people, and it looked as if our efforts were in vain.

By chance we then had one piece of good fortune. I was sitting in an ERDF committee meeting with Mark Reynolds from KPMG, when it became apparent that some of the local schemes promised ERDF funding had not got off the starting blocks. There was a tranche of unused money in the pot that would go back to Europe unless we applied for it as additional funding. In July 1999 we were awarded an additional £150,000 by ERDF, on the proviso that we let the main building contract by 31 December – just five months away. This raised our ERDF funding to a total of £450,000 – not a fortune, but a very positive success. It didn't matter that IMG dropped out, deciding they no longer wanted to be involved in fundraising. I felt we were finally on our way.

Then an extraordinary thing happened: Northumberland Estates' agent Rory Wilson made a complete U-turn. Perhaps the ERDF money made him sit up and take notice, but he told the Duchess she ought to start building the Garden. But how? she said – we don't have the cash. Rory said, yes you do. The Duke's charity was prepared to release an additional donation of £5.8 million – making a total £8.8 million – to enable Phase 1 of the Garden to go ahead.

It was a very special moment. At any stage, the Duke could so easily have said: 'Look Jane, I appreciate what you're trying to do, but I am being advised by my agent, solicitors and trustees that we shouldn't be getting involved in this commitment.' But he didn't. Jane was hugely grateful, but had mixed feelings about agreeing to the donation. On the one hand, she recognized Ralph was doing an incredible thing. 'What a gesture from someone who isn't remotely interested in gardens,' she said to me in amazement. It was patently obvious our fundraising efforts had been a disaster: over three years, we'd raised less than half a million pounds ourselves. If Jane genuinely wanted the Garden built, she had no choice but to accept Ralph's offer.

On the other hand, she felt Northumberland Estates had always been lukewarm about the Garden, and agreeing to take the money would compromise her vision. 'The Estates never believed this thing was going to happen,' she said, 'and now here they are pushing me to build. How close am I going to have to be to them – are they going to try to run the project the way they want? If so, it's going to be impossible – we are coming from completely different angles.' She was wary that Rory wouldn't listen to her. She wondered what he hoped to get out of the project, and was convinced he was only interested in the 'bottom line'.

That evening, Jane thanked Ralph for his incredible generosity and his faith in giving her the money to start Phase I. Ralph replied that he was glad to help and knew that she would see the project through. 'But please,' he added, 'I don't want to hear about the Garden day and night.'

Though she was happy at the time, Ralph's comment came back to haunt her. She could understand his point of view: as Duke, he had many commitments of his own and didn't want his family time to be dominated by conversation of her big business project. He'd backed her with a huge act of faith, but from that moment on their boundaries were defined: Jane looked after the Garden, Ralph the Castle and Estates, and she shouldn't discuss the Garden with him. It made the project a very lonely one for the Duchess and meant that, in the years ahead, I was the only person she could confide in when times got tough.

CHAPTER 6

ONLY DEAD FISH SWIM WITH THE STREAM

The years from 1997 to 1999 weren't just characterized by our frantic hunt for sponsorship. It was also the time when we were trying to get planning permission for the new garden design. That is such a simple sentence to write, but behind those words is two years' worth of blood, sweat and tears, frustration and, at times, genuine distress. We locked horns not with the local planning authorities, but with English Heritage, the body legally authorized to be consulted in planning matters for listed buildings and registered gardens. Our dispute escalated into a frustrating and long-running battle that cost the Estates around £500,000 – half of it directly attributable to English Heritage's involvement.

We knew this was a listed environment and that English Heritage needed to be involved from the beginning. I went out of my way to consult them and the local planning office and pave the way towards consensus, for example by asking for advice to brief Tadao Ando on the Pavilion design. Early on I was given a quiet word of warning by Dr Rory O'Donnell, then English Heritage's Inspector of Historic Buildings for the North-East Region, not to go over his head on the planning application as this would be to our detriment. I always prefer to avoid conflict, and took this advice to heart. Still, many of English Heritage's requests and decisions seemed inconsistent to me, never mind to the Duchess, who had much less sympathy for their position.

In the early 1990s, before Ralph and Jane became Duke and Duchess, I'd been working with English Heritage concerning the Garden. Harry, the 11TH Duke, had plans to turn the lower area into a car park, picnic area and caravan park. By the nature of its layout, Alnwick is a traffic bottleneck beset by queues at Hotspur

Tower, which has only a one-lane road through the old wall. By allowing Castle visitors to park in the site, Harry hoped to lessen congestion in the town and improve facilities for visitors to the Castle. English Heritage North-East were prepared to go along with the car park scheme, and hardcore had been laid in preparation. So imagine my disbelief when English Heritage, on receipt of the Duchess's planning applications during November and December 1996, suddenly decided the walled Garden was a treasured piece of national heritage that had to be saved for the nation at all costs.

Since the 1980s, English Heritage had been running a 'Register of Parks and Gardens of Special Historic Interest in England'. Parts of Northumberland Estates including the 'Capability' Brown landscape north of the Castle across the Aln, were Grade I Registered, which means they were considered of international importance. The derelict walled Garden, however, was Grade II Registered, considered of 'special historic interest' by English Heritage. In practice, this means that local planning authorities have to consult English Heritage before approval for changes to the site can be given.

This is a good thing: most of us would want to prevent the owners of registered gardens and parks from destroying important landscapes. But the old walled Garden at Alnwick was not a glamorous Heligan-type restoration waiting to happen. It was a wilderness, and had been in decay since I started working for Northumberland Estates. In the 1930s, forty gardeners had worked the plot, growing vegetables and flowers for the Castle, but it had been in decline since the Second World War and was growing more dilapidated with every decade. In 1953, the eastern part of the Garden was converted into a nursery of larch and spruce trees. The two blocks of peach houses were almost entirely dismantled. For some reason, the stone in the peach houses had been laid bed-faced, so it weathered quickly, accelerating the deterioration. As Estates Clerk of the Works I further contributed to their destruction, because whenever a building on the Estates needed repair, we'd use the good stone from the peach houses. By the 1990s there was none of the Garden's previous grandeur to be seen.

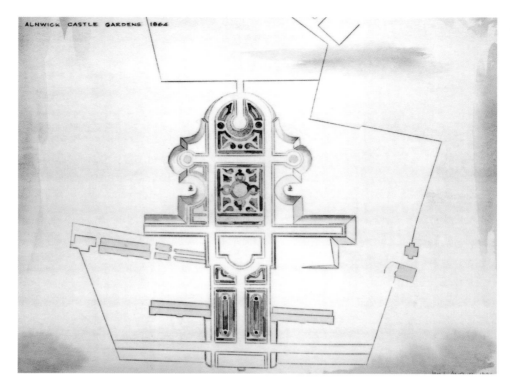

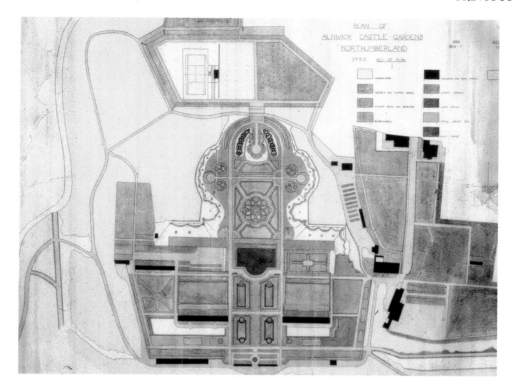

TOP RIGHT: A plan of the garden dating from 1864 and showing its Italianate features. The 4th Duke, Algernon the Good, brought his love of Renaissance Italy back to Northumberland and commissioned a team to redesign the garden with parterres, walkways and a sunken area in the shape of a Maltese cross.

BOTTOM RIGHT: The garden c. 1900. Here again we see the Italianate features. The Chestnut tree in the centre is still part of the modern-day garden.

TOP: A plan produced by Alec Smith in 1932.

THE HISTORY OF A GARDEN

On one point English Heritage was right: this was a terrible comedown from the Garden's heyday. In the eighteenth and nineteenth centuries, Alnwick Garden was famed for its innovative design, hothouses and exotic produce, a result of the horticultural enthusiasm of four successive Dukes of Northumberland. The Garden was created by Sir Hugh Smithson of Stanwick in Yorkshire, who married the heiress Elizabeth Seymour. In 1750, the couple became Earl and Countess of Northumberland, made the 'Gothick' Castle habitable and started transforming the landscape around it. The couple, who became the first Duke and Duchess of Northumberland in 1766, commissioned 'Capability' Brown to remodel the landscape, aided by the Duke's head gardener, Thomas Call. Meanwhile, across the river but near to the Castle, a piece of land called Barneyside was laid out as a kitchen garden full of walkways, flowering shrubs, espaliered fruit trees and hothouses stocked with melons, pineapples and grapes. The garden was so renowned by the time of the 1st Duke's death that John Busch, gardener and designer for Catherine the Great at the imperial palace of Tsarskoe Selo near St Petersburg, came to visit.

The 2nd and 3rd Dukes consolidated the kitchen garden, buying adjacent plots of land and building new walls and grand hothouses, vineries and mushroom houses that used the latest in horticultural design and technology. In 1825, six pineapples from the Garden were shipped to Paris to grace the table of the 3rd Duke at the coronation of the French King Charles X. The 3rd Duchess, Charlotte Florentia, was a keen painter and plantswoman, who built fashionable rockeries and stocked the garden with exotic flowers. So keen were the people of Northumberland to see the famous plants and produce that in 1842 the garden was opened one day a week for the local gentry.

With the arrival of the 4th Duke, Algernon the Good, in 1847, both the Garden and the Castle were radically altered. He had travelled the world and become fascinated by the culture of Renaissance Italy. He brought in English architect Anthony Salvin to remodel and consolidate the Castle buildings, and Roman designer Luigi Canina to recreate the interiors in Renaissance style. In the Garden, meanwhile, the Duke bought land along the back of Bondgate Within to straighten out the irregular perimeter, and purchased a plot alongside Denwick Lane, called Gooseknows Field, that doubled the Garden's size. His team redesigned the space as a formal Italian-inspired garden with parterres, ponds, walkways and a sunken area in the shape of a Maltese cross, to complement the Italianate restoration of the Castle. Algernon Percy was also a generous and enlightened man, and opened the Garden to the general public every Thursday. This tradition of public opening was one that the 12TH Duchess was delighted to re-establish in the twenty-first century.

By 1996, Alnwick Garden was what English Heritage called a 'multi-phased site'. This meant there was no one original garden design: multiple additions and alterations had been made over the generations as fashions and interests changed. 'With such sites' – and I quote from English Heritage's *Register of Parks and Gardens: An Introduction* of the late 1990s – 'it is the sum of the development as seen in the landscape today which is considered.' In Alnwick Garden in 1997 there was, in my opinion, very little in the landscape left to be considered. It still had its beautiful bones, which Wirtz International elegantly incorporated into their design, but few other structures remained.

Still, that didn't stop battle ensuing. We first got an inkling that planning permission was going to be one long headache in February 1997, when we woke up to headline news in the local press: 'Castle Garden restoration plan hits opposition'. The Garden History Society, one of seventeen pressure groups the local council planning office was legally obliged to consult, had asked the Government Office for the North-East (GONE) to appeal to John Gummer, the Secretary of State for the Environment, to block our car parking and access application. It seemed an unduly aggressive move by the Society, whose conservation officer, David Lambert, called our plans 'profoundly damaging'. The Society and English Heritage said the proposed car park for 208 cars and six coaches was too big, and would ruin the views from the 'Capability' Brown

LEFT: The Capability Brown landscape forms a backdrop to bulldozers excavating natural sand and gravel deposits. These deposits were used to aid drainage in the main Garden.

BELOW: The original car park, landscaped with beech topiary hedging and interplanted with oak trees. This space proved too small and is now used for disabled parking and coach drop off/pick up point.

landscape: they wanted us to cut it back by 126 spaces. Their preferred option was to site a smaller car park inside the walled garden – where it would be visible only to the Castle's inhabitants and visitors. They also considered, quite rightly as it turned out, that the car park would not be big enough for our needs and that on busy days we would spill over on to the eighteenth-century landscape.

The district councillors, who had been minded to grant the application, were furious, not just at the high-handed way the Garden History Society had gone over their heads to John Gummer, but also at the lateness of their intervention – well past the consultation date. In the *Northumberland Gazette*, Councillor Hugh Philipson was reported as saying: 'This [Garden] will be one of the best things to happen to the district and to the North of England. If we turn this down, we want our brains examined!' But the local council had no alternative: Gummer postponed the decision.

The Duchess, meanwhile, wrote to Lord Lambton with heavy irony: 'The Garden History Society would prefer me to put the car park *in* the garden (seriously) which I suppose would mean that I didn't need quite as much money because half the garden could become a great car park!'

These overwrought reactions and responses came to characterize our relations with English Heritage and the Garden History Society. I always felt that below the surface we were fighting them, and I was never quite sure why. Perhaps our approaches were just too different. The Duchess and I had a philosophy, 'Only dead fish swim with the stream', which summed up our approach to the Garden and is now inscribed on a boulder at the entrance to the Labyrinth. It meant simply that we refused to go down the easy, conventional route and instead wanted to question the norm and look for new ways to produce an innovative design, while still respecting the historic elements within it. That was radical enough to put us at loggerheads with those who wanted a 'restoration' of the old garden.

Our original planning application for the Garden and Pavilion used Dominic Cole of Land Use Consultants' design and my Queen Anne Pavilion. Once the Duchess was committed to using the Wirtzes, we decided to withdraw these applications and wait until we were ready to resubmit their new Garden plans. Still, the car park application was keeping us busy. Anthea Taigel, assistant conservation officer of the Garden History Society, again objected to the site and the size of the car park. But more importantly, her letter of 15 September also raised a new spectre that came to haunt us: the name of William Andrews Nesfield.

ENGLISH HERITAGE SEE THE PLANS

William Nesfield was a nineteenth-century painter, soldier and garden designer who worked on over 200 gardens in England including the Royal Botanic Gardens at Kew and Regent's Park. His style was to create complex parterres and vistas that harked back to an earlier age. Along with Joseph Paxton, he was one of the century's gardening greats, and if he had a hand in the 4TH Duke's Italianate garden, English Heritage and the Garden History Society might indeed have legitimate reason to halt our development. The indication from Northumberland Estates' archivist, Dr Colin Shrimpton, was that there was no proof Nesfield had been involved in the mid-nineteenth-century redesign. In the archives, Dr Shrimpton found an unsigned drawing in Nesfield's hand, dated 1860 and with his address on it, but few of Nesfield's proposals seem to have been implemented. However, Anthea Taigel, after looking at an 1851 Ordnance Survey map, suggested that an old drive to the north of the walled garden had been moved between 1851 and 1867 and that these dates were of relevance because:

> It was within this period that William Andrews Nesfield is known to have been involved on the site. The further information, that Nesfield's surviving plan for the walled garden was only one of a series, suggests that he may also have introduced the concept of the open sweep of lawn to either side of the drive ... We feel the proposal both to contour the ground and to impose tree planting close to the line of the drive is in direct conflict with design intention.

At this stage, nothing more was made of the Nesfield connection. Dominic Cole made substantial changes to the car park design to meet the Garden History

Society's objections and by the fourth resubmission, in November 1997, the car park accommodated 254 cars and six coaches – a plus for Alnwick District Council, which hoped this measure would relieve traffic congestion in the town. The application was passed on 4 February 1998 but it was an empty victory for us. There were so many conditions attached concerning specific landscaping details, a woodland management plan and the phasing of the works that we knew we'd be designing amendments and fighting further objections for a good while yet.

The Wirtzes' design was by now complete, and as a pre-emptive strike before applying for planning permission I went to London in January 1998 to show the plans to English Heritage. My hope was that we could save time by discussing and negotiating details before submitting the application and also get English Heritage on our side. When I arrived at their Savile Row offices, there was no offer of tea, coffee or even a glass of water, despite my long journey on the train. Lorna McRobie, English Heritage's Director of Gardens and Landscapes, greeted me by saying she knew I'd come from Northumberland, that was hunting country, wasn't it, and she wanted me to know that she was completely against blood sports of any kind. I was taken aback: why did she feel the need to tell me this on our first meeting? Perhaps she assumed the Duke and Duchess hunted – in fact, they don't – but I immediately sensed antagonism from her. It was one of those defining moments, as if she was setting out a rule saying 'don't expect much from me because I don't agree with you on any matter of principle'.

Dr Rory O'Donnell joined us and I presented the Wirtzes' designs, but neither of them showed much interest: they wanted to talk about how the historic details would be incorporated into the new Garden. They asked for an archaeological study and historic report to be carried out – which we were happy to do, and would have done for the Estates archives. They said they would prefer the derelict peach houses to be retained, and wanted the lily pond to be incorporated into the new Cascade. They also pointed out that the Wirtzes' plan did not exactly follow the contours of the banksides along the Cascade. I realized then that they were looking for a rebuilding of the historic garden. They weren't interested in innovation: they wanted restoration. A week or so later, Lorna McRobie wrote thanking me for showing her the proposals and saying she was concerned the development might destroy the fabric of an important registered garden. 'Relict Nesfield designs of this grandeur are rare,' she wrote, ' and every attempt should be made to conserve the surviving historic features and to incorporate them in the new design.'

I replied saying how disappointed I was at her views, arguing in favour of removing the peach houses and lily pond (which leaked terribly anyway) in order to build the bold new Cascade. I also tried to debunk the Nesfield myth, pointing out that our archivist, Dr Colin Shrimpton, said there was no evidence that the Garden as finally laid out was to Nesfield's design. Our records showed Nesfield visited Alnwick at the time that architect Anthony Salvin – Nesfield's brother-in-law – worked on the Castle renovation, and it is recorded that he worked at the Duke's home at Stanwick in Yorkshire. But the 1860 Nesfield plan I'd left with Lorna showed a design that was never implemented. Moreover, I explained, none of the parterre designs from the 1864 restoration now exist and, in any case, the 1932 plans showed these as having been substantially ploughed over and sown to trees as a seed orchard. I continued:

> It is certainly our intention to demonstrate how conservation and innovation can be combined where appropriate. But in a Garden which has run into such disrepair over a very long period of time, here we have a wonderful opportunity to create a world-class garden for the twenty-first century ... If similar decisions had not been made in the past, we would not now enjoy some of the wonderful gardens that exist in this country. There must surely come a time when change is the answer and I believe that situation is with us at Alnwick now.

Despite the deadlock, we put in a new planning application for the Garden and Pavilion on 17 March 1998. Two days later, Lorna McRobie and Rory O'Donnell visited Alnwick to see the site. Lorna wrote thanking me for our hospitality, then added that she was very impressed with the 'grand survival' of the Nesfield design but 'rather saddened' that the designers of the proposed new garden 'had not taken the opportunity to use creatively and positively these remarkable features …'.

I felt as if I was hitting my head against a bureaucratic brick wall. How many times did I have to explain that this was not a Nesfield garden? On the principle that a softly, softly approach might defuse the situation, I asked Lorna McRobie exactly what 'relicts' she considered to be from the Nesfield garden and what priority she attached to them. Her response was vague, but stated that she had found even more evidence of Nesfield's involvement, including the 1860 OS plans and an appendix in a 1997 Northumberland Estates' analysis of the walled garden. 'The Estates acknowledges that on the basis of archival evidence, these gardens can be classed as a Nesfield garden. Their surviving fabric is therefore without doubt of national importance,' she wrote, with what I thought was a hint of triumphalism. (In fact, our Estates' report was in error, as Colin Shrimpton later confirmed.) She concluded that once an archaeological survey of the site was carried out, 'We [English Heritage] would be pleased to help you in assessing how these important historic features could be incorporated in to a modern design worthy of the twenty-first century.'

You can imagine the Duchess's response to this offer: it was rich and fluent, and certainly can't be printed in these pages. She knew that if English Heritage's advisers and designers got their hands on the project, all her hopes for the Garden would be dashed.

I compiled an update of the planning situation for her, outlining all the objections, major and minor, from all interested parties. The Victorian Society had also jumped on the Nesfield bandwagon and objected to removing the Nesfield features (even though neither we nor they had any idea what they were). They also considered that the 'themed' gardens designed by the Wirtzes were not appropriate to the site. 'Whereas its previous use as a car park was?' scrawled Jane viciously in the margin. She was getting very frustrated. She wanted to respond more feistily because she thought English Heritage were treating us very badly, but she had to remain discreet. As she wrote to Lord Lambton:

We still haven't had this passed by English Heritage. I'm told not to say anything to the newspapers on this subject or I would become a target myself. I think that's blackmail. A lady from The Times asked me what I'd do with the Garden if I didn't get planning consent and I said that I'd turn it into a wonderful car park for the people of Alnwick. I told her it had been a car park when we arrived here and that English Heritage didn't seem to mind that. So wouldn't it be lovely to park 500 cars within the walls of an eighteenth-century garden? She didn't put that bit in the article.

In April and May, Tyne and Wear Museums archaeology department carried out the archaeological survey; Robin Kent, a local architectural and historic buildings specialist, the historic buildings survey; and Fiona Green an evaluation of the historic development of the walled garden. We hoped the results of these surveys would give English Heritage and the Garden History Society all the information about the historic gardens they required to facilitate planning permission.

But we were still left with one central problem: W. A. Nesfield. However much we protested that this was not a Nesfield garden, everyone seemed to believe it was. What could we do to change their opinion? Robin Kent suggested asking Shirley Evans, acknowledged as Britain's leading Nesfield expert, to assess the site and give her opinion on whether this was a Nesfield design. She had visited all 250 Nesfield gardens in Britain, and written a book on him: surely she would be able to tell the hand of the master? I thought this was a great idea and commissioned her to do a report that I hoped would sort out the dispute once and for all.

We were thrilled when she presented her findings. She had looked at Nesfield's 1860 plan, the 1864 plan and a 1902 newspaper photograph and article about the garden. She confirmed that the 1864 plan was not by Nesfield, who was then seventy years old, but was probably drawn up by his son, Arthur Markham Nesfield. She looked at the 1902 photograph and found the planting, use of architectural features and earthwork mounds to be out of sympathy with Nesfield's other designs and philosophy. She concluded:

Even if he did have a hand in the Conservatory Garden, whatever he did is long gone and altered out of all recognition … My conclusion, therefore, is that the 1864 plan was drawn up, incorporating features from William Nesfield's original 1860 plan, and put into place at some time, with variations, possibly by somebody employed on the Estate. It would be very risky indeed to assume that William Nesfield was responsible for the garden shown in the 1902 article … the hand of the Master is missing.

That, we thought, was surely the end of that.

MODIFICATION AND DELAY

Of course, the Nesfield saga was not English Heritage's only concern. We and Fairhurst, our planning and structural engineers, were working hard to address all their objections, including modifying the design of Paul Robbrecht's Tower. Colin Barnes of Fairhurst and his team were doing sterling work, amending the drawings and providing all the new elevations, revised layouts and extra overlays that English Heritage required. Once the archaeological and historical surveys were in, we hoped we'd be able to move fast towards a successful conclusion. I commissioned a local metal detector expert, Peter Proctor-Cannon, to go over the site. He found sixty artefacts, including a large nineteenth-century brass tap, copper coins from the reign of George II onwards, gunshot pellets, and many lead fruit-tree tags hand-stamped with the species and date of planting. He also found a small silver whistle, a seventeenth-century pewter spoon handle and a Victorian silver teddy bear, probably from a rattle. The Garden had obviously been used as a play area by children of previous Dukes of Northumberland.

All this time and work proved very expensive. In fact, the Duchess's major worry was not about getting planning permission – she didn't for a moment dream the Garden wouldn't happen – but about not having the cash to pay for the time-consuming and expensive changes and modifications English Heritage required. As she wrote to Tim Smit:

LEFT: The Ornamental Garden in early summer. The purple delphiniums create a stunning visual effect.

English Heritage are being difficult. They have cost us £200,000 so far, according to Rory Wilson. They refuse everything we put in front of them. I have decided if they don't pass this, I'm going to sell our designs to America. That way, at least the Wirtzes will see their plan come to fruition ... a great garden will be built in the States and we can recoup our losses.

Meanwhile, the Garden History Society was still complaining about the car park application. They didn't like the siting of the coach spaces and thought there was no 'historical precedent for beech hedging ... and together with the proposed lines of *Gleditsia*, [this] will present all the appearance of a municipal car park ...'. These kinds of petty complaints seemed mere stalling tactics to me by now. Whether or not their aim was to waste time and make life difficult for us, that was certainly the effect of their interventions, and I was getting heartily sick of it. Sometimes, despite their historical knowledge, they were downright wrong. We found out that the beech planting they protested about had been used by 'Capability' Brown himself, which debunked that objection. It was around now that I read a joke in the local press, which made me laugh out loud: 'Why does it take four preservationists to change a light bulb? One to insert the new bulb, another to record the event and two more to lament the old bulb's passing.' My feelings entirely.

In August 1998 we got the final go-ahead for the car park – twenty-one months after we'd first applied. The Garden History Society were still complaining, of course, but the local planning officers overrode their objections. I remember going to the council meeting at which approval was finally given. I was sitting in the public gallery, the only person there, listening to Colin Barnes's short presentation in support of our plans. There were a couple of comments from the floor, then the application was unanimously approved. The whole procedure took five minutes, and walking back to the Castle through the streets of Alnwick, I was aware of a strange feeling of anti-climax. The first fight had been won. It had taken almost two years of discussion, argument, negotiation and compromise, but we had finally got the car park application through.

We'd been immensely buoyed by the support of many local groups who'd written to cheer us on, including the District Council, Alnwick Civic Society, the Northumberland and Newcastle Society, and the North-East Civic Trust. They were on our side, but that didn't seem to make any difference to our progress: already it had been six months – the agreed time frame for a decision – since we put in the new Garden and Pavilion application, and we hadn't heard a whisper. What on earth, Colin Barnes wrote to ask the District Council, was going on?

Then came the bad news: simultaneous letters arrived from English Heritage, after their Advisory Committee meeting, and the Garden History Society, putting their objections to the Garden and Pavilion application in the strongest possible terms. Although English Heritage remained 'enthusiastic in [their] support for the opportunity and concept of a new and innovative garden ...', they explained that the Wirtzes' design failed to respect and incorporate the historic features of the registered garden. This meant our plans were, they said, 'therefore unacceptable to English Heritage as they are excessively and in our opinion unnecessarily damaging and destructive to the surviving historic fabric...'.

Nor, as we had hoped, had the Nesfield saga been put to bed by Shirley Evans's definitive report. To English Heritage, her words confirmed that Nesfield had had an influence on the Garden, however oblique, and that seemed to be evidence enough for them to demand more investigations. They suggested again commissioning another consultant – someone like designer Arabella Lennox-Boyd, who'd been an adviser to English Heritage's Historic Parks and Gardens Committee since October 1993 and was restoring a Nesfield parterre at Eaton Hall – to 'adapt the exciting new Wirtz concepts into a reality which is achievable on the ground within the historic restraints necessary ...'. In other words, we could build a garden provided English Heritage oversaw the design. This, of course, was completely unacceptable to the Duchess.

The letter left us reeling in disbelief at English Heritage's inconsistency. At the beginning they'd been happy for us to tarmac over the Garden and use it as a car park. Now they'd upped the ante and it had somehow become 'a development within a Grade I Registered garden of outstanding national importance'. To me, the supreme irony was that the 'surviving fabric' of the 1864 garden that English Heritage were so keen to preserve was buried underground where no living person had ever seen it.

Of course, the local planning authority couldn't grant approval in defiance of such strongly worded opposition. The Duchess was furious and wanted to go to appeal, but Colin Barnes of Fairhurst, Paul Gee, the planning officer of the District Council, and Lorna McRobie agreed it would provoke a public inquiry, which would not be in anyone's interests. I knew we had to keep the paths of communication open with English Heritage but we needed some leverage. Colin and I put our heads together and suggested approaching Sir Jocelyn Stevens, Chairman of English Heritage, and Lady Mollie Salisbury, Ralph's godmother, who had created the wonderful gardens at Hatfield House and who was, more importantly, a long-standing and influential member of the Garden History Society. She threatened to resign unless the Garden History Society modified its position. Meanwhile, Jane wrote a long and thoughtful letter to Jocelyn Stevens, explaining her aims and outlining her frustration at English Heritage's approach. But with Dr Rory O'Donnell's earlier warning ringing in her ears, she scrawled 'Too dangerous' across the page and instead sent him a brief and polite request to visit Alnwick and see for himself what all the fuss was about.

I thought a measured response might draw the sting from English Heritage's tail. I contacted Lorna McRobie, inviting her to Alnwick on Friday 9 October 1998 so we could talk through her objections to the plan well ahead of the next District Council planning meeting. Meanwhile, Jane's tentative approach to Jocelyn Stevens bore fruit: Richard Berry, English Heritage's Director of Regions, wrote offering his help in finding a way through the dispute. He was to join Lorna McRobie and Peter Bromley, English Heritage's regional director for the North-East, at the meeting with Jacques and Peter Wirtz, Paul Robbrecht, the Duchess, Agent Rory Wilson, Colin Barnes, planning officer Paul Gee and myself at Alnwick on 9 October so that we could thrash out the outstanding planning issues.

It was during the tense run-up to this meeting that the Duchess was invited to judge a function hosted by *Country Life* magazine in London. Lady Arabella Lennox-Boyd was also a guest, and at the end of the event the Duchess and she started discussing the plans for The Alnwick Garden. The two had never met before, though at an earlier stage Arabella Lennox-Boyd had contacted the Duchess about designing the Garden herself – an offer the Duchess refused as she already had the Wirtzes in mind. Tempers were short and the discussion grew heated – in fact the Duchess told me it turned into a 'row' – in which it became apparent that Lady Arabella thought we were wilfully destroying a Nesfield garden. She said she was unaware of Shirley Evans's report debunking the Nesfield connection. To me it was astonishing that a key adviser to English Heritage's Historic Parks and Gardens Committee, someone who had influence over the planning decision, had apparently not been shown the Evans's report and thus could still believe it was a Nesfield design. I complained vociferously to Dr Rory O'Donnell.

I also wondered if the Duchess and Arabella Lennox-Boyd's mutual sensitivity at the *Country Life* event might have been triggered by another ongoing dispute, this time with the Wirtzes. In May 1998, Lady Arabella had won a gold medal and the award for best overall garden at Chelsea Flower Show for 'A Contemporary Water Garden', sponsored by the *Evening Standard* newspaper. The garden was beautiful: two placid rectangular ponds on different levels were linked by three long, shallow steps, with elegant hard and soft landscaping details. But many people at Chelsea thought the garden was very similar to one designed by Jacques Wirtz in 1976 at Hasselt in Belgium and photographed in various garden design books. Jacques Wirtz was sent a picture of the garden and was quoted as saying he thought it a 'blatant copy'. He wrote to the Royal Horticultural Society asking them to withdraw the gold medal because of the alleged plagiarism. His request was refused, so he then wrote to Arabella Lennox-Boyd personally, claiming she had infringed his intellectual property rights and threatening to sue her for breach of copyright under the Berne Convention. Her solicitors replied denying the allegations and pointing out that the garden had since been dismantled.

The *Sunday Telegraph* picked up the story – 'Top garden designer is accused of stealing rival's classic layout' – and ran a huge exposé the weekend before English Heritage were due to make their decision about planning for The Alnwick Garden. It made gripping reading. Although we felt sure that Arabella Lennox-Boyd's professionalism as a designer and adviser would enable her to rise above her dispute with Jacques Wirtz when asked to comment to English Heritage's Parks and Gardens Committee about The Alnwick Garden, we couldn't help but have a nagging worry about it.

Meanwhile, we were working hard to make sure everything would run smoothly at the 9 October meeting. Frances Berrigan of Cicada Films and Rosemary Forgan of Bamboo Productions were filming the development of the Garden as a joint production for the BBC. One day they rang and the Duchess said: 'Look, you can't do much filming until we get planning permission. Why don't you contact the people we're dealing with at English Heritage, and ask them to be filmed discussing the matter.' On 2 October 1998, Rosemary Forgan wrote to English Heritage suggesting filming the Lorna McRobie meeting at Alnwick Castle a week later. The Duchess's hope was that, if they were put on camera, English Heritage would realize their procedures and objections were under public scrutiny, and might be more circumspect towards the Garden. This tactic might even have worked, as we later got a message from Frances saying Lorna McRobie from English Heritage definitely did not want to be filmed.

GETTING EVERYONE TO THE TABLE

The meeting took place at 2.00 p.m. in the Castle tea room after a hearty lunch. My immediate impression was that Lorna McRobie thought the heavy guns of English Heritage – Richard Berry and Peter Bromley – were behind her all the way, and that together they would dictate events. But perhaps surprisingly, things went in our favour. The Duke joined us, and the Wirtzes and Robbrecht gave short presentations. Then Lorna McRobie explained the rationale and approach of English Heritage, emphasizing that what was important was what was buried beneath the ground, and that the earth banks and the basin at the foot of the slope had to be retained.

She explained that the Garden had suddenly been Registered Grade I because it reflected an important phase of the architect Anthony Salvin's development. Then she asked us, with what I thought was some irritation, why we weren't prepared to leave the 4TH Duke's garden undisturbed. Pointing a finger at the Duchess and Jacques Wirtz, she said they were going to be responsible for the destruction of one of the most important gardens in England. The Duchess said, 'Come on, Lorna, look at what we're dealing with. It's derelict, a quarter of it is down to hardcore, there are cars parked all over it.' But Lorna said there was as much left underground as there had been at Heligan. 'But it's all been ploughed up,' the Duchess retorted. 'There are Christmas trees planted in rows on top of it.'

It was at that point that Jacques Wirtz, perhaps unable to contain himself any longer, said the reason we weren't restoring the 4th Duke's garden was because it wasn't good enough – it was 'bourgeois' in concept and design. Lorna looked at him in horror and said something like, 'So you think you can do better?' And the Duchess replied: 'Absolutely, we can do better. We're creating a new garden with the best design talent in the world, and with an improved understanding of technology and design. It would be a sad state of affairs if we couldn't do better.'

Perhaps that sounded arrogant to English Heritage, but the Duchess couldn't see the logic in dismissing a first-class, international team's attempt to create something new and great in favour of a third-rate historical restoration. Restoration is all very well if there's something excellent worth restoring but, equally, there is room in Britain for forward-thinking, creative and innovative gardening concepts, as the Eden Project was to prove. It was also hugely important to us – as it was to Tim Smit at Eden – that this new garden should have positive and far-reaching economic and social effects on the region. That wasn't an issue for English Heritage: their primary interest seemed to be to preserve the past in Mrs Beeton's finest nineteenth-century aspic.

Still, by the end of the meeting I felt we'd made real progress. Lorna was in retreat, which I put down to Richard Berry's benign presence. We agreed to make the required changes, including redesigning the Cascade and flanking pergolas to reflect the original form and outline of the earth banks, and revising the location of adjoining ponds to their footprint positions. We also agreed to commission another archaeological survey from Tyne and Wear Museum's archaeology department – the Duchess groaned at this one! – this time concentrating on the nineteenth-century remains in the Lower Garden. I didn't want to lose momentum so jostled everyone along to get new plans and layouts done before English Heritage's next Advisory Committee meeting on 3 November, to go before their Commission on 18 November.

SUCCESS

A couple of days after that date, with trembling hands, I opened a letter from Lorna McRobie. It was a long and detailed analysis of the situation, written in rather heavy technical language, but in the last section of the letter there were a couple of sentences that made my heart sing:

> English Heritage does not object in principle to the proposal for the new garden design …[provided there are] the highest levels of recording, analysis and rescue archaeology of all the nineteenth-century features … as part of a Section 106 Agreement.

We'd done it! Subject to the Section 106, our Garden plans had passed English Heritage's stringent Commissions and Committees. Now we needed approval for one outstanding item, the Pavilion Tower, which had been designed and redesigned, and was being considered by the Historic Buildings Committee on 3 December via their Inspector, Dr Rory O'Donnell, for Alnwick District Council's meeting on 8 December. Rory O'Donnell promised to provide the results of the Committee for the councillors well in advance. But nothing turned up. I tried to contact him on the 4 and 5 December. No luck, and nobody at English Heritage seemed to know where he was. By the morning of 8 December, I was desperate: we needed to know English Heritage's decision now. Mid-afternoon, I called Richard Berry's assistant for help, expressing my annoyance at Rory O'Donnell's silence. He might have gone AWOL, but surely someone at English Heritage must know the Committee's findings?

When I went to the Council Meeting at 6.30 p.m., I was unaware of any change in the situation. We were up against the wire, and worried that the application might not get through because of Rory O'Donnell's silence. I was heartened to see that the councillors were obviously in a bullish mood. They expressed their concern at English Heritage's approach to the application and the delays they had caused, and after some debate voted for approval of the car park and garden development subject to the same Section 106 Agreement. At this point that Claire Cardinal, the assistant planning officer, came over to me and said that the District Council had received a phone call earlier that afternoon from English Heritage saying that the Historic Buildings Committee had actually approved the application on 3 December. I was furious at Rory O'Donnell's silence.

But in the end, none of this mattered. We'd got planning permission for the Garden and Pavilion and the rest was only a rubber-stamping formality. (Though it wasn't until 24 August 1999 that we finally received the Section 106 Agreement, and planning permission and listed building consent for the Garden and Pavilion.) Our feeling was one of delightful and profound relief. Finally, we could start the build.

ABOVE: Visitors play in the Serpent
Garden. Torricelli is in the foreground.

CHAPTER 7

EVEN VERSAILLES HAD TO START SOMEWHERE ...

The Alnwick Garden was conceived as a water garden on a grand scale, with a cascade, fountains, jets, pools, rills and ponds giving movement, drama, sound and, the Duchess hoped, fun for all age groups. Jane had seen the wonders of classical water design at first hand when she visited the Peterhof Gardens near St Petersburg on the Russian Baltic, in the summer of 1997. These epic eighteenth-century water gardens were built by Peter the Great to commemorate the Russian victory over Sweden in the Great Northern War, and are a monument to military triumphalism. Complicated, gravity-fed hydraulic systems supply around 3,000 litres of water per second to an astonishing range of 150 fountains, canals and dramatic cascades. The Duchess's dream was that, by utilizing the wonders of twenty-first-century technology and the innovation of fibre-optic lighting, we could come up with something equally spectacular (though rather more modest in size!) in our twelve acres at Alnwick.

In Paris to meet the Wirtzes in 1997, the Duchess made a special trip to EuroDisney to see the high-tech water features created by the renowned Californian company Wet Design. Riding a roller coaster after eating a rich ravioli and cream lunch (courtesy of Lady Angelika Cawdor's friend Hubert de Givenchy) is never a good idea. On the rides, Jane was trying to hold on to her stomach while keeping her eyes open to see exactly how the water moved, as it jumped around and above her in fountains and jets. She came back captivated, saying Wet Design were 'genius' because they could make water move in a pure and clean way, as elegant and solid as steel, as if it was attracted to the other end of its loop by a strong magnet. The illusion was so powerful, you wanted to run your hand through it to make sure it really was water.

A friend of Jane's had an equally engaging encounter with a Wet Design creation in the Burj Al Arab Hotel, the sail-shaped architectural extravaganza in Dubai. He was due at an important meeting in five minutes, but the water feature in the lobby ran on a twenty-minute cycle, and he was so entranced that he had to stay and watch it end. The Duchess thought it astonishing that a hard-nosed businessman was prepared to risk being late just to see some waterworks. That was exactly the sense of awe and amazement she wanted to create in The Alnwick Garden.

Once we'd received the Wirtzes' master plan, we contacted Wet Design. The company had a reputation for doing high-tech glitz, but Jane knew the result needn't look tacky or theme-parkish. Instead of having twenty jets illuminated with multicoloured lights, our idea was to take a few jets with a blue or white light shining through so they looked elegant and beautiful. Two representatives from Wet Design came to the Castle and were commissioned to do proposals for twenty-one water features in the Garden. The Duchess was fascinated by the technology they'd developed: they could send balls of 'fire' into the fountains so that at night-time you would see light and water moving in the sky together; they could shoot 'marbles' of water into the air so children could catch them. A few months later, Wet Design returned to Alnwick to present their designs. We were bowled over. All the water features were drawn on a single roll of paper over twenty feet in length. As they unrolled it, they talked us through each individual concept, and twenty-one imaginative water features appeared before us, each exquisitely drawn.

Both the Duchess and I thought Wet Design's ideas were breathtakingly beautiful and sensitive to the *genius loci*. As the Duchess wrote to Peter Wirtz, 'They have totally respected your design and concept and have altered almost nothing ...' But Peter Wirtz disagreed profoundly. He wrote back:

> I opened the Wet Design roll and, I have to tell you, I am horrified by their proposals. Despite their sugar-coated language they do not respect our work, neither [do] they understand the spirit and the atmosphere we want to bring alive. It's really a symptom of the low self-esteem our profession

radiates in the US: apparently Wet Design think they can get away with changing and messing around in a creation which is not theirs. It's as if I would change windows in the Pavilion or propose to add some brush strokes on to your paintings. My answer is NO!

The Duchess wasn't prepared to get into a fight. It was too early in the design process to make a fuss with the Wirtzes, and anyway, the distance between our budgets and Wet Design's costings made compromise impossible. They estimated a $20 million build with running costs of $2 million per year. At the time, we estimated that we'd need 450,000 visitors through the gate each year just to run their water features. These were unsustainable figures and Jane knew we'd have to rethink. Meanwhile, however, she wrote back to Peter Wirtz:

> I will be wanting to make the water move. This was *always* my aim … We need to have some spectacular waterworks which will draw in all ages of people. You say the Garden stands in its own right and doesn't need embellishing but I disagree. To many visitors who already appreciate excellent garden design it will be utopia, but I want to bring in people who wouldn't normally visit a garden. Children, young mothers, teenagers, the unemployed, and they may prefer water to plants. Either way, the water is going to remain an important and integral part of The Alnwick Garden and we will have to be prepared to compromise.

In the summer of 1998, I sent the Wirtzes' master plan to Tim Smit in his role as director of the Garden. He had some reservations about the design: 'I feel I wouldn't be doing my duty to the Trust if I were to cravenly sing hurrah from the battlements. Jane expects frankness, if nothing else from me …' he said, and went on to list six failures, as he perceived them, stemming from the lack of a 'cultural glue' in the design. The Duchess always welcomed criticism. She felt that if someone she respected, such as Tim Smit, thought we could do things better, then we ought to discuss it. She sent Tim's letter to the Wirtzes for their comments. Peter Wirtz came back rebutting the criticisms and robustly defending his creation. The Duchess wanted reassurance from the Wirtzes that the Garden was a work of genius, but she also believed Tim couldn't see the whole picture because there was one vital piece missing – the waterworks. As she explained to him:

> I feel that this design is something very special. Unusual in England, quite European ... But what you haven't seen yet is the WATERWORKS. The BEST! Unbelievable things – world-firsts in water technology and just the most beautiful concepts imaginable ...

This was the last time Tim Smit gave us practical input into the Garden. In April 1999, Jane realized that his commitment to the Eden Project and Heligan made it difficult for him to have any real impact on the development of a garden 400 miles away, and she wrote to Tim – and to Lord Lambton, who lived in Italy and rarely came to Northumberland – relieving them of their duties as directors of the Garden. Tim wrote back the kindest letter:

> Dear Jane, I have thought of you often over the last 18 months and felt waves of guilt for my negligence as Trustee ... I hope my formal lack of a role won't prevent you from ever asking for any advice you feel I can offer. Actually sometimes it's not advice you want but someone to have a damn good whinge to when the pressure is on ... I've hugely enjoyed your company and sense of humour so hope we'll stay in touch and compare notes from time to time.

We couldn't afford Wet Design's 'beautiful concepts' so had to go back to the drawing board. I'd been negotiating with a British water engineering company, Invent Water Specialists (later renamed Lurgi Invent), to plan the technical procedures – the pumping systems, pipes, pressure and plant room infrastructure – needed for the Cascade waterworks. They were a highly regarded company and in the end we decided to work with them, hoping we'd be able to incorporate some of Wet Design's sensational features at a later phase, when we had more cash.

The water was our first point of difference with the Wirtzes and the problem arose largely because of the Duchess's *modus operandi.* Wirtz International was the lead garden designer and created the overall framework of the Garden. But within that framework, the Duchess wanted each disparate area to be designed by the best specialist in the business. She thought no one, not even the Wirtzes, could be expert in all areas. In effect, she wanted to create a team of top specialists – for the water, the lighting, the Labyrinth, the Poison Garden – to work together without any one person dominating the project.

The Duchess's unorthodox approach caused much discussion and debate, and more egocentric designers than the Wirtzes might have walked off the project with a flounce. But Jacques and Peter were professional throughout. On the occasions when Peter Wirtz dug in his heels about a designer and said their work was ugly or wrong, we almost always agreed not to use them. We knew we were never going to get the best out of Peter if he didn't respect the people he was working alongside.

MAKING THE 'VISION' A REALITY

Our first design team meeting took place on 30 January 1998. This was a landmark moment in the Garden's development, and we asked Bamboo Productions to record it on film. There was a real air of excitement and anticipation as the Duchess, agent Rory Wilson, Jacques and Peter Wirtz, Paul Robbrecht, Colin Barnes, John Robinson and Brian Hardy (of structural engineers Fairhurst), Iain Ramage and Eric Tully (from our contract administrators and quantity surveyors, Summers & Partners), Robin Hugill and Keith Armstrong (from our electrical and mechanical engineering consultants, R. W. Gregory & Partners) and I sat round the big working table in the tea room of the Castle. All our project managers and contractors were from the North-East and we felt this was important: we might be using European talent to design the Garden, but we wanted local businesses to benefit from the build.

That first meeting was remarkable. It felt as if we were embarking on something momentous, partly because of the sheer size of the undertaking but also because none of the contractors except Wirtz International had built a garden before. What was important to me was that the Duchess could explain her vision and inspire everyone to pull together. She's a great talker and her enthusiasm is

ABOVE: The first design team meeting at Alnwick Castle, 30 January 1998. From left to right: Eric Tully, Iain Ramage, John Robinson, Robin Hugill, Pod the dog, the Duchess, Paul Robbrecht, Brian Hardy, Keith Armstrong, Colin Barnes and Ian August.

contagious. Most of the people in the room hadn't met her before and must have been worried about how to address her and how to behave, but she said 'call me Jane', and soon put everyone at their ease.

Still, she was in an unusual position in these big monthly design meetings: she was the client paying the bills and calling the shots, but also part of the design team and the engine that drove us to achieve. She'd suggest changes, and you could see the contractors scratching their heads and wondering how on earth to make them happen. Sometimes when things got too technical, I'd see her eyes glaze over and some fairly detailed doodles would appear on her pad. But then someone would say something interesting and she'd want an explanation or clarification and you'd realize she'd been listening all the time. She was rigorous about achieving the highest standards: she always wanted the best, and we decided early on that if we couldn't afford something, we wouldn't do it half-cocked. We'd rather wait and raise more money than compromise on quality or design.

After that first meeting, the Duchess said she felt a great sense of relief that things could finally start moving. She's a doer not a talker. In the Castle, I'd sometimes hear grunting noises from afar and find her heaving enormous pieces of furniture across a room – she'd rather do it herself than wait for help. On several occasions our snail-like progress during the preliminary planning stages got her down and she'd say to me: 'What on earth are we achieving here – couldn't we be doing something better with our time?' Whenever she wavered, I'd try to reassure her that this project was so big and complex it was bound to have teething problems. We needed stamina, commitment and belief to see us through this period, and luckily the Duchess had all three in spades.

THE LECTURE TOURS

We had one other secret weapon in our armoury, and that was our lecture tours. Since 1996, before we'd even laid a foundation stone in the Garden, I had been giving talks to small local groups, sometimes with the Duchess and sometimes alone. I've always been involved with the local community and knew we needed to get the people of the North-East behind us: the idea was to enthuse them about the concept as well as raise the Garden's profile. The Duchess and I gave our first talk to Alnwick district councillors in the Castle. We didn't have much to offer them except a few pictorial boards, a glass of wine and our own passion for the project. But once they realized the impact the Garden could have on the community, they were genuinely positive and supported us all the way.

From this small beginning, something absolutely magical grew. Our lectures were, and still are, enormous fun. We'd race off to village halls, theatres and hospitals, set up our slide show, and talk for an hour about the Garden before taking questions from the floor. The Duchess and I were in our element: she has a natural talent for enthusing people, and audiences always responded very positively.

Occasionally we'd get the odd sticky question. I remember once, at Berwick Conservative Ladies' Association, a woman stood up and said: 'It seems to me that this Garden is all about children. I don't like children, so why will I enjoy the Garden?' As a mother of four herself, Jane was taken aback. She said impetuously, 'Well, I don't think this is the sort of Garden you're going to enjoy. I don't think you'd better come, because there will be lots of children around.' My instinct is always to take the diplomatic route, so I added, 'Of course, what the Duchess hasn't told you is that there are many quiet spaces where you can enjoy The Alnwick Garden and reflect and contemplate.'

What our lecture talks gave us was contact with ordinary people, and their responses were always so upbeat that the Duchess and I knew we were on to a winner. People loved the idea of a public pleasure garden, and their enthusiasm sustained us during low points when Press coverage was vicious or personal about Jane, or when planning permission seemed as far away as the Emerald City. The talks raised our morale because we felt in touch with grass-roots opinion – and in the end we knew it was ordinary people who were going to help this Garden succeed or fail. To date, we have given over 300 presentations around the UK, which I believe have been instrumental in our success.

But meanwhile, we had to sort out our teething problems with the Wirtzes. Peter Wirtz was keen to be involved in all aspects of the process. Jane, on the other hand, wanted him to look after his own areas, but leave the rest to her and the other specialists she chose. When Peter sent us an estimation of the overall garden budget, Jane scrawled on it:

> Will you please make sure that Peter is *not* involved in the overall budget of the Garden. He does not need to be involved in costings for a) Water b) Belinda Eade's grotto. Can he be given his own budget and that is that. Otherwise we end up with a total Wirtz experience which I don't want. This is very important. Thanks.

This became a recurrent theme. Peter wanted to maintain the integrity and discipline of his design and worried that the garden was becoming a mishmash of heterogeneous features. In fact, the Duchess was always enormously respectful of the Wirtzes' footprint within the Garden, but she had the audacity to ask for various improvements, for example on the Labyrinth. She felt the Wirtzes' design was not complex enough and brought in Adrian Fisher, an accomplished British maze builder; Peter, meanwhile, thought the Wirtzes' team could work on improving the Labyrinth themselves. Jane wanted more child-friendly features in the garden; Peter disagreed. Peter worried, needlessly in our view, about the competence and efficiency of some of our contractors. On many occasions he wrote to the Duchess expressing his fears. Eventually Jane lost patience. On one of Peter's letters, she added a note to me:

> This makes my blood boil. It's crap – the Wirtzes knew this was always going to be a team effort. Pay no attention to them. Peter wants to do it all but isn't going to. I have been ultra careful not to 'spoil' the Wirtzes' design but it is boring for children. We have to make this garden pay. It must be exciting, fascinating, incorporating the *best* in latest technology. The Wirtzes are not the experts in this case. They must be prepared to compromise.

I wrote a tactful letter back to Peter, saying how magnificent we thought their design was but how it had always been our intention, as well they knew, to bring in other specialists to produce unique features that would lift the Garden to a higher level. I sent my draft letter over to the Duchess for her comments and at the bottom she wrote: '10/10 for diplomacy Ian. I don't know how you do it. I would like to kill them.'

RISING COSTS

If tempers were fraying, there was little wonder. Budgets had risen again, to £14 million – comprising £7.5 million for the gardens, £2.5 million for the Pavilion, £2 million for water features, and £2 million for specialist features such as grottoes, lights and fittings. We had money to finance Phase 1 of the development – to build the Cascade, the Ornamental Garden and the Rose Garden in the lower area. But the Pavilion and specialist features such as lighting had to be moved into Phases 2 and 3 – for which we had as yet raised not a penny. Meanwhile, the pressure on the designers and contractors to finalize drawings and costings to meet our one immovable deadline of 31 December 1999 was intensifying. To fulfil the requirements of the £450,000 ERDF grant funding we had to let the building contract by the end of 1999, advertising for contractors in European construction journals so anyone in the EC could quote. We hoped to start building in April 2000. We needed to start motoring.

Structural engineer Colin Barnes and I prepared the contract documents, invited tenders and received several estimates from contractors in the North-East by our due date of 20 December. Contract administrator Iain Ramage and I looked through the submissions, then put them to the Lovaine trustees for a final decision. In the end, we went with the contractor who provided the lowest tender: the Newcastle branch of builders Sir Robert McAlpine Ltd, under regional director Andrew McAlpine. They are a long-established and highly successful construction and civil engineering company, and we felt we were in good hands. On 23 December 1999, I hand-delivered the required information to the Government

Office for the North-East. It was a close-run thing, but we met all the ERDF requirements and Sir Robert McAlpine Ltd officially became The Alnwick Garden's building contractor. We had planning permission, finance and now a builder. Finally, work could begin. Everyone in the team set off for their Millennium celebrations in high spirits, feeling that the start of the new century was going to bring more just than a date change in our lives. The year 2000 was truly the start of something momentous and new.

LOOKING FOR SPONSORSHIP

But first we had other money matters to sort out. We were still looking for private sponsorship for Phase 2 – the most expensive phase, taking in the Pavilion and Visitor Centre – and our resounding lack of success in Britain made the Duchess think the US was the only realistic source of hard cash. Why not give one of our lecture talks in the US to assess sponsorship interest in the project? Our lawyers set up the Garden as a registered charity in the US and one of our US fundraising advisers organized a gala evening at Sotheby's in New York, hosted by Mrs Judy Taubman, wife of Sotheby's chairman, Alfred Taubman.

At once, events turned against us. In February 2000, just days before our talk, we heard that Alfred Taubman and Sotheby's president and CEO Diana 'DeDe' Brooks had resigned over allegations of price fixing between Sotheby's and Christie's, the two largest international auctioneers. It was safe to say that our PRs and contacts at Sotheby's – and presumably just about everyone we met on the trip – would have more pressing things on their minds than raising funds for an unbuilt garden 4,000 miles away.

Then further catastrophe: we found out that because of a mix-up there wasn't an up-to-date guest list for the event. Of the British Press in New York, it looked as if only the *Daily Mirror* – not our first choice for reaching potential sponsors – had been invited. Of the US Press – well, we had no idea who was coming, though an exclusive lifestyle interview with the Duke and Duchess had been agreed with the fashion magazine *W.* Unfortunately, this meant no gardening magazines or other

publications could get near us, which infuriated Jane. In these circumstances, the Duke was understandably reluctant to make the journey, but the invitations had been printed with his name on, which made his appearance something of a *fait accompli*. We decided to go as scheduled, and make what we could of the trip.

Things got more surreal when the Duke, Duchess and I were collected from the airport in a flashy limo and deposited at a vast Manhattan hotel. The couple's luxurious suite was piled high with presents and teddy bears, and the Duchess immediately said: 'Dammit, I think we're paying for this.' Our purpose in coming had been to raise funds, not fritter away money on big cars and stuffed toys. We were also apprehensive about the presentation. We'd been persuaded to change our normal lecture routine, showing instead a short video about the Garden followed by a question and answer session. We didn't understand the US approach to fundraising, and had agreed to this against our better instincts: our talks had always been highly successful so changing the formula was a risk for us.

The evening was impressive, if a bit rushed. Alfred Taubman himself turned up, which raised the temperature a few degrees and caused a lot of rubbernecking among the guests. Judy Taubman introduced the Duchess and me to the assembled company, then everyone watched the video, and we answered questions from the floor. People seemed interested, but it's easy to be enthusiastic over a glass of wine at a party. Unfortunately, we couldn't follow up contacts because there wasn't any way of contacting possible donors who'd attended the event.

By the end of the trip, the Duchess was grumpy, furious about how vulnerable she and the Duke were to reporters' questions about her family when she wanted to talk about the garden. The journalists wanted to know intimate details of their life, asking them for stories about their children, their family life in the Castle, what they ate for breakfast ... The Duke and Duchess are intensely private people, and the Duke was particularly appalled, as Jane wrote in a private letter to a friend:

> The fundraising is a total horror. Ralph is getting stroppy about the 'prostitution element' and the final straw for him was having to accompany me to New York to give a talk at Sotheby's. I thought I might have to drug

LEFT: The Woodland Walk in spring.

him and stick him on a chair in the corner so that he didn't say anything flippant which could have been taken seriously. He says to me at least once a week if anybody else asks me about your bloody garden, I'm going to kill them! The quicker it's built, the better!

We decided to cut our losses and leave New York. The Duke and Duchess went home, but I took the opportunity to visit Longwood Gardens in Pennsylvania with Gil Truedsson. These wonderful gardens are set in over 1,000 acres of land and have the most spectacular water fountains I've ever seen. There are over 1,350 fountains and the 750 illuminated jets in the main water garden use 10,000 US gallons per minute, at pressures high enough to shoot water 130 feet in the air. The gardens come alive at night. To give some idea of the scale, there are over 400,000 lights running across forty miles of wire over trees, plants and displays. The effect was subtle, not theme-parkish, and the lighting enabled Longwood to operate day and evening. In Britain gardens shut from October to March, but despite the cold and short daylight hours, Longwood was open all year round and made an event out of Christmas and the winter landscape with daily entertainment. This, we decided, was exactly what we wanted to do at Alnwick.

Overall, the Duchess thought the US trip was interesting but that the timing was wrong – it was too early in the Garden's development to go looking for foreign investment. We were still selling a concept not a 'product', and couldn't offer any validation about the success or social and economic benefits of the Garden. One well-meaning person at the Sotheby's event told us that before any British project can take off in the US, it has to have massive regional and national support in the UK. We took those words to heart and wrote the trip off as part of our learning curve.

MORE CONTENTION AT HOME

In the run-up to the start of the build, relations between the Wirtzes and the Duchess were still tense – though this was expressed in the politest and most respectful way. First there was the restaurant issue. It's a little known fact that the seas off the North-East coast provide some of the best seafood in Britain. The Duchess wanted to make an asset of this local resource by establishing a seafood restaurant in the Garden. We commissioned beautiful designs from Clerkenwell architectural firm Patterson, Fenton-Jones Ltd and had been in discussions with Anthony Walford of the Mussel Inn in Edinburgh about catering. This wasn't going to be an English seaside fish 'n' chip shop, but an eating place of real quality and distinction. The Wirtzes had serious reservations about the idea. They believed a restaurant building within the Garden would detract from the design of the Pavilion, and that the attendant noise, smells and crowds would sit unhappily within the peace and tranquillity of this particular part of the Garden.

There was further contention over a muckraking article in the *Sunday Times* entitled 'Duchess under attack in her £15 million Versailles'. The piece suggested we were attempting to 'rival the seventeenth-century splendour of Versailles'. Actually no, though we were flattered by the comparison. Journalists often called The Alnwick Garden the 'Versailles of the North' – after all, it was an easy phrase to coin for a grand gardening project with lots of waterworks and connotations of aristocratic excess. The Duchess was used to taking these daft comments with a pinch of salt and didn't mind as much as Peter Wirtz, who fired off a letter to our poor PR, Philip Gregory:

> Please do not use the word 'Versailles' any more, it's clearly provocative in [journalists'] ears and spiritually so far away from what we are doing here ... [This] is about an excellent garden, about art, NOT about sloganesque flashy headings and spectacle that provides journalists with the ammunition to destroy the project and attack the family.

But the article had another sting in its tail. An 'unnamed local woman' was quoted as saying: 'It looks like something from Disneyland, quite unsuitable for here. It is a vanity for the Duchess.' It was obviously a tactless and untrue comment – how could she know what the Garden looked like when building work hadn't yet started? But the Wirtzes, sensitive about their reputation, were appalled that the word 'Disney' had been used in conjunction with Alnwick and made their concerns known to the Duchess.

ONE STEP FORWARD...

Things were further complicated by the entrance, stage left, of another key player. In July 1999 while on holiday in Greece, the Duchess had been approached by Mark Lloyd, a businessman who offered help finding sponsors. Back in Britain, he suggested meeting Eric Albada, a wealthy Dutch businessman for whom the Wirtzes, by coincidence, had built a garden. He was a great admirer of the Wirtzes and might be prepared to sponsor the first of their gardens in Britain. In November, Jane met him in London, where he seemed keen to donate £1 million to the Garden in sponsorship. Jane was delighted – if the deal came off, he would be the first private benefactor we'd attracted in the four years we'd been looking for funding. She invited him to Alnwick to attend a design meeting so he could see the Garden, meet the team, and appreciate how well everyone worked together.

Eric Albada came up to Alnwick in March 2000, and was extremely charming and enthusiastic. Our hopes were high – £1 million would kick off the Phase 2 funding very nicely indeed. Design meetings were long, and we always broke for a good lunch prepared by the Castle's chef Rod O'Brien. Over lunch, Jacques and Peter Wirtz, Paul Robbrecht and Eric Albada were placed near the Duchess. At one stage I heard them talking volubly in Flemish, which Jane couldn't follow. This behaviour was surprising, for the Wirtzes are always extremely polite and thoughtful about others. The Duchess told me later she thought it quite remarkable, as Eric Albada had very good English – and of course it made her wonder what they'd been talking about.

She soon found out. When she took Eric Albada to the station she expressed her thanks to him for coming, and said she hoped he'd seen how well everyone worked together and what a great team they were. She thought Eric Albada looked at her quizzically. He replied that during lunch Jacques Wirtz had said she was undermining the concept of the Garden by bringing in lots of other designers. In addition, he didn't like the idea of a seafood restaurant – he didn't want 'his' garden to smell of fish and chips – and he didn't approve of what she was doing with the waterworks. Jane was horrified. She knew Jacques Wirtz had reservations about some issues, but to air these grievances in front of a potential sponsor felt like a betrayal.

A letter soon arrived from Jacques Wirtz. Coming from an older generation, he was always more traditional in his approach to the Garden than Peter, and perhaps some of our early difficulties came from his different viewpoint. He said how well he thought the design meeting had gone, and how positive he was feeling about Mr Albada's involvement. However, he was very annoyed by the 'cheap and low' article in the *Sunday Times*, and said that now 'the word "Disney" has fallen it will accompany us for the rest of the project'. He added that the water features looked 'absurd', the idea of a hell grotto was 'anecdotal and boring' and, as a finale, he complained about the seafood restaurant again.

The Duchess had been furious with the Wirtzes ever since her conversation with Eric Albada, but until now she'd held her fire. Without telling me – she knew I'd counsel her against it – she wrote back what she called a 'filthy letter'. She told me later she'd thought very carefully about this letter, and had amended it with the help of her elder son, George. But she didn't show me a copy until she'd posted it. It's worth quoting at length to get the full impact of her fury. She wrote:

> I am pleased that you felt the meeting with Eric Albada went well. I was not so happy having heard from Eric that you had talked to him about my 'interference' with your designs. Had my language skills been as competent as yours I would have realized I was being discussed. You should understand that Eric has not actually put any money into the project ... My husband is the only person to be pouring money into the Garden Project at the present time. He has paid all the design teams' fees to date ... He is doing this because he has faith in what I am trying to achieve ...
>
> The garden ... has to produce income. So far the only guaranteed form of substantial income will be from a franchise for the fish restaurant. Please

give me a little credit for having looked nationwide for the best people to run this operation. I am not talking about a fish and chip shop. This will be an upmarket mussel bar serving locally produced seafood, lobster, crabs, etc. The restaurant will be in that part of the garden adjoining the pond which will make a good location. It will sit within the existing design, and I will work directly with the architect. The grotto is being designed by Belinda Eade and she will create what she feels is most suitable for the space and I will try to accommodate her wishes. That is all as I said it would be when I first met you in Paris ... The only comments I agree with in your letter concern the water. I am not happy with the designs ... I will leave the eight areas for water features empty until I decide what would be right. It is possible that I haven't met the most suitable water designer yet.

You have designed a wonderful garden which is what we commissioned you to do. The rest is my department. Final decisions regarding the pavilion designs, individual water features, sculptures, grottoes and other details will be taken by me. This is an important area to sort out ... We also feel that you are worrying too much about the press. Any unfavourable press will be directed at Ralph and me. We are used to this and tend not to pay much attention to it. It would be tragic to produce a garden purely with press appreciation in mind.

I would like to think that we will be able to continue working as a team and I would like to hear your final comments about the points I have raised.

The Duchess was prepared for the Wirtzes to walk away from the project, but was determined to stick by her convictions. Luckily, they saw sense. Jacques Wirtz sent a gentle, short note, saying that any criticisms had been made with the best intentions, because they wanted to be proud of the final result. As a result of this, the Duchess decided she was not prepared to accept any sponsorship money from Eric Albada. She was worried that the personal relationship between the Wirtzes and Albada meant they would dictate the development of the Garden and she would no longer be in control.

This episode, though difficult at the time, cleared the air with the Wirtzes. Perhaps they finally appreciated the fact that Jane was not like their usual clients.

She knew exactly what she wanted, demanded to be involved in every decision, and was fiercely hands-on.

This was a time of realization for the Duchess too. She had never been totally in awe of the Wirtzes, but it was a rude awakening to realize that everybody involved – however much you liked and respected them on a personal level – wanted to influence and control the outcome in their own way. The Wirtzes wanted to design a Garden to go down in history, while other designers and workers wanted money, acclaim or perhaps just to make a living. The Garden, Jane realized, was seen by most people as an opportunity and a business. Perhaps before, she'd believed people got involved because they were as enthusiastic about the concept as she was. Now she realized that everyone had their own agenda. I felt angry for her, that her dreams had been dashed again, but with hindsight it was better she lost her illusions about the project now. You need to be tough and clear-sighted when you're about to have a building site the size of Versailles on your doorstep.

CHAPTER 8

LET THEM EAT CAKE...

One of the best things about hiring contractors Sir Robert McAlpine Ltd was meeting project manager Aidan Harrison. Aidan is a great team player: an enthusiastic, funny, problem-solving person with mind-blowingly good leadership skills who has, over the distance, become a very good friend. Even when severely tested by the complexities and delays of the Cascade build, as we all were, he kept everyone's morale high. He was committed to the project from the word go and the Duchess loved working with him because he was always sensitive to her concerns about the quality of the build. On a personal level, too, he was a delight. You could always sit down in his Portakabin office with a cup of coffee and a chocolate biscuit – he had a hidden supply that the Duchess raided on a regular basis – and have a good moan about what was (or sometimes wasn't) happening on site.

McAlpines started work on 27 March 2000, and it immediately became apparent that Aidan was going to be an integral part not just of the construction team but of the design team too. Normally on a build, finished plans are passed to the contractors well ahead of schedule, so they can prepare themselves in terms of materials, manpower and equipment. But McAlpines were on site before our designs for the Cascade were anywhere near complete. Aidan and his team had to work on the hoof, helping us refine concepts in design meetings so McAlpines could crack on with the building work the next day. It was the only way we were going to meet our projected completion date of May 2001, just over a year away.

On the Wirtzes' master design, the Cascade was a virtuoso series of eighteen elliptic weirs with curved walls, all of different radii and with nearly 140 central and side jets. The water ran down the weirs like a staircase, before dropping under a terrace and erupting into another series of weirs, over a water wall and into the Lower Basin where there was a central fountain. The whole Cascade was built over

ABOVE: Aidan Harrison and I testing the
new furniture in the Ornamental Garden.

a vertical drop of ten metres. At the top of the hill in the ornamental garden there was an illusory 'source' pool – a black pond that bubbled gently to make children think it was full of scary denizens of the deep – from which a central rill divided to take a stream of water down each side of the Cascade.

The engineering skill needed to turn this concept into practical reality was phenomenal. Water features are like icebergs: what you see on the surface is about 10 per cent of the whole. Underneath the Cascade, we had to store and organize the movement uphill of over a million litres of water – enough to fill nearly 15,000 domestic baths. We needed pump rooms, drainage systems, irrigation pipes, an underground reservoir, filtering and cleansing facilities, computer systems and electricity. We had designers, civil engineers, water specialists, electronic and structural engineers – but no formal architect – on site trying to organize these disparate parts into a coherent whole.

Lurgi Invent was designing the water engineering. Hardworking Brian Hardy and his structural engineering team from Fairhurst were drawing up plans and cross-sections of each component of the build. It was slow, detailed work and technical problems arose every inch of the way. In design team meetings, Aidan's practical experience meant we could make quick decisions about the efficacy of one course of action over another, which saved us enormous amounts of time and money. Thanks to Aidan and Brian, it quickly became a tight operation. One day Brian Hardy would modify the drawings, the next day Aidan and his team would build from those plans. This is not an ideal way to work – there is no scope for error or time built in to deal with the technical problems that inevitably arise. We simply had no choice: our deadlines were non-negotiable. As well as the stringent construction dates we had to meet to sustain our ERDF funding, we had seasonal deadlines imposed by Mother Nature. To open in May 2001, the trees and shrubs needed to be planted at the optimum time during dormancy in winter 2000. This would give the plants a few months to bulk out by the time visitors arrived. The schedule gave us about eight months to construct the Cascade groundworks and water structures, and mark out the paths and

TOP LEFT: The archaeological excavation of the hothouse boiler room.

TOP RIGHT: A view from the top of the Garden, near the Ornamental gates, down to the area of the Pavilion. Contractors dig out the area for the lower basin of the Cascade, under which are the pump rooms and water storage reservoir.

RIGHT: The Grand Cascade under construction. The builders in the centre of the picture give a sense of perspective and reveal the enormity of the project.

LEFT: An aerial view of The Alnwick Garden under construction. At the bottom left we can see the Poison Garden under construction; centre bottom – where the Pavilion and Visitor Centre now sit; bottom right – the very beginnings of the Rose and Serpent Gardens and Labyrinth; to the sides of the Cascade are the new pergolas, not yet covered in foliage. At the top of the image is the Ornamental Garden.

other hard-landscaping areas in the Ornamental Garden, Lower Garden and Cascade area.

The Duchess, meanwhile, was coming to terms with the fact that she'd set something huge in motion and there was no turning back. One day, Andrew McAlpine wanted to update her on progress in the Garden. Wearing her regulation builder's kit – the hard hat, dayglo jacket and steel-capped boots which were always kept for her in McAlpines' Portakabin – the Duchess was walking towards the east corner of the Garden wall when she said: 'Where are we going? You don't get into the Garden that way.'

He said, 'You do now.'

We walked through the side entrance and on the lawn in front of us were huge diggers and earthmovers. The archaeologists were still working in the Lower Garden, but McAlpines were getting ready to dig out groundworks the size of a football pitch for the Cascade. It was a strange moment for the Duchess: even four years at the helm planning every detail of the process was no preparation for the sheer magnitude of the building works. At that moment, she said she felt physically sick. On paper, construction plans look straightforward: in practice the practical effort involved in making them reality beggars belief. The Duchess had the terrible worry of knowing she was ultimately responsible for the men, machinery and money.

REALITY BITES

When Jane took the Duke to see the diggers, the scale of the project must have concerned him too. The next day, she seemed distracted and I asked her why. Apparently, the night before, the Duke had said very abruptly, 'Jane, I know you're enthusiastic and committed to the project, but just because you think it's going to be so great, why should anybody else?' Then he turned over and switched off his light. Jane said she lay there for hours thinking: 'My God, what if I'm wrong? I'm spending £5 million on building work and haven't done any research to see if this project is going to work.' Then, in desperation, at 3.00 a.m.: 'You bastard, Ralph, how could you say that? You're fast asleep, but I'm so wound up I can't sleep a wink.'

What worried her, she gloomily admitted, was that he might be right. She and I were so caught up in the planning and dramas of the last four years that it never occurred to us the project might not succeed. This was one of the few moments when the Duchess's optimism failed. I did my best to reassure her, but once a huge building project like this is under way, things are outside any one person's ability to control them. The way I saw it, our only course of action was to stay positive and deal with the problems as successfully as we could.

Almost immediately, it became clear that these problems were going to be off the scale. The contractors told us that building the Cascade was the most technically complicated job they'd ever undertaken (this was before they'd started work on the Treehouse, but that's another story ...). One reason was the depth of the build – down to the height of a double-decker bus – in difficult terrain. The Garden was sited on ground prone to running sand, a fairly typical geological occurrence around Alnwick, which causes soil to shift in wet weather. Running sand occurs in seams at various depths below the surface, so we were never sure where we were going to find it. We were building about 400 metres from the River Aln, so the water table was high. All these factors make excavation hazardous and difficult, and unless the area can be stabilized, the foundations of anything built on it can literally float away – extremely dangerous when a million litres of water are involved. Before we could start building, the contractors had to 'de-water' the ground by putting straws into the area to be worked, and drawing out the ground water. This allowed them to excavate deeper and deeper until they could sink a concrete base with enough weight in it to remain secure.

Then there was the shape of the weirs. The Wirtzes had made each of the curved weirs on the Cascade of a different radius. Laying vertical concrete is difficult enough, laying vertical concrete on a slope in a curve is extremely testing, but laying vertical concrete on a slope in eighteen curves of different radii multiplies that difficulty by a factor of eighteen. Poured concrete needs to be contained by wooden formwork and shuttering until it sets hard enough to hold its shape. Each individual piece of formwork had to be made on site by McAlpines' joiners, and was horribly time-consuming. Aidan was always looking for ways to make the build less costly and more efficient, which was a huge bonus for us. He'd often come and say, 'Ian, provided Peter Wirtz is okay with this, I can save you £20,000 if we do it this way.' He wanted to rationalize the design and make the formwork stage easier by using curves of only four different radii. This meant his joiners didn't have to reinvent the wheel every single time, cutting costs and speeding up the job. The Wirtzes were happy to oblige, though this meant back to the drawing board for poor Brian Hardy.

On any build, there are challenging technical questions to be answered and decisions to be made every day. Which would last longer as facing on the inner Cascade walls: natural stone or concrete? What changes would occur in coloured concrete when it was poured on the most economical pour-sequence? What kind of lining coursing would match the coursing on the natural stone used on the outside of the Cascade? Which irrigation system would work best in the Rose Garden? We'd thrash through these and many more problems, alternatives and costings at our regular design meetings.

We wanted a warm, honey-coloured sandstone for the outer walls of the Cascade and Lower Basin and searched in northern Spain, France and Belgium, but in the end the perfect fit was right on our doorstep. Darney stone is from a quarry leased by Northumberland Estates in West Woodburn, and all royalties have been made over to the Garden. For the edgings and copings around the pond and rill edges in the Ornamental Garden, we decided to use blue limestone from a quarry in Kilkenny.

One of our biggest headaches was matching the concrete used to form the inner walls of the Cascade and Lower Basin to the colour and texture of the Darney stone used on the outer walls. Aidan and his team constructed flat 'stone' moulds made of Reckli latex, which were imprinted on the vertical wet concrete. These jelly-like moulds were very hard to manoeuvre and needed many practice runs to get a finish that looked authentic. Bobby Corkin, McAlpines' general foreman, was heavily involved with this, as he was something of an expert on concrete. He was a great chap, chatty and friendly when he showed the Duchess round the site. He loved the project – he always said it was history in the making – and would go out of his way to help. One time Aidan had a serious problem, and some of the builders, including Bobby, didn't finish work until 3.15 a.m. Bobby drove home to Sunderland forty-five miles away. Next day was his day off but he was back at 10 a.m. – his local club had organized a trip to the Garden and he'd come along. I found him asleep on the grass!

He was very keen on the royal family, so every time the Prince of Wales or the Duke of Edinburgh visited, Jane made sure he knew and had his camera handy. One time when Jane and I were giving the Duke of Edinburgh a tour, she saw Bobby standing nearby and asked Prince Philip if he'd have his photograph taken with him. Bobby was over the moon and apparently kept the photo in pride of place. For a long time, Bobby was our eyes and ears in the Garden, telling us to 'look at this', or 'try that'. He's a great man, and was an enormously important member of the team.

The banks the Cascade was sited on were of significant historic importance and English Heritage insisted we retain them. To avoid damaging them and compacting the area with foot and machinery traffic, we decided to use a tower crane to shift materials up and down the site. Tower cranes are huge and unwieldy – this one was about twenty-five metres high – and the water table sat a metre under its base, which caused Aidan some worries in case it slid. But in this confined area with lots of people working on site, it allowed McAlpines to lift and drop the wooden formwork into place, followed by 500 tonnes of steel reinforcements and 7,000 tonnes of concrete poured from ready-mix lorries, without turning the area into a stage set for the Battle of the Somme.

At this time, the build was being filmed by director John Thornicroft for a BBC1 *Ground Force* special called *Charlie and the Duchess*. The Duchess and Charlie Dimmock made a good TV team: one petite and dark, the other buxom and blonde. Jane had always loved the *Ground Force* concept of building a garden and changing people's lives in a weekend – in fact she used to do exactly that for friends before she became Duchess, loading up her van with big plants and trees and creating an instant transformation. So when Peter Bazalgette, then of Endemol, suggested she and Charlie make a film about the Garden together, she'd jumped at the chance. Charlie Dimmock was at the height of her popularity, and Jane wanted a big celebrity to take the project away from her and make people understand that this was a public garden. It seemed a perfect fit: just as Charlie Dimmock was regarded by some people as the unacceptable face of gardening – popular, but not a horticultural heavyweight – so The Alnwick Garden was seen as populist and 'theme-parkish' – 'Ground Force with a vengeance!' as Jane put it – by many of the English gardening élite. Jane appreciated Charlie's warmth and sense of fun, and from day one they got on like a house on fire.

One day Charlie challenged the Duchess to go with her to the top of the tower crane, saying, 'Think of the view – we'll be able to see the Castle.' Jane got about a metre up, then thought better of it. She's petrified of heights just couldn't do it. Charlie carried on to the top where the crane sways wildly in the wind and you can feel the torque, talking all the time to camera. It's only when she got to the cabin at the top that she said how wobbly and seasick she was feeling. I applauded her courage: she was nervous of heights too but said cheerily to me later, 'I had to do it. I had no choice – that's what I'm paid for!' Jane, meanwhile, had felt that she could be being 'set up', and asked John Thornicroft why the cameras had kept rolling. He told her seriously that it was not in their interests to make her look stupid, as it could backfire on Charlie.

Using a crane rather than manpower to shunt supplies and equipment up the slopes slowed us down, but it protected the banks and prevented the subsoil from getting compacted. That was Peter Wirtz's big worry. The very first time Peter met Aidan in spring 2000, he barely said hello before tearing into him, saying builders always compact the soil, kill trees, spill chemicals and leave huge lumps of concrete and rubble in the ground so nothing ever grows again. As a result, Aidan was terrified: on most building sites rubble is buried, but if a lump of concrete was left in the garden soil, anything planted near it would never realize its full potential. All the service ducts, pipes and paths around the Garden had to be laid so that future planting would not be compromised. Aidan and his team were fastidious about protecting the natural environment, which was just as well as in a few months' time we'd be planting hundreds of hornbeam (*Carpinus betulus*) hedging plants into the soil around the Cascade. Hornbeam makes a lovely topiary hedge; it's vigorous and fast-growing, and its fine-textured leaves are more elegant than beech.

There was lots of ancient rubble already buried on site. In the lower section of the Garden, I was expecting to find beautiful, loamy, high-quality earth that we could store for use later as topsoil. Instead, the archaeologists found that over the centuries builders had chucked their rubbish there, then levelled and covered it with a thin layer of soil – in essence, the whole area was a rubble fill. However, just beyond the car park area, Aidan discovered an area of sand and gravel to a depth of around ten metres. This was quarried and graded, and used as a drainage medium in the Lower Garden, which saved us money. In a neat exchange of resources, the unusable rubble from the Lower Garden was deposited into the big quarry hole.

PRACTICALITIES

Although we'd anticipated many construction difficulties, one problem hit us completely out of the blue. When we were planning the build, we'd blithely placed the lighting and other 'specialist features' into the Phase 2 budget of the Garden and promptly forgotten all about them. As soon as the build started, it became obvious this was impractical. If we didn't incorporate the underground service installations for the lighting at this stage, in a couple of years we'd have to dig up the Cascade to put them in – a damaging and expensive procedure.

Lighting design doesn't come cheap: the infrastructure was going to cost an extra £1.7 million for which we hadn't budgeted. The Duchess entered into lengthy negotiations with Philips Lighting to do a sponsorship deal. She was hoping for a

RIGHT: The shape of the Grand Cascade
reflects through the staircase, striped
detail of the lawns, the pergolas and
subsequently into the beech details on
the listed banks. This continuity creates
a visual panoramic effect that brings a
natural transition from the hard
structure into the treeline on each side.

donation in the region of £500,000, but unfortunately Philips could only offer less than a tenth of that, which wasn't enough for us to continue without contingency funding to tide us over. Aidan needed the go-ahead to continue work, and although we were hopeful that a sponsor would come along, we needed a fallback position. The Duke once again stepped into the breach and said he was prepared to underwrite the bridging work if no sponsors came forward. We were extremely grateful: if he hadn't pledged his support, the build would have been called to a halt.

WATER ENGINEERING

Perhaps our most serious problem was with the water engineering. Since December 1998 we'd been working with Lurgi Invent, pumping specialists from Rochdale who'd suggested a design with three plant rooms underneath the Cascade. Invent were an interesting company. We'd hired them during a period of massive international consolidation in the water industry: they were soon bought by the German company Lurgi Bamag, which was in turn taken over in September 1999 by the global water and waste company Azurix and its parent company, the US conglomerate Enron.

Quantity surveyor Iain Ramage and I had always felt Lurgi Invent's budget costings were high, and Summers (our contract administrators and quantity surveyors) advised me that in their opinion we should consider competitive tenders. By April 2000 when the build started, it became clear we needed underground infrastructure and storage facilities additional to those Lurgi Invent had allowed for, which was going to bang up our costs. Then in June 2000 they announced that they needed extra fees to make concept changes, even though we still hadn't had a peep of a design out of them. We agreed to pay, provided they gave us the completed technical drawings as soon as possible.

But Aidan was getting worried. He could see their approach was slowing down the project: our structural engineers couldn't move on until they knew the cable and duct routes, the size of the pumps and tanks, the hydraulic profiles and other general calculations on how to make the water design work. I could feel an air of mutual distrust beginning to hover over proceedings.

It was at this difficult stage in July 2000 that Tony Tibbott from the water engineers called me and Iain Ramage aside at one of our design meetings. He suggested to us that there was a possibility Azurix might sponsor the design and build of the project to the tune of £5 million. I was very excited: I thought we might finally have cracked the sponsorship problem, and rushed back to tell the Duchess. She was equally happy, and the possibility of their funding the waterworks swayed our decision to keep going with Lurgi Invent.

Whenever we met a representative from the company after that, I'd ask for news about how the sponsorship was coming along. No further details materialized. Nor, more seriously for our schedules, did the design plans. The Duchess was getting annoyed, and we began to wonder if the £5 million sponsorship deal was just a carrot they were dangling in front of us to keep us sweet. Perhaps, we thought, they were trying to delay proceedings for so long that they forced our hand into giving them the lucrative contract to build the water displays on top of designing them.

The year before, when we heard of their takeover by Enron, Jane had written to Kenneth Lay, the Chairman and CEO of Enron, on the advice of a friend in New York who knew him well. Mr Lay had replied telling us to brief Colin Skellett, chairman of Wessex Water, one of Enron's subsidiaries. On 30 October 2000, when the situation with Lurgi Invent was getting tense, the Duchess wrote to Mr Skellett inviting him and Lord Wakeham, the former Conservative Secretary of State for Energy and a director of Azurix, to Alnwick Castle. A week later she got a terse reply from Colin Skellett saying that he had been briefed by the managing director of Lurgi Invent and had discussed the project with Lord Wakeham, and they were not in a position to offer The Alnwick Garden any financial help. The Duchess was furious: we had allowed ourselves to be strung along for months because of the prospect of a £5 million handout, which had suddenly disappeared into thin air.

In retrospect, it was lucky we didn't rely on Enron's generosity. The company went into bankruptcy in 2001 amid massive debts and murky accounting practices, and Kenneth Lay and many of his colleagues faced FBI investigations in the biggest US corporate scandal ever.

At the end of 2000, however, we still had a problem. What was going to happen to our water features now? Luckily, Aidan had been researching other water companies, and asked Lurgi Invent and a Glasgow sewerage company, Ritchie MacKenzie Co. Ltd, to do a competitive tender. There was no contest: Ritchie MacKenzie's quote was £1 million cheaper and we considered it provided real value for money. When we told Lurgi Invent, they suggested 'off the record and without prejudice' that they might be entitled to claim loss of profit for losing the right to install the water features. I went down to speak to our lawyers in London, who looked at all the contractual evidence. It was watertight: Lurgi Invent had no justification in thinking they could construct the waterworks without winning it on tender.

So Ritchie MacKenzie joined our team. The bonus for us was that the delightful Gordon Murray – whom we nicknamed Jacques Cousteau for his joy at plunging into water features in a dry suit – was doing the water design. Like Aidan, he was a natural and enthusiastic problem solver and a delight to have around. Ritchie MacKenzie produced an alternative design proposal using two plant rooms instead of three. This met with the Duchess's wholehearted approval as it made the build simpler and substantially reduced costs.

Aidan and Gordon worked closely with two other highly qualified professionals: Robin Hugill of R. W. Gregory, who designed the electrical and mechanical systems, and Brian Hardy of structural engineers Fairhurst. None of them had been involved in building a garden before, but together they made a hugely committed and focused team with very high standards. Importantly for the Duchess and me, they were also great people to work with. There was no jockeying for position: everyone knew exactly what they were responsible for and respected everyone else's boundaries. The Duchess and I had responsibility for the aesthetic decisions; everything else was up for discussion. Looking back, we were running a dream team. Our guiding principle was never cost, and we never took the easy option to save ourselves effort or trouble. Instead, we focused on the quality of the finished product. We all pulled together and morale remained high throughout the whole of the Phase 1 build. It was a wonderful time.

CELEBRATIONS

At the end of August, aged sixty, I was due to retire after forty-five years working for Northumberland Estates. The Duchess and I hadn't discussed the future so I was delighted when, at a fundraising dinner in the Castle, the guest sitting next to me said he'd heard I was retiring soon, and before I could answer the Duchess, sitting at the far end of the table, said, 'That's what he thinks!'

My retirement party was in the Guest Hall in the Castle, and I remember making a speech saying 'As one door closes, and I should have been riding off into the sunset to paint in Provence, a garden gate has opened.' Jane offered me a new contract working solely on the Garden project, which was a big relief: my dream now was to stay on until the Garden was up and running.

Despite all the delays, by Christmas 2000 the team had made considerable progress. Reinforcement work had begun on the Cascade, concrete floor slabs had been laid on the Lower Basin, the brick paving in the entrance courtyard had been completed, the pools and paths in the upper Ornamental Garden were under construction, and the pergola and footpath lines were set out in the Rose Garden. At the top of the hill, the original Renaissance ornamental gates – one dating from 1560 – had been restored to their former glory by Ridley and Charlton Amos, blacksmiths from Heddon-on-the-Wall. We'd also built a public viewing terrace and kiosk, which was due to open in April 2001.

Morale on site was high and most of that was thanks to the Duchess. She was incredibly popular with the contractors: she'd come round a couple of times a week to check on progress and say hello to everyone. They were a great bunch and the Duchess would always stop and chat: 'Have you worked out that problem

LEFT: The Duke and Duchess of Northumberland present Ian August with an Alexander Creswell painting in honour of my retirement from the Northumberland Estates.

you had last week?' 'Did your son get into the school football team? 'Is your wife over the flu yet?' She always has such an interest in people, and they loved her for it.

That first Christmas, the Duchess wanted to give everyone some seasonal cheer and say thank you for their commitment to the job. On the day before Christmas Eve, we gathered together under the tower crane amidst the concrete reinforcements and with a prime view of the enormous hole in the ground – the culmination of eight months' hard graft. The Duchess and I brought down cases of beer and hot sausage rolls, and she made a speech thanking the team for their hard work, saying how much she appreciated their efforts and wishing them a very Happy Christmas. It was an occasion full of laughter and fun, and there was a real feeling of camaraderie. Her simple but instinctive gesture of friendship brought the whole contracting team together. Afterwards, site manager Ian Thomson walked off with the Duchess and me, and said: 'You realize they're not working for McAlpines any longer, Your Grace, they're working for you.' It was a great compliment.

If 2000 was exciting, 2001 was wildly unpredictable. It started badly and got steadily worse. First it was the weather. According to Aidan, this was the wettest year on record since 1762. The rain poured down for months upon the forlorn building site that was The Alnwick Garden. And when it wasn't raining, it was snowing – it was inches deep for a while in February and everyone was sent home. In construction, bad weather equals delays, and delays cost money. We were already three-and-a-half months behind schedule, and Aidan had to tell the Duchess that the Cascade works were far from finished and we'd have to delay the Garden opening. She took it well – she was determined to open when we were good and ready, and not a moment before. Our public opening day was put back to 1 October 2001, just within the time frame set by our ERDF funding.

LOCAL DISASTER AND SELF-DOUBT

Then we had some catastrophic news. An epidemic of foot-and-mouth disease had broken out, and the source was the farm of Bobby Waugh at Heddon-on-the-Wall, just thirty miles down the road. The Ministry of Agriculture, Fisheries and Food (MAFF) ordered the mass slaughter of the 800 animals on his farm and banned the movement of livestock around the country, but it was too late to stop the spread of the disease. Soon the countryside around us was in chaos. Footpaths were closed, cars had to be disinfected before and after entering farm areas, and pedestrian access to farms was restricted. Over 150 of the Duke's tenants were farmers, and their lives were shattered by the epidemic. In total six million animals were culled across the country with a devastating effect on the farming industry. The farmers of infected cattle did at least receive compensation for their losses. Others, however, were less lucky. Many near us were unable to move their cattle to fresh grazing, or sell them through the market and therefore income dropped substantially, without compensation. Prices were at rock bottom. People couldn't sell their livestock and we heard harrowing accounts of the stricken tenant farmers.

Flying from Newcastle to London that spring, the Duchess could see the thick, acrid smoke from the pyres at Ponteland floating up into the sky. For months, we had to drive over disinfected straw to get into the Garden. One day, the Duchess arrived on site and I started talking to her about some technical problem. I could see she wasn't taking in a single word. She looked at the scene in front of her and said, 'Ian, should we be doing this? I feel like Marie Antoinette spending £5 million on a water feature when there are farmers next door who don't know where their next meal is coming from.'

It was a time of terrible doubt for us. Alnwick is arguably more feudal in outlook than many British towns because the Castle has dominated not just the skyline but also the economy of the area for the past 700 years. That a Duchess was building a garden while the rest of the North-East was in desperate straits seemed a terrible 'let them eat cake' moment of insensitivity. The Duke had just given Jane a substantial donation, and now his tenant farmers could hardly eke out a living.

Jane had many sleepless nights over it, and a real depth of concern for the people and the future of the area.

It was only when we began to discuss how we could help that we started to see the bigger picture. We'd always hoped the Garden would bring jobs, money and tourists to a neglected but beautiful part of the country. Foot-and-mouth accelerated the process. Over the next year, farmers started to diversify and become more entrepreneurial: they let rooms in their farmhouses for bed and breakfast; they converted barns or outhouses into holiday cottages; their wives started baking cakes and other goodies, which we sold in The Alnwick Garden. In 2002, Alnwick District Council received over a hundred planning applications for tourism-related developments, compared with five or six in previous years. 'Diversification' was the buzzword and our plan to make the Garden a lifeline in the regeneration of the North-East was taking shape. In March 2001, Northumberland Estates issued a press release:

> After due consideration of the current state of the foot-and-mouth outbreak, the Duke and Duchess of Northumberland have taken expert advice and decided that it should be 'business as usual' at Alnwick Castle and at The Alnwick Garden site ...
>
> It was felt vital that visitors should be actively encouraged to continue to visit Alnwick, bringing much needed revenue to local businesses at this trying time. The Castle will therefore open as usual to the public on 1 April. At the same time, local people will at last be able to see what is going on behind the walls off Denwick Lane at The Alnwick Garden site. In opening these two areas, Northumberland Estates have kept necessary precautions in place. Visitors on foot or travelling by car to both the Castle and The Alnwick Garden must cross specially disinfected mats to help prevent the spread of foot-and-mouth disease. Access to Estates walks and farmland, however, will be denied until the outbreak is over.

Our public viewing terrace and kiosk opened in April 2001 – and during the Phase 1 build over 100,000 people came to satisfy their curiosity about what was going on behind the Garden wall.

LIFE MUST CONTINUE

Although a private visit by the Garden's patron, HRH The Prince of Wales, was cancelled because of foot-and-mouth disease, work otherwise continued in the Garden. Charlie Dimmock filmed the vertical concrete being poured on the Cascade. BBC2 started filming a documentary for the Open University about the technicalities of the build. The Duchess designed the garden seats, and the Estates' joiners set to work making around fifty benches and twenty chairs out of Douglas fir. The 'oversized' benches were classical in design, big and comfortable – the Duchess wanted people to feel they could linger in them, with a glass of wine or cup of tea, and watch the world go by.

The tree planting in the car park was finished; the gun sheds were approved as the site for public toilets. We'd chosen Raisby Golden Amber gravel, a magnesium limestone composition used at Buckingham Palace and Longleat. Although it was still giving Aidan sleepless nights, the main substructure work in the Grand Cascade was nearing completion. The two plant room service areas and reservoirs were in place and now McAlpines were laying the roofs on top, to form the base of the Cascade pools.

I'd been liaising with the highway authority about road signage, with Northumbria Crime Prevention Office about security, and with various bodies to discuss disabled access requirements and a Shopmobility scheme – the Duchess was keen that disabled and elderly people should be able to move around the Garden as easily as everyone else. We'd hired the Newcastle company Robson Brown as PR consultants, the name of the Garden was finally confirmed as 'The Alnwick Garden', and a new logo was designed.

PREPARING FOR PHASE 2

Now that work on Phase 1 was progressing apace, the Duchess and I had mentally moved on and started to consider how we were going to raise funds for Phase 2. In May 2000, after the Chelsea Flower Show, we'd visited fundraisers Jane Kaufmann and Kate Brooks of Jane Kaufmann Associates at Covent Garden opera house.

They'd raised a spectacular amount of money to rebuild Covent Garden, and we wanted to ask their advice about fundraising for Alnwick. They suggested we hire a professional fundraiser for a couple of years. The Duchess was reluctant – she'd always thought professional fundraisers were the 'dregs of the earth' – but we were getting nowhere with our own fundraising endeavours and realized we knew next to nothing about the complicated process of attracting public funds. The Duchess also wanted to take some of the fundraising pressure off me, so we decided to give it a try.

In spring 2001, we put an advert in the trade press and received just three applications (today, the Garden gets 200 or more replies for every job we advertise). We interviewed and eventually chose Elisabeth Smith, who'd previously worked for the NSPCC. She started on 13 August 2001 – a momentous day for me. For forty years I'd had my own office, and all of a sudden I had to share it with Elisabeth. It was in the Clock Tower part of the Estates offices, and she used to joke on the phone that she was now working in the Tower.

Elisabeth was the first full-time member of staff the Duchess and I appointed to work for the Garden. Jane couldn't wait to offload all her hated sponsorship files but unfortunately her arrival didn't mean an end to our fundraising activities. Before Elisabeth arrived we were still lobbying commercial and private sponsors. I'd met Alan Wann, director of Regeneration NCC, to discuss grant aid through Northumberland Strategic Partnership, and Jo Laverick to discuss aid through the Leader+ package via DEFRA. I'd written another begging letter to Suez-Lyonnaise des Eaux. On the corporate side, the Duchess invited Lord Blyth of Rowington, chairman of the global drinks company Diageo, to the Castle. Lord Blyth wrote that he didn't want to visit under 'false colours' as he would find it difficult to sponsor the Garden because of public perception – he thought questions would be asked about spending shareholders' money on behalf of the 'nobility'.

At lunch, Lord Blyth was also pessimistic about the Duchess's chances of getting a commercial 'big fish' to sponsor Phase 2. He thought we were going at this the wrong way and asked an obvious question: why didn't she borrow the money and run the Garden as a business, rather than waiting for sponsors to come along? The Duchess's reply was bullish: 'I can't borrow that much money. But even if I could, in order to pay back the interest I would have to set the entrance fees so high that the Garden wouldn't be affordable for local people, and that defeats all my objectives.' If people had to pay £15 or £20 to get in, it was obvious that The Alnwick Garden would become an attraction for the well-heeled instead of a vibrant, community-based resource used by people from all backgrounds.

It was at times like this that I took inspiration from Tim Smit, who'd just opened the Eden Project to great fanfare. Tim has what he called his 'Tinkerbell' theory: 'If you think enough about something it will happen.' The Duchess and I had put that principle into practice for years. I sent Tim a good luck card and heard that within three months the £86 million Eden Project had received its millionth visitor. 'Tinkerbell' had worked for him.

In a roundabout way, James Blyth was as instrumental in raising our morale as Tim Smit. Diageo then owned the Gleneagles Hotel and other tourist venues, and Lord Blyth offered to send Ian Wright, his head of visitor attractions, to the Garden to give us some advice. Ian Wright listened to Jane, walked round the site, and immediately saw the Garden's potential. KPMG's 1997 feasibility report had suggested we'd expect 67,000 visitors a year, about the same number as visited the Castle. But Ian Wright said the project was going to be huge. He thought that in the first year we'd be looking at around 250,000 visitors, and he was spot on. He was the only outsider in the early days who understood exactly what the Duchess was aiming to do, and who was as upbeat and positive about the success of the project as she was. And with his experience in running visitor attractions, he knew what he was talking about.

THE IMPORTANCE OF LOCAL SUPPORT

Having lived in Alnwick and been an active community member for forty-five years, I was always keen to liaise with local people about the changes the Garden would bring to the town. Some locals wholeheartedly supported it; others were naturally

ABOVE: Charlie Dimmock signing up to become a friend of the Garden.

ABOVE: The first get-together of The Alnwick Garden Volunteers, 2000.

LEFT: The Garden staff enjoy a team-bonding breakfast in the marquee.

apprehensive, fearing that noise, litter or crowds of tourists would descend on Alnwick's normally tranquil streets. I always felt it was important to have the town with us, to keep the local people updated so they felt part of what was happening.

As early as 1998, I asked the Duchess about setting up a Friends of the Garden scheme to get locals involved. On 1 April 2001, we offered an introductory rate of £10 per Friend and £25 per Family Friend, with unlimited access to the viewing area. My wife Ann rushed to make sure she got the very first Friend's membership – she is still proud to be 'Friend Number One'. Aidan and his family joined as the first Family Friends membership, and were awarded the number 1,001.

The scheme was a great success: four months later Charlie Dimmock became our 1,000th member and gave the Garden her official support. By the end of the year we had 4,000 Friends and that soon rose to over 10,000, a figure that is still rising to the present day. The membership offers good value: there are newsletters and special events, and Friends can visit the Garden every day of the year (except Christmas Day, when it is closed). Many take the opportunity to walk their dogs in the Woodland Walk where they have unparalleled views of the Castle, the River Aln and the 'Capability' Brown landscape. The Friends scheme has been very important for us because it created a core of loyal people, many of them local, who supported the Garden even before it was built.

COMMUNICATION PROBLEMS

But their support couldn't stop the flak flying in summer 2001, when we had our first misunderstanding with the town. The local water company, Northumbrian Water, needed to replace some of the town's three-inch water pipes with six-inch ones to give an enhanced supply – apparently there was greater demand as more houses were coming into the system. For some reason, the water company decided to do this in the peak summer season in late July. They switched off the town's water supply for a weekend and dug up the road around Hotspur Tower to replace the pipes, so traffic was at a standstill. This was at the height of the tourist season, so visitors staying in central B&Bs were unable to get a cup of tea, never mind a bath, and the town was in uproar. Everyone blamed the Duchess, saying that the water had been cut off to provide a new supply for the fountains at The Alnwick Garden. People saw a trench being dug by Northumbrian Water at the entry to the Garden in Denwick Lane, put two and two together and naturally made five, thinking this had everything to do with the town's supply.

There was a lot of resentment. Charlie Dimmock and her TV crew filmed locals complaining vociferously about the Duchess 'taking the town's water for her Garden', which wouldn't bring locals any benefits at all. The Press picked up on the story, and one national newspaper quoted an unnamed hotelier as saying: 'We think it's a damned disgrace to have our supplies cut off so the fountains will flow better at the Castle. It seems we've gone back to the Middle Ages when the aristocracy walked all over the peasants.'

This was laughable, but couldn't be ignored. We needed to defend our position and convince local people that this problem with the water was not a direct result of the Duchess's profligate 'fountains'. Jane and I gave many interviews to TV news channels and newspapers, trying to explain our position. But we couldn't tell the whole story. We were still in negotiations with Northumbrian Water about sponsorship – they were promising us a donation – and didn't want to compromise our relationship with them by blaming them for the débâcle, even though we believed it was largely their fault. We'd been asking them for months to lay the pipework for the Cascade, but they had delayed so long that they had to do the work in mid-summer to make the opening date. The Duchess now says that discretion in this case was the wrong decision, and we'll never again take that kind of flak for something that wasn't our fault.

THE PEOPLE'S TRUST

After this I was keen to get the town on side and prevent local criticism growing. There were some letters in the local newspaper complaining about the Garden – why did it have charitable status, what's in it for the townspeople, why isn't the money being spent to benefit the whole of the Alnwick district? We needed to address these issues. We made sure we had a representative on The People's Trust, which had been set up specifically to encourage commercial interests in the town. On our website we organized hyperlinks to the district council's site for places to stay, and to Northumbria Tourist Board's site for those looking for attractions beyond the town. We hammered it home that we were employing over fifty local builders on site, and that we would be delighted to listen to any ideas local people might have to help 'grow' the garden and the town in tandem. We also instructed our PR, Robson Brown, to let people know of local businesses we were using in the construction of the Garden, such as Bede Engineering Ltd from Birtley. They had constructed the steel frames of the pergolas that ran up both sides of the Cascade and in the Rose Garden, and had expanded their full-time workforce to fulfil the contract.

Meanwhile, building work on the Cascade, Ornamental Garden and Rose Garden was progressing well. The first frame of the pergola was erected on 16 July; the structural elements of the pools and rills in the Ornamental Garden were laid; the walls and weirs of the Cascade were finished; and the car park surfaces and planting were completed. It was beginning to look like a proper garden, much to Aidan's relief. Prince Philip, HRH The Duke of Edinburgh, made a private visit in August and wrote a delightful thank-you note wishing us millions of visitors. On 10 September the tower crane was removed. We were nearly ready to go public.

ABOVE: The Alnwick Rose in full bloom. The rose was specially chosen
for the Garden from a selection of newly developed David Austin varieties.
The Duchess chose it for its deep colour and subtle scent of raspberries.

CHAPTER 9

'A REVOLUTION IS NOT
A BED OF ROSES'

The Rose Garden has always been a world apart. Tucked into the west corner of the Lower Garden near the Castle, it is our one traditional 'English' garden. Serpentine paths lead visitors through the wide borders under rose-covered pergolas where 3,000 rose bushes and climbers provide an exuberant mass of colour and scent. What I love about it is the freedom and flow of undulating colour. Here, the roses are pruned at different heights and levels so the bushes intertwine and you can't see where one species begins or another ends. The result is a magnificent tapestry of flowing colour and rich greenery, with not a patch of bare earth below. The Rose Garden was also the easiest garden to create and, to my immense relief, the first to attract commercial sponsorship.

In March 1999, a month after the publicity generated by our website launch, David Austin Roses approached me about sponsoring the Rose Garden. At this time we were desperate for money. We'd spent three years hunting down sponsors, wining and dining and knocking on doors, with not a penny to show for it. We were at a low ebb, and this letter came like a gift from the gods.

David Austin championed old-fashioned, deliciously fragrant roses such as gallicas and floribundas in the 1970s when the fashion was for colourful, unscented hybrid teas. Crossing the old-fashioned varieties with new cultivars, he developed the 'English rose' – charming, subtly coloured, highly scented roses, with repeat-flowering and dense-cupped flowers. Working with a trailblazing British horticultural company seemed a reflection of our ethos. I was very pleased.

Later that year I visited nursery manager Michael Marriott at David Austin Roses' headquarters near Wolverhampton. I remember being unnaturally excited

RIGHT: An elevated view of the Rose Garden in summer. The picture was taken from the roof of the water tower, 2005. The garden contains over 3000 rose bushes and climbers, all planted close together to create a profusion of colour and scent.

by the thought of visiting the city. As a kid I'd been a passionate supporter of Wolverhampton Wanderers in the days of Billy Wright and here I was, forty years later, making my first visit. My spirits rose as we passed the football stadium en route to the Austin nursery in Albrighton, and I'm only sad I didn't have time to stay for a match. Michael Marriott – an immensely tall and charming man who is a walking rose encyclopaedia – introduced me to David Austin Senior, who set up the company in 1969, and his son, David Austin Junior, the commercial director. They gave me a tour of the nursery and I explained the concept of the Garden, showed them the Wirtzes' plans, and left hoping I'd planted a seed of interest.

They immediately wrote saying how excited they were about the project and offering us a sponsorship package of 3,000 roses, plus free planning time and site visits. This was a milestone for us: it was our first commercial sponsorship success, but I think compliments are also to due to David Austin Roses who showed great business acumen by approaching us at that early stage. Both the Duchess and I wrote thanking them: to us, their name was synonymous with excellent roses and their sponsorship supported our aim to ensure everything in the Garden was of the highest quality.

Then Michael Marriott had another good idea: he suggested the Duchess choose one of David Austin's newly developed roses and name it after the Garden. She loved the idea, and suggested 'a deep rich red rose – or any colour with an incredible scent – not a wishy-washy multi-coloured one'. So in July 2000 Jane, Peter Wirtz and I visited the nursery with a BBC TV film crew to choose what became the 'Alnwick Rose' from a selection of six new David Austin roses. We went for fragrance as well as looks, choosing a wonderful pink blush rose with full, cupped flowers and layer upon layer of petals blooming from early summer to the first frosts. But what lingers in the memory is its fruity, old rose fragrance with a hint of fresh raspberry. The 'Alnwick Rose' is a classic in the making and quickly became one of David Austin's top twenty bestsellers.

That year Peter Wirtz drew up a planting plan for the Rose Garden with Michael Marriott's involvement. At first I wasn't sure how Peter and Michael would get on, but as Peter showed his wide knowledge of the Austin roses – he'd used then regularly in other Wirtz International designs – the two of them clicked. The Duchess's aim was to make the garden a rose lover's paradise, with a profusion and flow of colour from May until November. She wanted people to be so overwhelmed by the range and quality of species that they'd be jotting down notes of their names.

The roses Peter chose range from pure white to deepest purple, through cream, yellow, apricot, pink and red. There are deep cup, rosettes, open cup, semi-double, single and tea rose blooms, ranging in size from the tiny creamy semi-double 'Rambling Rector' to the hand-sized, salmon-pink blooms of 'Morning Mist'. Climbers and ramblers such as 'Etoile de Hollande' and 'May Queen' twine over the pergolas and walls while the beds are full of old and English roses such as 'Tuscany Superb', 'Queen of Denmark', 'Winchester Cathedral', 'Graham Thomas' and 'Jude the Obscure'. In total there are over 180 named varieties, but pride of place on the corners and front of many borders goes to the profuse pink blooms and heady scent of the 'Alnwick Rose'.

A FOCAL POINT

It was sheer good fortune that Wirtz International had designed the Rose Garden in the west end of the Lower Garden, which was the first area to be constructed in McAlpines' organizational schedule. Although it needed irrigation and good drainage, the Rose Garden was otherwise a straightforward build and McAlpines made swift progress. By the end of 2000 the footpaths and pergolas, simple rectangular shapes made of matt black wrought iron by Bede Engineering, had been set out. In January 2001 the Duchess suggested we move a monumental lead Fox sculpture from Syon House to take centre stage in the arbour. At Syon, where it sat in a courtyard, it was only appreciated by the family. She felt it should be seen by a wider audience.

The Fox sculpture has a romantic history. Dating from the late eighteenth century, it's similar to an earlier Four Seasons monument designed by architect

ABOVE: The Fox sculpture. Formerly located at Syon House,
London, it now has pride of place in the Rose Garden.

Thomas Coke, now situated at Melbourne Hall in Derbyshire. According to Jane Johnson, the Assistant Head Gardener who researched its provenance, the Fox sculpture was made to the same cast as the Four Seasons at a lead works in Hyde Park Corner, possibly for Charles Hamilton of Painshill Park in Surrey. It was bought by Hugh, the 10TH Duke of Northumberland and Ralph's father, after he'd won a big wager on a good day's racing at Ascot. In all my years working for the 10TH Duke, I'd never once seen him blow money on anything as frivolous as a garden ornament – it seemed completely out of character! Jane thought he only bought the urn because he was a mad keen hunting man and loved foxes, and on top of the 200-year-old sculpture is a very realistic life-sized fox. Around the sides are several nasty-looking monkeys, which keep children enthralled, a row of plump cherubs running through a sylvan glade, and stern-looking heads of the Four Seasons near the top.

The urn was freighted from Syon, and placed in its permanent position in the arbour. We had to rebuild the stone base to provide a balanced plinth to support its massive weight.

Old artefacts like this often provoke memories and imaginings about times past. Jane sometimes thinks the ghost of her father-in-law, Hugh, is watching her as she walks among the roses, and wonders what on earth he makes of The Alnwick Garden now. Times have changed: the 10TH Duke that I knew had a very different concept of ducal responsibilities from Jane and Ralph's. I don't think he'd have understood either the landscape or the public-spirited aims of The Alnwick Garden. Forty years ago, this Garden wouldn't have been built.

CHELSEA 2001

In May 2001 the Duchess, Charlie Dimmock, my wife Ann and I went to the Chelsea Flower Show to launch the 'Alnwick Rose'. I always enjoy Chelsea, and this year was going to be something special. One of the advantages of working for the Garden has been the buzz of meeting interesting people from a wide variety of backgrounds. Some are famous, like Charlie Dimmock. She was at the height of

TOP LEFT: The part of The Alnwick Garden that has now become the Ornemental Garden, 1996. This area was formerly the kitchen garden and larch seed orchard.

BOTTOM LEFT: The triple arches of the Ornamental Garden and the flowers under a light winter frost, 2005.

TOP RIGHT: The Ornamental Garden during the first stage of construction, winter 2000.

BOTTOM RIGHT: Diggers start forming paths. The size of diggers used was determined by the width of the ornamental arches, being the only access into this garden.

her popularity in 2001, and it was a treat to see a real star in action. The Duchess enjoyed the fact that the crowds paid no attention to her as they mobbed Charlie for her autograph.

The sparky chemistry between Charlie and Jane turned the launch of the 'Alnwick Rose' into a big success. The rose's classic beauty and fragrance and long flowering season has made it a bestseller – in the Garden alone we now sell over 2,500 plants a year.

THE ORNAMENTAL GARDEN

As well as the Rose Garden, Wirtz International drew up planting plans for the Ornamental Garden and the slopes around the Cascade. Both Jacques and Peter are masterful plantsmen. The Duchess saw some of their plantings in 1999 when she visited six private gardens they'd created in Belgium. Her first impression was of the terrible topography of the Belgian countryside. 'If they can make places look so beautiful in this awful landscape,' she joked, 'we picked the right people to create something great at Alnwick.' She thought Jacques Wirtz understood and treated plants almost as if they were human. He didn't just care about the overall look, but about putting the right plants in the right conditions so that every single plant was happy and thriving.

Ann and I also visited the Wirtzes in Schoten a little later. I was overawed by the gardens Jacques Wirtz had designed thirty or forty years earlier. They still had a freshness and magic about them. The green architecture and floral abundance had matured around the pure linear structures to create visions of simple elegance.

The Wirtzes asked the Duchess if there were any particular plants she wanted to include or exclude from the Garden. Jane loves peonies and irises, isn't keen on big pompom dahlias – but felt that they were the experts and should be left to develop their own plant schemes. Although I spend a good few hours a week looking after my own one-and-a-half-acre garden, I'm no horticultural expert either and the planting was developed almost entirely by the Wirtzes.

RIGHT: One of two dovecotes in the Ornamental Garden, home to our tumbler doves.

For me, the Ornamental Garden is their horticultural *tour de force*, the jewel in the Garden's crown. They created a design using over 16,500 plants, laid out on a repeating square pattern, with rills and paths between. The central 'bubble' pond is surrounded by a wooden pergola covered by climbing roses, clematis and vines. Pleached crab apples above head height give a soaring three-dimensional effect and in late spring turn into a wall of white blossom that young children could imagine as fairyland. When I take people on tours round the Garden, they always exclaim with astonishment at the secret wonderland behind the sixteenth-century Italian gates. Each square is bordered by hedging of low box or tall *Cornus mas,* and filled with irises, delphiniums, Oriental poppies, euphorbias, hydrangeas and peonies. There are squares packed with unusual spring bulbs and the fruiting area contains red, white- and blackcurrants, gooseberries, strawberries and jostacurrants. On the walls are red dovecots. It's perfect. I go up there whenever I get ten minutes to sit and think. To me it's a place of quiet and contemplation, a welcome contrast to the solid green structures and noisy activity of the Cascade area below.

LANDSCAPE PLANTING

Before we could put a single plant into the Garden we needed a landscape contractor versatile enough to work with trees, shrubs, perennials and other soft planting. We put the contract out to tender and Trevor Atkinson & Co. from Barnard Castle, a family business run by Trevor and his son Richard, came in with the lowest bid. Peter, Aidan and I went to assess some of Atkinsons' planting at Durham county cricket ground and the Royal Quays in Newcastle. Then Richard took us to see the private garden of Neil Tennant, formerly of the pop group the Pet Shop Boys, in County Durham. Unfortunately, we didn't catch a glimpse of the man himself but his gardens were beautifully landscaped and planted. Atkinsons started work in November 2000, building up the subsoil and preparing and levelling the top soil under Peter Wirtz's beady eye. One of Peter's obsessions is the quality of soil cultivation and he wanted a nutrient-rich, well-structured tilth before planting started, and no quarter to be given!

Atkinsons went straight into top gear. The conditions were testing: to meet our deadlines they had to work flat out in all weathers – and that year it rained so hard we were at one point seriously worried that the top of the Cascade was going to float down the hill. On 18 December the Duchess and Charlie Dimmock ceremoniously dug in the first tree in the Ornamental Garden. A momentous occasion – and, as Jane reminded us, 'Only 64,999 more to go!' By the end of the year Atkinsons had finished planting the oak and beech whips in the car park area. The Garden planting was done with factory precision. As soon as McAlpines finished building one area, the Atkinsons team moved in. By the time McAlpines had laid the steel pergola half way up the west side of the Cascade, Atkinsons were at the bottom planting it up with hornbeam, methodically following them round like ants carrying a tasty dinner. They tracked McAlpines up the west side, then up the east. Some trees were dropped in place by the tower crane to speed things up.

TREES AND SHRUBS

All the trees and shrubs were supplied by two European nurseries, a choice that later became a bone of contention. One of the stipulations of receiving ERDF money to finance Phase 1 was that we put the contracts out to tender in other EU countries as well as Britain. We had little response from English nurseries, but were very impressed by the deals offered by the Dutch tree nursery Van den Berk and the Belgian shrub and perennial nursery Jan Spruyt, who could supply high-quality plants in the large quantities and at the prices we needed. I met up with Jan van Vechel from Van den Berk and thrashed through a sponsorship deal that we calculated saved up to £50,000 within Phase 1. Meanwhile, Jan Spruyt jumped at the chance of supplying us: Peter Wirtz was confident they could do the job, and they too offered us a very generous discount.

The Duchess, Charlie Dimmock, Peter Wirtz and I went out to Van den Berk's to watch the trees being selected. Charlie went on Eurostar but Jane and I got the 6.00 a.m. flight from Newcastle to Brussels. We met up with Charlie, Peter Wirtz, director John Thornicroft and his cameraman and sound recordist at Brussels

ABOVE: The pergola framework soon after it had constructed.

ABOVE: It took four years for the hornbeam to grow over the pergola. Windows were cut into the hornbeam and can be seen by the light shining through. Visitors can look through the windows to the Cascade.

RIGHT: A view of the Grand Cascade through a pergola window.

airport, and piled into a big van to go over to Van den Berk's 500-acre nursery. I'd never seen such an expanse of incredible specimens – tabletop and peach trees, cloud junipers, and vast Scots pines that were being moved to the middle of Paris to make an instant wood. We watched as Peter and the Van den Berk team selected the 166 'Red Sentinel' crab apple trees for the Ornamental Garden. They pleached these as standards on the spot, tying in and pruning the branches along a cane frame so they would grow to give a wall of greenery above head height.

We chose the tall, thin, fastigiate oaks – Peter Wirtz's favourite 'northern European alternative to the Italian cypress' – to form the sacred groves around the Cascade side pools. The trees were then loaded on to huge container lorries to begin their journey to Alnwick. Over the next few months packed container lorries would turn up once or twice a week delivering the rest of the trees and shrubs.

In total the two nurseries supplied about 62,000 trees and plants: 850 hornbeam for the Cascade pergolas, nearly 15,000 evergreen box, 32,000 beech trees and 10,000 perennials, as well as other specimens. The hornbeam trees were ten years old, but still had root balls smaller than a football because they had been grown using the spring-ring root technique, which aids successful transplantation. When the hornbeams were a year old, Van den Berk's lifted them out of the ground, clipped the roots and replanted them, repeating the process on a three-year cycle. When the trees arrived with us, we stored them in the reception area of the nursery and planted them individually in perforated pots containing a special growing medium. As the roots grow through the holes in the pots and hit light and air, their tips shrivel and die and the remaining piece of root divides. This produced exceptionally strong fibrous growth within the root ball. Normally when transplanting trees you expect to lose around 25 per cent; with the spring-ring technique we were warned we'd lose up to 3 per cent. In the end we lost just one tree, even though they were planted in difficult conditions between the concrete foundations of the pergola. This was a real tribute to the quality of trees supplied and the resourcefulness and care shown by their planters.

'A revolution is not a bed of roses,' Fidel Castro once said, but it soon transpired that even creating a bed of roses is not a simple task. Michael Marriott of Austins announced that the volume of roses we needed was creating stock problems for the nursery: he'd be able to deliver a third of the roses in spring, but the rest would have to wait until autumn. This was a blow as we'd have a half-empty Rose Garden on opening day, but there was little we could do about it. The first delivery of 1,000 roses, including the climbers for the pergola, came in April 2001, and were planted out. Peter Wirtz was concerned that when we opened there should be no bare patches of earth, so he decided to plant radishes at the base of the roses. When the public walked in, they saw a bright green carpeting of radish leaves in the Rose Garden: an unusual combination, but it worked. The advantage was that before planting the next batch of roses in November the gardeners simply forked the radishes in to add a lovely lot of nitrogen into the soil.

WHO WILL MANAGE THIS?

Now planting was under way, my next job was to hire a head gardener to run the horticultural side. In a 1998 estimate of the running costs of the Garden, Peter Wirtz had suggested we needed one head gardener, six full-time gardeners and five part-time students to maintain the twelve-acre site. Peter had strong ideas about the kind of person he was looking for, as he wrote to the Duchess and me:

> We need an excellent technician to come to grips with the Garden
> and all its aspects and diversity: roses, pleaching, fruit, delphiniums,
> peonies, hydrangeas, annuals, vegetables, perfect clipping of geometric
> shapes, spraying pesticides and fungicides AND being a pleasant person,
> although excellent gardeners are often eccentric and great introverts with
> love for the job.

Jane had been staying with Harry Henderson, a good friend who'd helped with fundraising. She had noticed a wonderful smell from some cut flowers and said to Harry, 'With flowers like that, you've obviously got a great head gardener.' Then turning her back, she cheekily added: 'Let's hope he applies for a job at Alnwick.' Harry, of course, was mock furious and said, 'If you dare...!' She knew she was going to be in the doghouse if – as was entirely likely – she poached a head gardener from someone she knew.

Richard Atkinson, Aidan and I drew up a shortlist of ten candidates. For the first year, the head gardener was to be employed by Atkinsons so they were heavily involved in the process. Eventually, we whittled the numbers down to two, whom the Duchess, Peter, Rory Wilson and I interviewed. We were very taken with Chris Gough, who'd worked for fourteen years as head gardener for Sir Philip and Lady Isabella Naylor-Leyland at Nantclwyd Hall in Ruthin, and later at their Humphrey Repton-designed landscape at Milton Hall near Peterborough. Chris was a larger-than-life character, very hands on and practical, a good talker and leader. I immediately took to him and thought he had every quality we needed in abundance. The only difficulty was that the Duchess was going to be pinching the gardener of someone she knew: Isabella Naylor-Leyland is one of Lord Lambton's daughters. Lord Lambton thought it hilarious that Jane was 'stealing' his daughter's head gardener and has joked about it ever since, though Isabella Naylor-Leyland doubtless has her own views on the matter. The Duchess knew her a little, and wrote to say she was sorry if Chris's appointment caused her inconvenience.

Chris was due to start on 1 October 2001, the Garden's opening day. Although we were far from ready, we needed to open to the public to fulfil the demands of our ERDF funding. The plan was to have a preview opening for the Friends of the Garden on 29 September, followed by a day free of charge for the people of Alnwick, followed by the public opening on 1 October. Patron HRH the Prince of Wales couldn't be there but sent a very supportive letter and promised to attend the official opening the next year.

HOW MANY VISITORS?

We weren't sure how many people to expect over the weekend, but we knew we'd need to supply refreshments and had been talking to Anthony Walford of

Edinburgh's Mussel Inn about on-site catering facilities. Before a catering meeting in the Conference Room, Northumberland Estates' agent Rory Wilson took Jane aside and said that, although the Garden was opening in autumn, he didn't want her to do a deal with the Mussel Inn until next spring when the Castle season started and visitor numbers would be higher. But Jane was adamant and said, 'I think he's wrong – the opening weekend is going to be busy, and I'm going to ask the Mussel Inn to start now.'

We went in, and when Anthony asked how many people we were expecting on the opening weekend, Jane said calmly, 'Oh I think we'd better plan for about 5,000.' Rory blanched and said, 'Duchess, with the greatest respect, that is not going to happen. The Castle only gets 1,000 visitors on a busy summer day, so what makes you think you'll get 5,000 in a weekend?' At that moment, I felt incredible sympathy for Rory. This was dealing with new territory and he was trying to protect the Duchess from what he perceived as her over-confidence: Alnwick is dead in the winter, and he thought our figures were pie in the sky. But Jane was closer to the project and had been getting positive feedback from locals and Friends for months. She gambled that people were interested enough in what was going on behind the Denwick Lane wall to make the opening a success.

Despite Rory's entreaties, we hired Anthony Walford and erected a marquee where the Pavilion now stands. To me there's something enticing about marquees: this one had a small kitchen area and a larger seating area where people could sit with a sandwich and coffee and watch the works going on. The Mussel Inn team moved in and started to get ready for the promised thousands to turn up on the big day.

VOLUNTEERS

At this stage, there were still only four of us working full time in the Garden: office administrator Karen Daniels, who'd been my assistant for years, fundraiser Elisabeth Smith, a part-time student helper called Rob McNally, a charming lad who'd had a bad time working for a big bank in London and returned to Alnwick, and me. We knew we couldn't cope with thousands of visitors by ourselves. So Ann rallied a team of eighty Volunteers, local people who were prepared to give a few hours a week to help in the Garden on an ongoing basis. I'd always been keen to set up a Volunteer system. An old friend of mine, Martin Dawes, is a volunteer at Holehird Garden in Windermere and had often talked about how the team of volunteers run this forty-acre garden without a permanent gardener in sight. I thought there was a similar opportunity for us at Alnwick.

In July I gave a presentation at Holehird about the Garden, and in return picked their brains about how their system of volunteers worked. In Alnwick so many talented professional people were keen to give their time and energy to the project that we were spoilt for choice. Before the opening, I wrote a three-page potted development of the Garden so that Volunteer guides were equipped to answer any questions. Two days before the opening, I led an orientation around the Garden, showing the volunteers the key features and explaining the history and development of each area. We roughly divided labour: Carnegie and Marjorie Brown were to lead the plant room tours; Tom Pattinson, a great man with an incredible knowledge of horticulture who writes the gardening page in the *Northumberland Gazette*, and who later became the Garden's second Lifetime Friend in honour of his great contribution, helped with guiding and horticultural queries. Support came from so many Volunteers, without whom we couldn't have coped that day, nor on many days in the years to come. They are a committed and enthusiastic group who assist with gardening, guiding, hosting and administration.

SCRABBLING BEHIND THE SCENES

Meanwhile, Aidan and Gordon were working flat out for the big day. Twenty-four hours before, the paths and cobbles in the rills were still being laid. Although the Rose and Ornamental Gardens were looking good, the area around the Cascade was a mud bath and we didn't have a drop of water in the pipes to fill the weirs and basins. We weren't expecting the Cascade fountains to be running but we wanted a few working jets and fountains to show the Friends the whole thing wasn't a damp squib. Northumbrian Water had promised us our water supply by mid-September, but it only began to materialize a nerve-wracking twelve hours before the opening in a very, very, very slow trickle. We realized it wasn't going to fill a bath, never mind the whole system, before morning. In a panic, Aidan contacted the water company who suggested bypassing our pumps and opening the valves so that the water flowed straight in. At 7.00 that evening, Aidan and Gordon were anxiously watching and waiting: they still didn't know if there'd be enough water by the morning to get any fountains working.

On opening day Aidan arrived at 4 a.m., an hour later Gordon turned up, and by 8.00 a.m. when I arrived, there was enough water flowing down the rills to count as a small stream! When I went up to the Ornamental Garden a little later Gordon was still in his Jacques Cousteau dry suit, jumping into the fountains to align the nozzles and adjust the height of the jets. Our hydraulics and IT engineer, Steve Tellwright, was in the lower plant room fiddling around with the computer system. The Duchess and I were doing the final clean-up on site, moving chairs and benches into position, sweeping up debris and getting the dustpan and brush out to give the Marquee a final spruce before the hordes arrived. By the time we had finished it looked nearly perfect.

FIRST VISITORS

It was pouring with rain, but that didn't put off the queues waiting to get in. I couldn't believe it: all day there was a long line of people outside the Marquee desperate for a cup of tea and a bite to eat. The Duchess brought the Duke and family along. It was a great day, and amongst the Volunteers something of the Blitz spirit prevailed.

There were two film crews on site: one for *Charlie and the Duchess*, the other filming *The Challenge*, the BBC2 Open University production directed by Jane Dibblin about the technical difficulties of building the Cascade. They got a lot of footage that day! I was trying to be everywhere – coordinating Volunteers, welcoming people, checking the facilities and making sure everything was running smoothly.

There were mile-long queues for the underground pump room tours Aidan and others were giving. The pump room was still classed as a building site so for health and safety reasons visitors had to don hard green hats before they went underground. The tour was a one-off opportunity: visitors were amazed that it takes eighteen pumps the size of domestic baths to create the water displays, with electronic control panels running from floor to ceiling for each pump. There are filter systems, cleaning systems, chemical dosing systems and complex pipe works. The technology is remarkable: the wind strength is electronically measured and in high winds the height of the fountains is automatically lowered to stop the water blowing across the Garden. I think the pump room is the only place where you get a true understanding of the sheer engineering feat of the Cascade. Even today people come up to me and Aidan and tell us that the highlight of their visit years ago was touring the underground plant room.

I was astonished at the enthusiasm of the visitors – they seemed to get such a buzz from wandering around what was in reality still a construction site. The success of that first weekend took us all by surprise. Although the Duchess and I had always been optimistic, we hadn't expected this level of interest. People collared me in the Garden to say how wonderful the project was, and to chat about the past, and what they wanted from this new Garden on their doorstep. What thrilled the Duchess was that over 5,000 visitors came through the gates that first weekend. We couldn't have hoped for a better start.

JETS

Seven weeks on, the jets in the Cascade were running – better late than never – and we decided to have a special opening to celebrate at the end of January. In the run-up to this, Steve Tellwright, the electronics engineer, damaged his hand in an accident at home so was trying to program the computers and fine-tune the displays with a duff finger. It was freezing cold and dark in the plant room, so we brought him soup, coffee and heaters to keep him going while he prepared us for the big event.

PREVIOUS PAGES: The pump room beneath the Grand Cascade. It takes eighteen massive pumps to keep the Grand Cascade flowing and create its water displays.

At the test run, Aidan and I were both hopping around like schoolboys, jumping for joy as the water flowed through the jets. I was completely emotional: we'd been working for five years to get to this point and it felt like the culmination of our efforts. It was a fantastic moment. I called Jane on her mobile and asked her to come down to the Garden. 'You're not going to believe what you see,' I told her.

She arrived, looked at the fountains in full flow and said, 'That's great, it works. Fantastic – it does just what we wanted it to do.'

A bit surprised that she seemed lukewarm, I said: 'Isn't this the best moment of your life?'

She looked at me and laughed. 'To be honest, Ian, no. I'm glad it's running, but for me it's done and dusted and in my head I'm on to the next phase.'

Our roles were reversed: normally she's the impulsive, exuberant one, while I'm calm and cool-headed. But at that moment she was two steps ahead, focused on the future and the finished product. Aidan and I always got a buzz from the technical achievements in the Garden, but for the Duchess the thought of seeing 150 OAPs tea-dancing in the Pavilion was more enticing – and that reality was still a long way off.

The fountains' opening day must have been one of the windiest of the year, with gusts of up to 60 m.p.h. The Marquee was billowing wildly and I was worried it was going to take off as we walked past to the Cascade where the Duchess was to give her welcoming speech. While Jane was talking, a huge gust blew a wall of water from the fountains all over her, drenching her thoroughly – a moment picked up by all the Press photographers.

'The water displays are every bit as good as I hoped,' she told reporters. 'I was worried about the wind but it has added to the overall spectacle and made the volume of water appear almost two-fold. It's easy to make a garden look beautiful in spring and summer, but this really proves it can be fantastic even in a gale-force wind in January.' Talk about looking on the bright side!

After everyone left we decamped to the Marquee for a cup of tea. The wind hadn't abated and the guy ropes were straining. Aidan was ready for it to go up like a balloon, and sat us away from the walls, which were billowing dangerously with every gust. It would be a bad opening day, he joked, if we lost the Duchess to the elements. 'You know, I really think we should evacuate,' he said five minutes later in a rather strained voice, but the Duchess only laughed and said, 'I'm staying to finish my tea.'

END OF PHASE 1 – OPEN AND BROKE

We finished Phase 1 at the end of February 2002 at a cost of £9.26 million, and McAlpines moved temporarily off site. That summer we were open to visitors. Poor Chris Gough, our head gardener: he'd come to this high-profile, multi-million pound Garden to find he had no team, no equipment – not even a wheelbarrow, a hose or a spade – and no money to buy supplies. We'd spent all our funds and didn't have a penny to run the Garden.

Jane went down to Chris's house one evening to have a drink with him and his wife, Elaine. 'I promise you we'll make this work,' she told him. 'We'll get the money together and it will happen – please just stick with us for a while.'

Begging and borrowing basic equipment is way beyond the call of a normal head gardener's job, but Chris didn't let it phase him a bit. He immediately set to work in the Garden with the help of Tom Pattinson and other horticulturally-minded Volunteers, who brought their own spades and forks with them. Then Chris began to work on sponsorship for tools and equipment and was very successful.

One of Chris's most generous contacts was the agricultural manufacturer John Deere, who came to me a little later offering us six children's tractors. The Duchess wasn't sure about having plastic toys in the Garden, but I thought it was a great idea. The Garden was only a third built and it would give children the chance to muck around and have fun in a big outdoor space. In the end Jane agreed, provided we asked for diggers with a dumper at the front so at least children could play at picking things up and carrying them around. We placed the diggers in the Lower Garden and watched what happened. Instantly, every child under nine made a

RIGHT: Resting on the oversized benches in the Ornamental Garden.

FOLLOWING PAGES: The Grand Cascade in full display during the official opening. In the background guests linger by the arches of the Ornamental Garden.

beeline for them. They drove up to the wall of water beside the Cascade, filled the scoop with water then pedalled back to tip it all over their parents' and siblings' feet. Within minutes there was a half-hour queue for these tractors.

HISTORY IN THE MAKING

Many visitors wrote praising the Garden, but we also got a few complaints: 'I am still brooding about my visit to your Garden and why you think it is appropriate to charge £4 for the privilege of walking round what is, in effect, a building site ...' was a typical refrain. I always wrote back offering complimentary tickets so that people would come back and see the Garden at a later stage. The Duchess coined a good marketing phrase, 'history in the making', which we started to use on our website and correspondence. People read newspaper articles and thought the Garden was finished, then arrived and were disappointed to see that it wasn't. When this happened, the Volunteer guides would say, 'Ah, but you're seeing history in the making here. It's a real opportunity – nothing like this has been built for the last 100 years,' so people started looking at it with fresh eyes. What makes this Garden unique is the fact that people have watched it develop over a ten-year period. Visitors come back and can't believe how much it's changed, and that can be as interesting and rewarding as experiencing the finished product itself.

One change that year caused a bit of a fracas with Peter Wirtz. The Duchess is a big champion of the region, and growing leeks and onions is a historic North-East tradition. Indeed, the Castle annals show that in 1822 it was the head gardener's responsibilities to provide the town's soup kitchen with leeks. Nowadays there's a leek and onion show in the town every year, and in pubs and clubs across the county there are fiercely fought competitions to grow the biggest leeks. Without telling Peter Wirtz, the Duchess and I gave over some big terracotta pots and a small area in the Ornamental Garden to leeks and onions. Then Chris Gough mooted the possibility with Peter Wirtz of permanently removing some delphinium beds to accommodate the leek and onion brigade. Peter was horrified and wrote back almost incoherent with alarm:

Leeks and onions don't have the class of delphiniums, despite their beauty, it's impossible ... Chris, I cannot understand, you take this so lightly, it would be a strong weakening of the garden, admit, you can't compare them!

Poor Peter: he couldn't understand what all the fuss was about. These prize leeks and onions grew to mammoth proportions and the interest from the public was equally as enormous, but I agreed with him that they stuck out rather amidst the delicate colours and geometric shapes of the Ornamental Garden. In the end, though, his delphiniums didn't have to be sacrificed – but the threat is not over yet. The Duchess still talks fondly about giving over a special corner of the Garden to leeks and onions ...

OFFICIAL OPENING

The Garden's official opening took place on 2 September 2002 at noon in the presence of HRH the Prince of Wales. I planned for this occasion with military precision: over 2,500 local people were invited, including contractors, designers, Alnwick district councillors, local business people, North-East regional government officials, hoteliers, Brownies and Cubs, local schoolchildren and the national Press.

Whenever a member of the royal family attends a public function, the security is phenomenal, so I was liaising with the police chief inspector and his team for weeks before. The Prince of Wales was arriving by helicopter, so we needed a landing pad: the rest of the visitors came by coach or car, so we had parking facilities and traffic flow to organize. The Garden Café was open, the water displays were running continuously, and the Alnwick Pipers Society was providing musical entertainment. Charlie Dimmock and John Thornicroft of the BBC were filming, as was Trevor Hearing of Studio Arts TV, for our own archives.

The day dawned bright and sunny and passed off without a hitch. The Duchess met HRH the Prince of Wales on the landing strip and introduced him to various

dignitaries, including the Mayor and the chief of Alnwick District Council. I was last in line, and led him off to be introduced to some of the Volunteers. The Duke and Duchess, their family, Sir John Riddell, Lord-Lieutenant for Northumberland, and I took the Prince of Wales on a tour of the Garden, meeting Jacques and Peter Wirtz in the top Ornamental area, where the Duchess gave her speech:

> Your Royal Highness, Friends of the Garden and Ladies and Gentleman, today is a day for celebration. We began this project six years ago and our homework has paid off ...
>
> The Alnwick Garden now has 10,000 Friends and eighty Volunteers who help with a variety of jobs. They understand this is their garden: a great park in the North-East for the people of the North-East. Visitor numbers have exceeded all expectations and we are on target to receive over 250,000 visitors during our first year and we are only one-third built ...
>
> His Royal Highness the Prince of Wales has been extremely supportive of the Garden project. He has watched it evolve from concept to reality and I am honoured and grateful for his help. He is a wonderful patron and has played an important role in the development and success of The Alnwick Garden.

HRH the Prince of Wales stayed for two hours and gave a very complimentary speech praising Jane's determination in the face of opposition and misunderstanding. He said it was a terrific achievement to bring the Garden back to life – then cut the ribbon and switched on the Cascade water fountains to great cheers. He had to leave a little later to open the charity Cancer Bridge, of which Jane was also a patron, and offered her a lift. As the helicopter rose into the sky, the Duchess saw the Garden from the air for the first time and said it was the most wonderful moment of an extraordinary day.

LEFT: September 2002, the official opening of The Alnwick Garden. HRH the Prince of Wales accompanied by the Duchess and Ian August is introduced to Marian Foster, a TV and Radio presenter for *Look North* and *Marian's Gardens*. When the Prince met her he said, 'I believe you are the Charlie Dimmock of the North'.

CHAPTER 10

DUCHESS, PUT YOUR HARD HAT ON!

My role as project director during the building works of Phase 1 had been to lead the design team for the Duchess. The job suited me down to the ground: because of my background in art and technical drawing, making aesthetic decisions was always a joy and what the Duchess jokingly called my 'August diplomacy skills' received a thorough workout on a daily basis. But once the Garden opened and we moved into Phase 2, the project altered dramatically and my role with it.

What changed everything was how successful the Garden suddenly became. Four times as many visitors as expected were piling up at the Garden gates each day, but we hadn't the infrastructure to cope or the money to fund the increased running costs. The Duchess was worried about the big financial hole that seemed to be opening up in front of us: we'd spent £9.3 million out of our £14 million budget to build Phase 1, which left just £4.7 million for Phase 2. But the Duchess was planning for a Pavilion, Visitor Centre, the largest Treehouse in Europe, a new car park – the one we'd built was overflowing by 11.00 each morning – plus seven or eight more garden rooms. All for £4.7 million? It was impossible, and Jane realized we needed expert financial advice to re-evaluate the Phase 2 budgets and move us towards a viable future.

And so John Lovett entered the team. He's a chartered accountant and businessman and a good friend of the Duke and Duchess. In early 2002, Jane asked him to look over the proposed Phase 2 finances and tell her precisely how much the rest of the Garden was going to cost. He had no concept of the size of it because Jane was always reluctant to talk about the Garden when she had dinner with friends. After the first week, he said to her: 'Jane, this project is huge – I had no idea,' and warned her it would take three months' work. We didn't have the money to pay for the Head Gardener's spades and forks, never mind three months' professional consultancy fees. Showing enormous faith in the Garden's future, John agreed to keep a tally of his working hours for payment once we'd raised some cash, and set up camp at the big table in the meeting room of our Portakabin office. I felt very comforted that someone with his professional and financial understanding was coming in to take the project forward.

John Lovett had been dropping heavy hints along the way that our £14 million estimate was too low. One day he sat the Duchess down, said he'd calculated the project down to the last paperclip, and it was a £42 million build. Jane's first reaction was to swear loudly: 'How am I going to explain this to the Press?' It was a big story. The papers had been outraged at the Duchess and her £14 million extravagance. How were they going to react now that figure had not just doubled but tripled?

John said he was full of admiration that the Duchess and I – complete amateurs – had embarked on such a bold project in the first place. But for us to have achieved Phase 1 and opened the Garden to the public with our limited resources, a team of part-time, ad hoc helpers and with only cautious, half-hearted support from Northumberland Estates completely astonished him. He quickly realized that the small, dedicated team who'd brought the Garden this far were not going to be able to run things any more: we were too inexperienced and lacked the necessary professional skills to take this brand new business any further. A £42 million budget is big business by any standards, and it was clear we needed proper management structures and staffing levels to be put in place.

PHASE 2: NEW TEAM

John moved into top gear, and organized an economic impact study funded by Northumberland Strategic Partnership to assess the Duchess's plans for the future phases. The Garden had already brought visitors and jobs to a depressed region, and many government bodies were keen to get behind us. Siân Johnson and Marc

Mallam duly arrived. I remember a stormy meeting in the town's council chambers at which Siân asked a group of us about the viability of future developments in the Garden. The day started badly: she went round the room asking our names, and when the Duchess answered 'Jane', blustered, 'Is that all, just Jane?' 'It's my name,' the Duchess replied. I sensed hostility in the air.

Obviously thrown a little, Siân started barking questions: was the Treehouse going to be a white elephant? What about the Pavilion? Where was the cash cow in this project? The Duchess shot me a look as if to say, 'What *is* this woman talking about?' This was the first time we'd been exposed to someone who thought of the project solely in commercial terms and it came as a shock. To us, the Pavilion and Treehouse were two separate attractions with different aims and functions and neither was going to be either a 'white elephant' or a 'cash cow'.

The Duchess's tolerance for this kind of business-speak is low and she started doodling ferociously on her pad, obviously trying to keep her temper under control. Siân then asked us to think seriously and prioritize every future development in the Garden by giving them marks out of five. The Duchess, in her usual optimistic manner, gave everything five, saying every aspect of the Garden was going to be brilliant. She got a ticking off for that.

Then Jane was asked why she was building a Pavilion and Visitor Centre with a large space for corporate entertainment when there were already too many such spaces in the North-East. Jane answered, 'It's irrelevant how many there already are. Ours will immediately go into the top six venues because of its outstanding beauty, extraordinary vistas and top quality.'

The gloves were well and truly off. Jane passed me a note saying 'They're all morons. They have no idea what we're trying to do.'

I got the feeling Caledonian Economics thought we were unprofessional, letting our enthusiasm run away with us. They liked a back-up business model in case things went wrong, and it seemed to make them nervous that, so far, the Garden's success was down to the Duchess's gut instinct rather than meticulous planning. Coming out of the meeting, Jane was upset and I felt alarmed at the way things were going. I was concerned that these new advisers were making generalized assumptions about the Garden from a box-ticking exercise. It was a sad day: the business suits had arrived, and nothing would be the same again.

A RADICAL MOVE AHEAD

What came out of the EI study was that there were no 'white elephants'. But to turn the Garden into a well-run visitor attraction our small team was inadequate and we needed a proper management structure. It made sense: we had no experience of running visitor attractions, and this way we could leave the running of the Garden to business leaders while the Duchess and I concentrated on maintaining standards of design and craftsmanship in the rest of the build. John brought in Joan Louw as finance manager, an ex-ballerina from South Africa who is dynamic with figures and brings passion to her analysis of spreadsheets and bottom lines.

To raise the outstanding amount, we needed to access public funding – no corporate knight on a white charger was going to give us £32 million. Elisabeth Smith and John were in talks with public and charitable bodies and it became clear that, to receive public money, the Garden had to split from the Lovaine Trust and set up as an independent charity. John Lovett wrote to the Duke explaining the situation, saying that the Garden needed to be run as a completely separate entity from the Castle, with its own independent trustees. This posed an interesting conundrum: although Northumberland Estates had never been fully behind the Garden, we were still part of their set-up, using their financial and legal expertise under the aegis of the Lovaine Trust. Although their support had always, in the Duchess's eyes, been lukewarm, they certainly didn't want to lose what was fast becoming the brightest toy in their toy box. The Garden was successful, a golden goose bringing tourists and money into the area, and the Castle was benefiting from the reflected prestige and increased visitor numbers. Although they hadn't wanted us in the first place, now they didn't want to let us go.

At its heart, the dispute was a clash between feudal and modern. There were two very different systems of patronage here: the 900-year-old Castle was used to

RIGHT: Aerial shot of the Labyrinth.

TOP LEFT: A meandering path leads visitors through dense *Fargesia rufa*. Lights in the peat beds and on top of tall vertical stakes combine with the rustling bamboo leaves to create a dramatic light–sound effect.

BOTTOM LEFT: The Labyrinth under early morning frost.

funding and running things its own way, without taking into account the wider public interest or any notion of democracy. By contrast, the Garden needed to be run as a modern entity, publicly funded, democratic and accountable. The two systems were obviously incompatible.

John Lovett immediately set the wheels of separation in motion, battling hard with Lovaine's trustees every inch of the way. He was effectively the intermediary between Jane and Ralph. Northumberland Estates, having first believed the Garden wouldn't work, now fought to hang onto the more lucrative parts of it, and wanted to charge large rents and consider profit sharing. John had a difficult job fighting over matters such as the ownership of the car parking area on the other side of Denwick Lane. It made him unpopular in the Castle but he shrugged it off, saying someone had to do it.

The process of separation took a year, during which, unable to ask for money from the Lovaine Trust, John had to convince lawyers and accountants to work on a contingency basis. Finally, in March 2003, the Garden was granted independent charity status. The Alnwick Garden Trust (AGT) was to run the Garden, its commercial subsidiary Alnwick Garden Enterprises to oversee retail and catering, with all profits going straight back into the coffers of the AGT. The trustees had to be important figures in the North-East: the Chairman was economist and OneNorthEast chairman Dr John Bridge, supported by a team consisting of the Duchess, Sir John Riddell, at the time Chairman of Northern Rock bank, author Matt Ridley (later to be replaced by Lord Stevens, a retired Commissioner of Police), local businessman Phillip Deakin and accountant Richard Middleton. Jane has always joked that John Lovett has surrounded her with accountants but we were all grateful that the Garden had a sound business footing at last.

During these manoeuvrings I took a back seat. Iain Ramage, a great friend who'd been working on the Garden from the start as contract administrator and quantity surveyor for Summers & Partners, now took over the title of project manager and was seconded to us four days a week. With Iain taking over project management and John Lovett the financial side, my role inevitably changed. It was decided my job title would now formally become Garden Liaison Director. In reality, it meant I got the opportunity to concentrate on what I really enjoyed: working with designers. At once, the Duchess and I put our heads together and started progressing plans for Phase 2.

THE LABYRINTH

In the Labyrinth, maze expert Adrian Fisher had already drawn up a design with a meandering path 'stream' surrounded by two-metre-high planted 'walls'. Adrian is a very interesting character: he has a great mathematical brain and talks very eloquently about the rationale behind his complicated maze designs. But he's not an expert on planting, and he and Peter Wirtz had to work together to find the best way of producing the dramatic light and sound effects the Duchess wanted. Peter was keen on using tall grasses to give a background rustling, but I worried about how this would work in winter when the grasses were cut back. Eventually, we came up with the idea of using *Fargesia rufa,* a dense Chinese bamboo that didn't lose its leaves in winter and would give an eerie, rustling effect all year round. It would be planted in waist-high beds of peat, sourced from an existing peat site in Poland, and densely planted with ferns. The maze would be underlit by lights in the peat beds, and tall vertical stakes carrying light on top would sway with the bamboo, giving a panoply of light and sound movement even in the lightest breeze.

THE POISON GARDEN

The Duchess had always planned an apothecary garden at Alnwick, and she came back inspired after visiting the infamous Medici poison garden in Padua with Lord Lambton. At the entrance to the Padua garden, there's a sign on the gate saying, 'Don't touch the plants, they kill.' This fired the Duchess's imagination: she believed that children would be more excited by evil potions and venomous intrigues than by 'healing' plants. Children want to know the gory details behind the events, such as how someone died

ABOVE: The ivy-covered tunnel entrance into the Poison Garden.

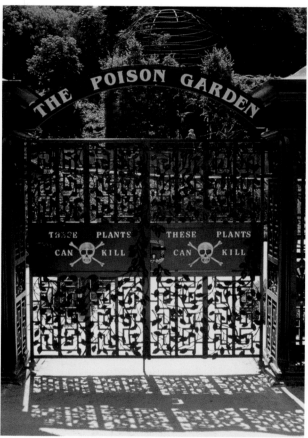

ABOVE RIGHT: To create a suitably deadly atmosphere the Amos Brothers designed big black gates with a skull and cross-bones and spine-chilling sign.

ABOVE LEFT: A close-up picture of the gates reveals snakes hidden within the ivy leaves.

TOP LEFT: *Cannabis sativa* (cannabis) and, TOP RIGHT *Ricinus communis* (castor) growing in the Poison Garden.

BOTTOM LEFT: the tunnel that leads visitors through the Home Office-licensed garden.

foaming at the mouth in agonizing pain after being poisoned by *nux vomica* from Lucrezia Borgia's ring.

I'd been in touch with Caroline Holmes, a garden designer and lecturer who'd been bringing groups of horticultural enthusiasts round the Garden for several years. She'd worked on many apothecary gardens and her knowledge of the subject was vast. I asked her to become our poison plant consultant, to create a poison planting within the framework of flame-shaped beds designed by Peter Wirtz. We discussed how to make the garden fascinating to children and adults: poisonous plants don't necessarily look frightening or unusual, but the myths and stories about them chill the blood. Their names tell their dark histories: Satan's cherries (the berries of deadly nightshade – just three will kill), death warrant (briony), the 'inheritance plant' (strychnine, used in Renaissance Italy to despatch errant spouses), mandrake (a narcotic), henbane (probably what Shakespeare had in mind for Juliet – the right dose gives the appearance of death, without actually killing you) and hemlock (paralysis stops lung function so death occurs from suffocation, while the mind is fully alert). The Duchess also visited Soutra Aisle, the site of an old monastery and the largest hospital in medieval Scotland. Archaeologist Dr Brian Moffat told gory stories of finding 'blood rivers' full of bones and 'soporific sponges' on the site. These sponges, infused with a dose of henbane, opium and hemlock, were fitted over the mouth and nose as anaesthetic so the monks could carry out amputations. The Duchess was fascinated by these stories of medicinal gore and knew they would grab the interest of our visitors, and also that of the Press and a wider public too.

To create the right atmosphere, we decided to make the Poison Garden a secret place, locked behind big black gates with a skull and crossbones warning 'These Plants Can Kill'. The deadliest plants would be grown in protective cloches and there'd be a strict 'no-touch' policy. Originally, we wanted a fine, spooky mist to emanate from the beds, with storytellers leading groups through the miasma telling them horrific tales of murder and intrigue. In the end, the mist didn't happen – it would have caused plants to die – but the storytelling became an integral part of the Poison Garden's allure. The idea was to inspire people verbally, not send them round with written fact sheets. Jane was definite the stories should be about kill, not cure: 'We want to inspire and educate our visitors without anyone realizing it. Please – no boring stories about fairy spirits,' she said on more than one occasion.

Caroline was completely inspiring and even persuaded Peter Wirtz to use plants he'd normally burn for their ugliness because they had such gruesome histories. Eventually, our education officer, Alison Hamer, liaised with the police and received Home Office approval to grow cannabis, coca and other drugs for educational purposes. Our aim was to complement the school curriculum and teach kids about drug use and abuse by stealth. This would be a safe place to learn about the dangerous side of plants.

THE SERPENT GARDEN

The Serpent Garden turned into the most challenging of the Phase 2 gardens. The area had been designed in a series of serpentine paths by the Wirtzes, but our early idea of using Wet Design's dramatic water sculptures was scuppered by their high cost. The pressure was on to find a designer with the same understanding and passion for water, and the technological expertise to create sculptures that made you stop and stare.

Lots of people were talking about William Pye, a British water sculptor who'd created *Slipstream*, the cone in the departures lounge at Gatwick Airport, and *Charybdis*, a vast acrylic cylinder with a vortex of corkscrewing water in a wine-glass shape, at Seaham Hall Hotel near Durham. One day the Duchess and I were in her kitchen flicking through a book of William Pye's work that a friend had lent her. It was noisy, the children were running about, but looking at his water sculptures I felt a moment of still pure calm. Jane looked up at me, grinned and said, 'This is genius – he's just the man we're looking for.'

His phone number was in the back of the book and she rang him on the spot. 'You won't have heard of me,' she said, 'but I'm building a garden in the north of

England and I'm looking for someone who really understands how to make water work. What I've seen in your book is exactly what I'm looking for. Would you be interested in coming up to have a look?' He replied simply, 'Duchess, I've been waiting for this phone call for five years!'

It is a joy to work with Bill Pye. He's a gentle man, with a lovely dry sense of humour. He has the brain of a physicist and the language and passion of an artist, an unusual combination that makes him stimulating company. Even Peter Wirtz, who sometimes rebelled against new designers being brought into the project, found him easy to get on with. Bill Pye's designs for Alnwick are captivating: the stainless steel and acrylic sculptures make water spiral, ripple, whirl and seemingly defy gravity. Torricelli, named after a seventeenth-century Italian mathematician, is the biggest and most dramatic of the sculptures and uses hydrostatic pressure to power ninety vertical jets. In action it's so remarkable that complete strangers stand and watch the twenty-minute cycle, chatting excitedly to one another about it.

Bill Pye and Peter Wirtz created a wonderful garden full of flowing curves, round pools and dramatic water sculptures. Then, one day, eight years after the overall plans were agreed, a square water feature arrived in a set of revised plans. The Duchess said, 'Ian, this looks strange. Everything else in the Lower Garden is round, then we suddenly get a square water feature. It doesn't work, and it's an alteration to the agreed plans.' I agreed: looking down at the Serpent Garden from the Cascade pergolas, the square pool would stick out like a sore thumb.

The project director talked to Peter, who said he was happy with the square pool. Bill Pye said, 'If Peter's happy, I'm happy.' This went on for months, until the Duchess put her foot down for the first and only time in the project's history. She asked me to let Peter and Bill know that if they weren't prepared to make a circular pool, she would leave the space empty and commission a separate design from another designer. They immediately agreed that a round design would be more in keeping with the rest of the Garden. Sometimes, the stick works better than a carrot.

William Pye's astonishing water sculptures in the Serpent Garden. The combination of stainless steel and moving water create a mesmerizing effect.

ANTICLOCKWISE FROM TOP LEFT: Vortex; Canyon; Torricelli; Waterglass; Starburst; Coanda; Meniscus.

TAKING THE MESSAGE TO THE PEOPLE

In 2002, the Duchess and I started an ambitious lecture tour around the country. The aim was to raise public awareness of the Garden at grass roots level and, hopefully, pave the way for more successful fundraising. My assistant, Karen Daniels, had pointed out that whenever we gave a speech, Friends' applications flooded in from the area: the lectures seemed to help people understand what the Garden was about, and made them want to support us.

By now we'd got our lectures down to a fine art: Jane stood on the right of the screen, I stood on the left, and we had a chatty dialogue across the stage to give an informal atmosphere. The presentation was interactive, done from a script with the Duchess ad-libbing at various points. We brought our own projector, screen and two illuminated lecterns so we could read our notes while the hall was darkened. I operated the projector's remote control and screen pointer light, and we used lapel mikes to link into the hall's sound system. Our driver, Ian Tate, was an old colleague with a long family history of working for the Percy family. After he left school he worked as an apprentice painter, his brother was an apprentice joiner, and his father worked on the Estates too. Ian married my secretary Lorna; and they now have three children. He changed jobs about the time I retired, becoming the Percy family's chauffeur and handyman. He used to help me set up the projector while the Duchess put Friends' leaflets on all the chairs. He also commandeered a table at each talk, and charmed guests into buying guide books about the Garden.

People get nervous inviting a duchess to speak, but their preconceptions about Jane are never borne out. They imagine they have to lay on a smart spread and reception so everyone gets a chance to meet the grand lady. In the early days, whenever we were invited to one of these events we'd say yes – many were ladies' lunches that I enjoyed immensely, often as the only man in a group of 250 women – but the Duchess grew to hate them. She was happy to talk about the Garden, but after a lecture she wanted to switch off.

From our point of view, it was always the bigger the audience the better, but however small the venue, you never knew what was going to come of it. Once we were invited to talk at Edinburgh Botanical Gardens. It was freezing cold, we had a terrible journey and when we arrived there were only about fifteen people in the audience. 'What a waste of time,' commented Jane in the car afterwards. I too was surprised that this was the best the Botanics could do. When the organizer thanked us at the end, he said, 'It's remarkable you already have 7,000 Friends of the Garden, while here at Edinburgh we only have a tiny percentage of that.' That comment sparked our interest, and we found out why: their membership was vastly more expensive than the £15 we charged.

In 2002 Sotheby's invited us to give a lecture in a series of garden talks they were holding in London. We decided to set aside a week in May to travel south and speak in each area from London to Cornwall. To us this was like entering the lion's den: people up north have always taken a fierce pride in the success of the Garden, but southerners seem at best indifferent and at worst highly critical of both the Duchess and the Garden. Being faced by a sea of cynical London faces was a daunting prospect that made us both quake.

Making the preparations felt like setting off on tour: we piled all the sound and lighting equipment into the car, and were ready for long distances and late nights. When the Duchess is on the road she likes to get from A to B as quickly as possible with no deviating or stopping – she's like a travelling salesperson, focused on the job in hand. On one leg of the journey down, Ian was driving and we were all hungry. The Duchess saw a big yellow 'M' at the side of the road and said, 'Do you mind if we pull in there?' I'd never been to McDonald's before: as the Duchess pointed out with a grin, I hadn't lived. She loves the whole drive-in concept: the fact you get your food, tea or hot chocolate in five seconds flat without even having to get out of the car is her idea of heaven.

The Sotheby's lecture was to 500 of the nation's great and good. Even Jane was worried: her biggest critics have always been those from her own social class, not Joe Public, and she knew they'd be out in force tonight. Friends kept coming up to her saying, 'You'd better be careful. I've heard two people really having a good bitch about you in the corner there. "Ask her why the Garden is so expensive," they were saying. "Ask her if anyone could have built this without their husband's money."' Jane doesn't normally drink at all, but she downed a couple of glasses of champagne to steady her nerves – a fact that made me even more nervous. Nodding towards her glass as diplomatically I said, 'Er, Duchess, we might have a problem if we're not careful.' It was water off a duck's back. 'Right, Ian, let's go and face the enemy,' she said, and strode off down to the podium with me tagging along behind.

The Duke and Duchess of Devonshire – a great lady who'd created the gardens at Chatsworth – were sitting in front of me smiling benignly. This set the tone for the evening and the talk was much more positively received than I expected. By now, the Duchess and I could read an audience pretty well. Jane has an instinct for seeing problem areas and can target the one or two people in an group of 200 who might cause trouble – they always nudge each other at a crucial moment in the lecture. The classic time is when Jane starts talking about the money the family has given to the Garden or – another hot topic – the plastic tractors. When she sees the nudge, the Duchess goes straight on the attack, looks directly at the person and ad-libs: 'There may be people in the audience here who don't like the idea of plastic tractors. But although we' – and she stares straight at the quivering offender – 'may be lucky enough to be able to afford plastic tractors for our children's garden, many of the people who visit the Garden live in flats and welcome the chance for their children to have fun in a safe outdoor space. Surely that's better than being inside watching TV and playing computer games?' Jane's not someone who thinks in terms of class, but she always says the worst dissenters are the 'pie-crust collar' brigade, the conservatives with a small 'c' who dislike the idea of a Duchess creating a public garden with plastic tractors and shooting water jets that soak visitors to the skin.

At the end of the talk, some of the guests were invited for dinner in Sotheby's private dining room. The Duchess of Devonshire said she thought what Jane was doing was wonderful; it was refreshing to see someone of her generation grasping the nettle and creating something big and bold, and she shouldn't bother her head about criticism or what anyone said. We didn't raise any money at the talk, but that one generous comment made our night.

Ralph played a joke on Jane after the Sotheby's talk. The auction house sent a sheaf of photographs of the reception to the Castle. The Duke, who in private loves nothing more than taking the mickey out of the project, superimposed rude speech bubbles on them on his computer. 'God, she's not still banging on about that bloody garden, is she?' he added on photos of friends chatting to Jane, then sent them out to everyone he thought would be amused. The Duchess took this in very good part.

The Duchess has several close friends who, almost as a way of relaxing, play practical jokes on each other. At one very tense time when we were desperate to raise money and the Garden's profile, her friend Ginny called Jane up pretending to be a US journalist, to ask if she would be interviewed for a US magazine. The Duchess said yes and after lengthy negotiations over pictures, Ginny called up again and said her 'editor' had now decided he wanted the Duchess to be photographed naked in the Rose Garden. At which Jane smelled a rat.

I was party to one of the Duchess's practical jokes on this trip. After our talk at the Eden Project, we set off bright and early for Brecon in Wales where we were giving an afternoon lecture organised by one of Jane's oldest friend, Fiona Lowes, known as Flossie. In the car, the Duchess – in need of some light relief – suddenly decided to play a trick on Flossie. She called her and said we'd had a puncture and were waiting in Cornwall for the AA to arrive. An hour later, when we were nearly at the Severn Bridge, Jane called again, saying bad news, the tyre can't be fixed and we're going to be late. Flossie is the sweetest person in the world, and said it didn't matter, she'd move tea forward, so we had a couple of hours' grace.

We were sitting in a pub just ten minutes away from the Brecon Theatre when Jane called for the third time saying we weren't going to make the talk – we were being towed off to a garage and wouldn't get to her before nightfall.

Flossie had never organized an event like this before, so was understandably on edge. 'Oh my God,' I heard her shrieking at the other end of the line. 'What am I going to do? There are 300 people coming to this event – we've sold out, it's huge.' I was expecting Jane to say: 'I'm just teasing, we're five minutes down the road.' But instead she put on her most persuasive voice and said: 'You know about the Garden, Flossie, you've heard me bang on about it. You do the talk. Just tell them where the water is and that there's a lovely Ornamental Garden at the top, and some nice flowers – tell them about the Rose Garden. You can do it, you'll be brilliant.'

This went on for some time and it was clear Flossie was in a complete panic. When she put the phone down, I said, 'Duchess, I can't believe you're doing this,' but Jane was over the moon with glee. We turned up at the theatre half an hour later, walked in to the restaurant and found Flossie's mother and father sitting with some friends after lunch. Their faces completely stony, they said: 'What on earth are you doing here, Jane? We thought you had awful car trouble.'

'Oh,' said the Duchess, laughing, 'it was a joke.' They didn't think it was funny.

Luckily, Flossie is a loyal friend and wasn't as cross as she should have been. We went off to find the theatre manager who, when told it was all a joke, looked at the Duchess as if she was completely deranged. He said, 'But I've sent everyone away because the talk wasn't going to happen – now I'm going to have to ring and ask them to come back.'

The Duchess thought this was the most amusing trick she'd played in her life. It wasn't until she saw Flossie doing her opening speech – ten lines introducing 'her oldest friend, the Duchess', which she'd been practising for a week – that she realized what an enormous trauma it would have been for Flossie to stand up and talk off the top of her head to 300 people about the Garden.

After a lecture in West Sussex, we went to Gloucestershire, to a talk and sit-down dinner organized by Michael Stone, a close family friend and supporter of Jane's. He's a successful businessman and Chairman of the sugar trader EDF Mann, and has backed her the whole way. He'd invited the Prince of Wales to attend, as well as the cream of Gloucestershire society and local dignitaries – our hope was that they'd be inspired to give some generous donations. He was enormously hospitable, and invited me to stay in the house as well as the

Duchess. He set up a marquee full of wonderful flowers, with a lobster dinner and the most delicious wines, the sort you get to taste on only a few occasions in your life. The Duchess wanted to introduce the Treehouse concept into the talk, so I added a second row of slides with some artist's impressions of how it would look.

It was a surprise when Michael Stone told us afterwards that many people he'd invited hadn't wanted to come, saying The Alnwick Garden was not a popular cause with southerners and that they were unwilling to support it. Some people had responded almost rudely, saying it was too much of a theme park, and 'Your garden and mine are much more charming.'

The next day we set off to Rupert Hambro's house and barn for our final talk, a lecture as part of Newbury Spring Festival. Rupert Hambro was an appeal patron of the Garden, a good family friend who has always been supportive of the Duchess. The other talks at the event were hugely entertaining, and the whole day went with a swing. At the end of the festivities, Rupert Hambro led us out of the barn and into his garden. 'You might be interested in seeing this,' he said. There laid out before us was Arabella Lennox-Boyd's award-winning Chelsea garden from 1999, which he had bought and transported down to Berkshire. It's the first time I've ever seen the Duchess speechless.

Over the ten years we've given the Garden lectures, the Duchess and I have talked to 42,000 people and raised over £500,000 for other charities, a fact that pleases me immensely. Now if someone asks us to talk at a fundraiser for their local charity, we have a formula to help them raise the maximum amount. The secret is the venue: they need a space that holds at least 300 people. Evening talks are better because both men and women attend. If they organize a sponsored champagne reception beforehand, so much the better – drinks are free, and they can then charge around £30 per head – which raises £8,000 to £12,000 for their charity, depending on numbers. One time we'd driven to Dorset to find that the organizers were charging only £6.50 a ticket. 'They could have tripled it,' the Duchess muttered darkly, 'and raised so much more money.'

At the beginning we gave our talks free, then started charging £100 to cover travel and hotel bills. Now we charge £500 a talk, but any money left after expenses goes straight into The Alnwick Garden charity – neither the Duchess nor I have ever received a penny for our talks.

In the year after the Phase 1 opening, publicity about the Garden was at an all-time high, none of it due to our own marketing efforts. Out of the blue, Alnwick was voted *Country Life* magazine's 'Best Place in Britain to Live' in 2002. According to *Country Life*:

> Alnwick's vitality was greatly boosted by the opening of the Castle's Garden project last autumn. Business in the town is booming, according to the local chamber of commerce. When the Garden's giant treehouse complex is completed, the town will enjoy another fillip.

When the award was announced, television crews and newspaper reporters arrived in force but the tourist office was closed! 'Twas ever thus in sleepy Alnwick: some of the shops still have half-day Wednesday closing and don't open at all on bank holidays. In desperation, the reporters contacted the Castle to get some quotes. The Duchess, always a great champion for the region, found herself in the Garden at 6.00 a.m. talking to camera about why Alnwick was such a great place to live.

We were also basking in the glow of the 'Harry Potter effect'. In 2001 Alnwick Castle shot to fame as Hogwarts School of Witchcraft and Wizardry. The first two Harry Potter films were set amidst the medieval towers, turrets and courtyards of Alnwick Castle. The Castle and grounds have long been a popular backdrop for many historical dramas but Harry Potter was the only movie to have a noticeable effect on visitor numbers. For the twenty years before, about 60,000 'skulls', as Rory Wilson jokingly calls visitors, visited the Castle during its six-month opening period. Over the next couple of years that figure rose to 175,000, then 275,000 visitors a year, an increase we put down to the simultaneous opening of the Garden and the sensation surrounding the Harry Potter films. Hordes of children must have pestered their parents to take them to Alnwick, and their parents agreed because they wanted to visit the new Garden they'd read about in the papers.

In January 2003, our cup was overflowing when *Charlie and the Duchess* was shown on TV and over six million people tuned in. The response was astonishing: the Garden website received 74,000 hits in the forty-eight hours afterwards, and we were inundated with letters and congratulations from the public. Director John Thornicroft told me that even Alan Titchmarsh had rung him to say how much he liked the programme. The Duchess replied to all those who'd written in:

> I am overwhelmed by the response the programme has received and it almost makes those many sleepless nights fade into oblivion! Although your letter was addressed to me, The Alnwick Garden project was very much a team effort. The team included garden designers, structural engineers, building surveyors, water technologists, stonemasons and many more individuals without whose expertise and support the Garden would not be so magnificent.

It was a very exciting time, but intense highs – or lows – never last long in my experience. We had a week's grace before the backlash started. This was over an article in the *Sunday Times* about the Duke's mooted sale of Raphael's *Madonna of the Pinks* to the Getty Museum in Los Angeles. The Press had picked up on the story that the Getty Museum had offered £32 million for the painting, provoking national outrage about the Raphael leaving the country. The National Gallery couldn't match the figure without lottery money, but Britain's Heritage Lottery fund administrators were apparently 'balking at the thought of handing over £20 million to one of Britain's richest landowners'. The fear, continued the *Sunday Times*, was that the money 'could help [the Duke's] wife complete her dream of turning the family's manicured gardens at Alnwick Castle into the "Versailles of the North".'

'Duchess,' I thought, reading this at home on a peaceful Sunday morning, 'put your hard hat on if you want to avoid the flak!'

The *Sunday Times*'s interpretation was nonsense, of course, but it started a huge public debate. Newspaper columnists, art critics, economists, social commentators and MPs of all parties weighed in, some worried about losing the Raphael, others angry at the idea of the Duke receiving lottery money, others saying he was doing the right thing – regenerating the local region was more important than one tiny painting. The outcry was so overwhelming that Baroness Blackstone, the Arts Minister, put a temporary export ban on the Raphael to give the National Gallery time to raise the cash.

The real story behind the Raphael is both more complicated and less sensational than these reports suggest. The *Madonna of the Pinks* used to hang in a passage outside the family's private apartments in the Castle. People say it's a masterpiece, and I remember passing it often and always admiring it as a beautifully painted little jewel, in an impressively carved wooden frame. It was bought by the 4TH Duke of Northumberland in Rome in the mid-nineteenth century, but its provenance was later discredited. In 1992 it went off to be cleaned, and new techniques showed it was indeed a genuine Raphael, painted by the master in around 1507. Suddenly the painting was too valuable to hang in the Castle, and was loaned by Duke Harry to the National Gallery. I remember it being earmarked then by him as a likely candidate for sale on a 'rainy day'.

That rainy day arrived sooner than expected. Foot-and-mouth hit the region, agricultural prices and rents plummeted, and the Duke's farm tenants needed financial support to diversify. It was at this bleak moment that the Getty Museum's 'silly offer' for the painting looked most attractive. Jane soon got wind of trouble in the air. When Ralph told her about the Getty's bid, she asked 'How much?' and he said '£32 million'. She called me later on my mobile. 'Ian, can you believe it? That's exactly what I've just announced we need to finish the Garden. This is horrendous. I'm going to be crucified.'

When the Duchess senses a crisis in the offing, she acts fast. She raced down to London and interviewed four PR agencies, asking in particular how they'd deal with the story: 'I am building an enormous garden that needs funding of X amount, my husband is selling a painting for the same amount. Even though I am a charity, he is a business, people think this is not a coincidence.' Of course, it did seem unbelievable that Ralph could be selling the Raphael for exactly the amount Jane needed to raise for the Garden, at exactly the same time. But truth is stranger than fiction.

There was another irony: the Duchess had always told everyone from Jacques Wirtz to Diageo boss James Blyth that she couldn't take a picture off the wall to pay for the Garden. Now here was Ralph apparently doing exactly that. It made Jane look, said one newspaper, like the 'Imelda Marcos of gardening'. The Duchess thought she and Ralph could weather the storm, but the scandal could have a very detrimental effect on fundraising efforts for the Garden.

She hired Citigate Dewe Rogerson, the PR company that came up with the most thorough strategy to ensure that the public knew the Garden and the Castle were entirely separate entities. A PR campaign started, and even the Duke went on the offensive, writing to the *Daily Telegraph*:

> It is untrue to say, as some have said, that the Raphael is being sold to pay for the new garden at Alnwick. The Garden is a public regeneration project that my family has placed in a charitable trust for public benefit, backed by a £9 million injection of private family capital. This ensures that we receive no direct benefit from it, and that all money raised for it and produced by it circulates back into the Garden itself.

The story rumbled on until 2004, when the *Madonna of the Pinks* was bought by the National Gallery for £22 million after tax, with over half the money coming from the Heritage Lottery Fund. The Duke used the funds to regenerate the Estates and Castle, and the Garden received not a penny.

MORE FLAK

The next public scandal wasn't far behind, this time provoked by an innocuous comment Jane made on *Charlie and the Duchess,* about British plant suppliers being more expensive than foreign nurseries. 'UK growers enraged over TV slur,' ran the headline in *Horticulture Week.* This started a furore in the horticultural industry, asking why The Alnwick Garden had been unpatriotic enough to buy its trees and shrubs from Holland and Belgium instead of Britain. British nursery growers wrote in saying how appalled they were, and we even got complaints from the environmental lobby that the pollution and greenhouse gases generated by transportation was a cost that had to be absorbed by British society and the NHS!

I put our case as straightforwardly as I could: we wanted massive quantities of mature trees and shrubs quickly and at competitive prices, plus tiny quantities of rare specialities. No nursery in Britain offered a comparative service or better price, so we went to the cheapest and best source. Van den Berk and Jan Spruyt nurseries had gone out of their way to offer us sponsorship and a good discount – something no tree or shrub nursery in Britain had.

The matter got confused because Peter Wirtz is Belgian and many people in the industry thought he'd favoured his own country's nurseries over their own. Of course, he was comfortable using a Belgian supplier – he'd used them before and knew they could deliver the goods – but in fact the Duchess and I made the final decision to go abroad. The Alnwick Garden always tried to source materials and stock from the North-East, but we were not approached by any British nursery carrying the stock we needed. Add to this the fact that the pound was at its highest value, making British nurseries uncompetitive compared to other EU countries, and the final decision was made resolutely on price.

The fall-out was bitter and hit deep into the horticultural industry. When the Duchess and I were giving a garden talk in the Isle of Man – a great trip, where we went round the TT course at top speed with the Governor in his brand new Jaguar – one man stood up and said he was a local nursery grower. 'Here we go,' I thought. 'Better duck!'

He said he'd read about the controversy over plant material coming from Europe. He agreed it was a shame that England didn't benefit from the huge orders, but he could see exactly why we had come to our decision. It made good commercial sense to cut out the middlemen. Jane was very grateful that a grower publicly stood up to defend her: it was always easier for people in the industry to keep their heads down and avoid the controversy.

As a result of these media hot potatoes, the Duchess suddenly got a storm of newspaper requests for interviews. One such, a handwritten note from garden journalist and designer Mary Keen, arrived asking for a tour of the Garden for the Saturday gardening section of the *Daily Telegraph*. 'Do I do this, Ian?' the Duchess asked me. 'She is a well-known writer and it would be good to have her on side. But she has been negative in the past, and I've been told she dislikes the Garden.' In the firm belief that all publicity is good publicity, both James McDonald of Citigate and I advised her to go for it.

Mary Keen is a grande dame of English gardening. She is the daughter of an Earl, and has often written about liking atmosphere and quiet spaces in a garden. She wasn't going to be an obvious supporter of The Alnwick Garden, but nothing ventured ... This was an opportunity for us to have a major article in a premiere gardening publication written by a recognized writer – it was too good to miss.

Mary Keen turned up one morning, and the Duchess took her on a tour of the Garden including the underground pump rooms. Jane can read people well, and could immediately sense that Mary Keen was not a fan. As usual, the Duchess was wearing baggy combat trousers – far from the tweeds and pearls expected of the aristocratic classes. They stomped around the Garden, Mary Keen complaining about the uncomfortable stride length of the steps beside the Cascade and commenting unfavourably, the Duchess felt, about everything from the cement facing inside the Cascade, to the oversized garden benches in a 'weak' traditional design.

By the time they got to the top, Jane was quietly fuming. Mary Keen mentioned that Lady Mollie Salisbury had consulted her years before about the planting in the herbaceous borders and the Duchess said in her most charming tone, 'I think we've both had a lucky escape.' Mary Keen asked her what on earth she meant. 'Well,' said Jane, 'you've hated everything you've seen so far, and I couldn't have worked with someone who dislikes the Garden as much as you clearly do, so it's probably better for both of us that you're not involved.'

Mary Keen was also due to interview Chris Gough about the maintenance of the Garden, but Jane rushed to the loo and secretly radioed him: 'Be careful, this lady hates everything!'

Before writing the article, Mary Keen phoned Peter Wirtz to discuss the design, raising eight or so points that she found problematic. He, independently alarmed by her approach, faxed the Duchess to express real concerns about what was going to be written.

He also wrote a detailed rebuttal of the points Mary Keen had raised: the 'absence of place'; the 'Cascade perspective'; 'the Cascade staircase and water levels'; the 'noisy children and water turbulence'; the 'cost'; the 'plant imports'; the 'narrow paths'; and the idea of the Garden as a 'public park'.

Goodness, by the time her article came out we were ready for anything! It was hardly a surprise to read her personal piece, saying the Duchess 'looks like Posh' [Spice] in her 'fashionista combat cords' and the project was full of 'showbiz and razzmatazz'. She ran through her objections then concluded: 'I feel like the ultimate party pooper ... I suppose it is the money, the feeling that what you see costs so much, that makes me wonder whether this is just vanity gardening.'

Anyone who knew the Duchess would find the 'vanity gardening' concept laughable, but of course most people reading the article in a quality national newspaper would take it at face value. The Duchess was even more alarmed when Michael Stone, who'd organized the Prince of Wales's talk in Gloucestershire and was helping with fundraising, wrote to her saying that the article by Mary Keen, who lived locally, had undoubtedly spread an anti-Garden feeling among the design fraternity.

Jane still hoped Mary Keen's objections could be 'contained', and wrote to PR James McDonald at Citigate:

> I met a lady gardener yesterday who lives in Gloucestershire near Mary
> Keen. This lady is a good gardener and she told me that ... anything written
> by her [Mary Keen] will, in gardening circles, be pretty much disregarded.

But this was wishful thinking: as the furore over the Raphael and Jane's attempt to raise £32 million in public funding heated up over the summer, Mary Keen wrote an article that seemed calculated to inflame matters. In *The Spectator*, she launched into a fierce and personal criticism of the Duchess's aims. 'To him that hath shall be given, and to the Duke and Duchess of Northumberland hath been given quite a lot. We are talking public funding here ...' her article started, and went on to criticize the Garden and question whether it was deserving of public subsidy. She concluded: 'Should those who are savvier and nobler than thou attract so much more money than those who are perhaps more deserving?'

As soon as I read that, I knew we were in choppy waters. The Duchess doesn't often hit back at Press criticism, but this made her see red because it could have a detrimental effect on our fundraising efforts. When the newspapers rang next day to get Jane's reaction, she let rip. The resulting headline – 'Duchess hits out at "bitchy" garden critics of the south' – said it all.

> It's a southern problem [the Duchess was quoted as saying]. I have very few critics in the north where they have embraced my work and think of it as their own ... I think it's jealousy and people saying: 'Who does she think she is?' It's also the snobbery element of gardening, which I absolutely loathe.

It's not fair to say everyone in the south was against the project. The eminent garden historian, writer and lecturer Penelope Hobhouse has always stood up for the Duchess's concept and written very positively about the Garden and the Wirtzes' 'triumphant' design.

However, the reaction from people in the North-East to *The Spectator* furore was astonishing. I remember thinking, 'Pride of the North!' as hundreds of letters of support came rattling in. Lalage Bosanquet, who runs a local school, wrote to the letters page of *The Spectator* and her eloquent and heartfelt response in support of the Duchess was typical of many responses we received:

Having read Mary Keen's article, I must defend our Duchess. We have watched the community become increasingly depressed as agriculture has declined and the economic base of the area has been destroyed ... We have emerged from the final catastrophe of the foot-and-mouth crisis battered and bruised. We have been the forgotten county of England sandwiched between well-funded Scotland and the former industrial areas of the North-East where much public money has been made available to counter deprivation.

Now at last the rural area is on the move. The Duchess has given us an attraction that actually works. People are coming from far and wide, we are getting news coverage as never before, local accommodation is booming and suddenly the area is on the map...

Northumberland has always been a feudal county and has been controlled to a certain extent by a Duke and Duchess for centuries. Now we have a young woman who is no snob, who understands exactly what the people want to do in order to enjoy a day out and she has welcomed them into the grounds of the Castle benefiting us all.

If the Duchess has the wherewithal to prime the grant-aiding pumps, press the correct PC buttons, take on English Heritage and extract millions from public bodies where all the rest of us have failed, good luck to her. She deserves our thanks and admiration and not the carping criticism of southern-based gardening experts who live in well-funded leafy areas of the South and who are unfamiliar with the needs of the rural north of England.

In this case, the oft-repeated adage that any publicity is good publicity was quickly realized. The scandal was picked up around the world and generated an unprecedented amount of interest in the Garden. Mary Keen's articles might have put a spoke in our wheels, but the reverse turned out to be true. She had actually done us a very good turn.

ABOVE: *Malus Evereste* crab apples bring autumn colour to the Ornamental Garden.

CHAPTER 11

ALL OUR PROBLEMS ARE THOSE OF SUCCESS...

The debate and publicity that arose from the Mary Keen affair swelled visitor numbers enormously. In 2003–4, around 535,000 people visited the Garden – and it was still only half built. Northumberland has always been regarded as a tourist corridor, bypassed by visitors heading from York to Edinburgh. But so many people were now visiting the Garden and surrounding areas that it was fast becoming a primary holiday destination. It was no surprise to me that Northumberland had finally been discovered. One of my favourite parts of my old job as Estates Clerk of the Works was driving across the remote byways and backwaters of the county, through undulating, wooded countryside with romantic views north to the Cheviot Hills and the Scottish borders, sometimes not seeing another car for hours. At weekends, Ann and I would walk our Norwich terrier, Tiffin, along the wide, deserted, golden sandy beaches. Great beaches and stunning scenery, plus the pretty towns and historic castles and monuments, make a holiday in Northumberland varied and interesting.

As a result, the rail station four miles down the road in Alnmouth was renamed 'Alnmouth for Alnwick' to great fanfare, and twenty-seven trains a day stopped on the direct London–Newcastle–Edinburgh route. Our building site had somehow become the third most visited garden attraction in Britain after RHS Wisley and Kew Gardens, and we were as amazed as everyone else.

Including contractors, we now had 153 people working in the Garden, and the Duchess joked that most of them seemed to be accountants. I remember bumping into her in the Garden one evening, after she and John Lovett had spent the day interviewing for a senior finance position. She looked completely exhausted and said it had been the most boring day of her life. Not that she meant to do down accountants: she knew as well as anyone that the Garden needed great financial people in the team. But it was a moment of recognition and some regret: in Phase 1, we'd all mucked in and done whatever we had to do. Now the project was becoming so big that the business specialists and experts were outnumbering us ten to one. 'At least that means we can get back and do the artistic side,' said Jane with a sigh.

By this time we'd moved into bigger Portakabin offices, generously funded by money from Northumberland Strategic Partnership. They were spacious compared to our old ones, but they had to be. The management team soon swelled to twenty-five: we hired a wonderful education officer, Alison Hamer. She's a ball of fire, an ex-headmistress who loved the idea of facilitating education and 'teaching by stealth', and immediately set to work creating dynamic programmes for the Poison Garden and other areas. Peter Gaynor came in as operational manager to run the day-to-day business of the Garden, and Deborah Germaine, who'd worked at Warwick Castle, was taken on as retailing consultant with the brief to get a retail outlet up and running as soon as possible. With extraordinary energy, she designed and stocked the shop in a little wooden hut, and it opened just six weeks later.

There was marketing manager Rachel Johnston, performing arts manager Esther Hingle, Dawn McCaig, who co-ordinates the organization and newsletters for Friends of the Garden, and Leigh Stevenson, who took over from Deborah as retail director. Marc Mallam, a delightful man who first came in with the Caledonian Economics study on visitor attractions, was still around, trying to persuade us to increase our revenue by whatever means we could. Head Gardener Chris Gough had hired a staff of seven full-time gardeners, all of whom had to be trained, the Duchess insisted, to understand the Wirtz approach to gardening so that they could explain the concept to visitors.

John Lovett was at the helm of this massive upscaling of the project. He's been a great influence on the evolution of The Alnwick Garden: the Duchess always says that if I was responsible for Phase 1, Phase 2 should be credited to him. John's commercial expertise and management skills have been central to the Garden's development and growth. At times tensions arose because of the inevitable disparity between his budgets and our aims. As Jane kept saying to me in her finest Lady Bracknell tone: 'Never forget we are a social enterprise, Ian.'

The Duchess's policy was to build the best, down to the smallest detail. But that costs money, an awful lot of money, and everybody was trying to get us to compromise. John Lovett and Marc Mallam were worried about running costs and wanted to upsize the Treehouse restaurant and kitchens so they would be self-sufficient, Elisabeth had to make sure we were meeting the different demands of funders, the retail manager wanted a larger area for the shop, and so it went on. The meetings were interminable: in one, Jane pushed her notebook over to me where she'd scrawled: 'Meetings are very boring and go on for too long. What shall we have for lunch? Avocado and prawns or egg mayo? On white or brown?'

Occasionally, she'd try to spice up meetings in order to return to the friendly, fun dynamic we'd had in Phase 1. Once, when new catering kitchens were being discussed, she asked the design team what the point was of having movable units on wheels. Iain Ramage explained it was to facilitate cleaning. Jane said in a clear voice: 'You mean so that we can get at the rats easier, Iain?' The room went silent and poor Iain replied, 'We're not really anticipating rats, Jane.' At which point the Duchess just smiled at him and he suddenly realised he'd been taken in.

Everyone had their own agenda and people were holding meetings and sub-meetings that neither the Duchess nor I was invited to attend. It wasn't malicious: we were a huge team and not every micro-decision could or should be approved by a full committee. But Jane was concerned at the way control seemed to be slipping away from us and at one meeting passed me a note.

> Ian, what's happening with the Treehouse? Everyone is trying to commercialize it to maximize revenue. This is wrong – the venue has to be more important than the food. People say it's not a big enough 'cash cow', it's only going to bring in £100,000 p.a. – CRAP! Has anyone accurately predicted the numbers that will come?

The main trouble was that Marc Mallam, being both charming and persuasive, was starting to pull the project his way. His main concern seemed to be that the Garden covered itself financially, whereas the Duchess was adamant that we should offer a quality visit with great service and facilities you didn't get anywhere else. 'Consultants come and go,' Jane said to me after one cost-cutting meeting, 'but none of them understands the project as we do. Quality and standards need to go hand in hand with finances.' We were in a stasis of debate and discussion about the best way to proceed, and when Jane and I weren't around, decisions were being made for financial reasons. It infuriated both of us but was increasingly hard to control.

'I'M ABSOLUTELY FINE'

Perhaps because we'd lost our earlier sense of cohesion and fun, everything seemed more exhausting and stressful. I'd noticed the Duchess had been looking tired and wan for a while, and the weight had dropped off her. The year before, she'd been rushed into hospital with acute stomach pains: everything had packed up in her tummy and she couldn't eat. They did a battery of tests but the doctors eventually said it was stress. Jane, being Jane, said, 'It's not stress, I'm absolutely fine,' and carried on as before. But continued pressure takes its toll, and during Easter 2003, she collapsed again. The Duke rushed her to Borders General Hospital on Easter Monday, where the only spare bed was in an all-male ward. She was stuffed with drips and painkillers while they tested for various stomach problems, including Crohn's disease. She had to stay in for over a week, and called John Lovett and me daily on her mobile, desperate to know how the Garden was doing, how many visitors we'd had over Easter and were the new ice-cream machines still working?

One evening there was a repeat showing of *Charlie and the Duchess* on the television, which apparently everybody on the ward watched. When she rang next day she said, 'I was lying there thinking how on earth can this be happening? I had so many drips and lines in me I couldn't even hide in the loo.'

Luckily nobody recognized her. When she was admitted to hospital she was wearing desert army combat kit, and probably looked so white and ill in her hospital robes that they would never think she was a duchess.

Typically, she turned her hospital bed into an office, and used the enforced rest to address the problems we were having about control of the Garden. When she came out, she read me a list entitled 'What's Gone Wrong?':

1. Ian and I need to be left alone to get on with final designs.
2. No Elisabeth, Siân or Alison at those meetings.
3. At this moment we aren't in a position to move and yet we have never had so many staff or so much money. Why?
4. Ian must be at every design meeting.
5. We need to have a weekly meeting with designers and Ian and I will arrange those ...

...and so on.

The problem was undiagnosed and she left hospital on steroids which she hated. The doctors said she'd have to continue taking them for the foreseeable future. She said, 'But I can't jump.' They specialist said, 'Why do you want to jump? You're in your forties and your body is telling you to slow down.' Jane replied, 'I want to be able to jump up two stairs at a time instead of walking up them.' Needless to say, she binned the steroids and went to any clinic she could find which specialized in digestive disorders. And she didn't give up until she was told exactly what was wrong with her and how the problem could be treated.

When she got out of hospital she talked at length to John Lovett about her concerns, and he cleared the air with the rest of the team. That gave the Duchess and me a breather to concentrate on the design briefs for Phase 2.

Elisabeth Smith, meanwhile, was working to access public funding for the second phase. Public funding is complex, time-consuming and at times completely frustrating. It's like trying to build a house of cards or three-dimensional jigsaw from scratch: it's only when you've got the final piece in place that the whole thing comes together and you can move forward. The good news was that, for the first time in the Garden's history, public funding bodies were very receptive to us. The success of Phase 1 made the government realize the Duchess meant business and they saw the Garden had the potential to become a magnet visitor attraction for the North-East.

Slowly, slowly, Elisabeth built up her jigsaw, with ERDF funding from Europe, regional funding delivered through the government's Northumberland Strategic Partnership and OneNorthEast, and the rest from private sources such as the Northern Rock Foundation, the Barbour Foundation and the US Claire Bell Fund. I'm full of admiration for her steadfastness under horribly intense pressure – the Garden simply couldn't have been built if she failed to deliver. She's charming, efficient and professional, a devastating mix that works wonders with funders. Sometimes with private individuals or companies, the Duchess and I made the initial approaches to lay the groundwork, before Elisabeth came in to take over. Overall, she raised promises of £23.5 million to fund the building of Phase 2 – an astonishing amount compared to the paltry £450,000 we'd managed to attract in Phase 1, and a tribute to her dedication and persistence.

The success of Phase 2 fundraising was also partly down to the Labour government's willingness to put its money where its mouth was. I always remember the 10TH Duke, Hugh, telling me that, in his experience, the Estates never suffered under a Labour government. At the time I was very struck by the statement: it seemed strange coming out of the mouth of a member of the aristocracy whom you'd expect to be a dyed-in-the-wool Conservative.

The same anomaly seemed to be happening with the Garden. A couple of years ago, Jane and I were sitting in the family kitchen talking about some details of the Treehouse design when she suddenly and said she had something funny to tell me. The night before, she'd gone to a friend's party and after dinner, when everyone had drunk a bit, a well-known Conservative MP had came up to her and said jovially, 'Oh Jane, you know we all call you the Red Duchess!' When she asked him why, he had replied: 'Because you're all over Labour like a rash!'

The Duchess retorted: 'But you'd have been running scared! You'd never have

funded the Alnwick Garden because you couldn't have seen past me as the Duchess.'

'You could be right there, Jane,' he replied urbanely. 'But rest assured we'll be fully supportive if we get in at the next election because of the great success of the project.'

Jane snorted as she recounted this tale to me: 'That just about sums them up!' She paused for a moment, then added: 'But when you think about it, Ian, you have to admit the Labour government has been fantastic for the Garden. They've never shown the same prejudice as the Conservatives about me or what we're doing. Do you realize that our biggest critics have always been right-wing, establishment people.'

At the time, the countryside lobby, including much of rural Northumberland, was marching and rioting against the government's proposed hunting ban, and most of the Duchess's friends would happily have seen Tony Blair hanged, drawn and quartered. Because the Garden's agenda matched the government's agenda of rural regeneration, and they saw that we were delivering the right economic and social benefits for the region, they were happy to give us generous funding – for which we are eternally grateful.

CATERING FOR LARGE NUMBERS

At the beginning of Phase 2 our plans didn't include the Pavilion build, but we soon recognized we needed extra infrastructure to cope with the influx of visitors, and fast-forwarded the Pavilion construction into Phase 2. That left us with a problem: Paul Robbrecht's Pavilion had been designed in 1998 to cater for KPMG's estimate of 67,000 visitors a year, and was far too small. In 2002, an independent economic study estimated that we could expect 230, 000 visitors a year. We needed an additional visitor centre and I wanted to discuss this with Paul Robbrecht. I thought I had asked for plans but none arrived. Perhaps he did not receive our instructions or misunderstood them but it led to the end of our partnership.

The new Pavilion brief was dramatically different: it would have to quadruple our support services and create a multi-functional space with admission facilities, cafés and conference and exhibition rooms. A building this size would take up

LEFT: Aerial view of the Pavilion and
Visitor Centre under construction.

too much room within the twelve-acre garden, so for the first time the local planning office agreed to let us build outside the walled area. Our idea was to design two interlinking buildings: visitors would enter the Garden through a grand Visitor Centre on the site of the original courtyard outside the wall, then walk through to the interlinked Pavilion building, which overlooked the Cascade and Garden.

It had been near impossible to find an architect for the Pavilion before, so it was with some trepidation that I approached the task again. This time we wanted to engage a British designer, and with help from RIBA I drew up a shortlist of five candidates. Each architectural firm came to the Garden offices and gave a presentation, all of extremely high quality. In the end, it came down to a decision between Foreign Office Architects and Michael Hopkins & Partners. Using wacky computer graphics, Foreign Office showed a series of strikingly innovative buildings they'd designed for other sites. 'If I'd had the guts,' the Duchess told me later, 'I'd have gone with them. They're amazing.' But in my opinion the Garden didn't call for such an unusual building – it needed a simple, beautiful structure to set against the complexity of the Wirtzes' design, and one that was in historical sympathy with the site.

Michael Hopkins presented with his wife, Patty, co-founder of Hopkins & Partners. He was quiet, gentle and thoughtful, she was upbeat and very energetic. Their presentation was excellent: their portfolio included the bold new Parliamentary Building at Westminster and the Mound Stand at Lord's cricket ground; they had wide experience both designing public buildings and working within the historic environment. The Duchess instinctively felt she could work with them and in January 2003, the appointment was confirmed: Michael Hopkins & Partners were designing the Pavilion and Visitor Centre for The Alnwick Garden. We all breathed a sigh of relief: we'd finally found an architect we could trust.

THE TREEHOUSE

There's something magical about treehouses. The Duchess loved the idea of a hidden, secret world high up in the trees that would enchant the child in all of us.

RIGHT: Sir Michael Hopkins. Hopkins and his wife Patty were commissioned to design the Pavilion and Visitor Centre in January 2003.

BELOW: View of the Pavilion towards the end of its construction stage.

When she visited Disneyland Paris on that freezing cold February day in 1997, she caught sight of a steep walkway through the trees with a tiny treehouse room at the top. 'This is what people love,' she thought as she climbed up the steps and walkways and saw the excited faces around her. 'I've got to create something like this at Alnwick.' She didn't tell me about her treehouse idea immediately, but a couple of years later asked me to research who was rated in the world of treehouse design, which is when John Harris's name came up.

He is a director of PearTree, a small company based in Ayrshire in Scotland that creates bespoke treehouses. We first met up at Chelsea Flower Show in 2000, where PearTree had a stand. As soon as he started telling us about some of the extraordinary treehouses he'd built, I could see the Duchess's mind going from nought to sixty faster than a Ferrari. Yes! We were going to build the biggest wooden treehouse in Europe and it was going to be a complete winter wonderland, with incredible fairy lighting, aerial walkways and a restaurant. It was to be somewhere to educate and entertain children, adults, the disabled and the elderly, with classrooms in the trees. It would look old, wooden and witchy, built on many different levels as if it had evolved over hundreds of years. It was going to take people's breath away!

Back at Alnwick, we identified an area of mature woodland outside the walled Garden and John Harris progressed a concept design built across sixteen mature lime trees – the British lime is ideal for treehouse construction because it is strong, slow-growing and long-lived. His design looked like something from Rivendell in *Lord of the Rings*, full of higgledy-piggledy towers, wonky windows, turrets and balconies, and not a straight line in sight. It was perfect.

Now we needed planning permission. The Duchess was concerned that this would be refused by English Heritage: after all, this bold and ambitious Treehouse could be seen from the 'Capability' Brown landscape. It's not surprising she was wary: in October 2002 we'd had another extraordinary encounter with English Heritage. The Duchess and I had been asked to give the keynote speech at an all-day gardens conference called 'The Pursuit of Excellence: New Design in the Historic Environment'. The Duchess was worried about it: London is where we

ABOVE: The Treehouse under a sheet of winter snow. Designer John Harris created the largest wooden treehouse in Europe, where visitors can enjoy a meal, listen to jazz in the evenings or even go speed dating!

always found our greatest critics, and we knew that many of the historic restoration lobby would be attending the event. But I persuaded the Duchess that we needed to confront these people and show them exactly what was going on at Alnwick.

We bust a gut to get down to London for the 10.00 a.m. start, and walked into the room to find Lorna McRobie and many other members of heritage groups with whom we'd had dealings. We had a good chat with Dominic Cole of Land Use Consultants, but Lorna McRobie didn't say hello or acknowledge us in any way. In the morning, she gave a paper about innovation and restoration, which seemed odd given her approach to The Alnwick Garden three years before. We sat through the morning's papers but at lunchtime Jane couldn't face eating with all those people, and so we went to a café round the corner. She sat worrying about the speech saying, 'What on earth are we doing here? Do we have to go through with this?'

'Come on,' I said, 'let's go and show them what this Garden's about.' We went back to present our talk about the development of The Alnwick Garden, only to find that Lorna McRobie had left. We thought this was a bad omen: if she hadn't stayed to hear what we had to say, it didn't augur well for any future planning application we might put in.

So when it came to the planning application for the Treehouse, Jane decided to go straight to the top. I was still pleading caution and a softly, softly approach, but she overrode me completely and flew down to London to show the plans in person to Sir Neil Cossons, the new English Heritage Chairman. She arrived too early and, sitting in a café outside the EH offices, drinking coffee with Colin Barnes, called me on my mobile. She made me laugh out loud: she said she felt as if she was outside Gestapo headquarters and didn't want to go through the door. After many jokes, she finally plucked up her courage and bearded Neil Cossons in his den.

She told him the long and sorry saga of the original Garden planning application, and explained how she was anticipating big problems with English Heritage's Park and Gardens Committee this time round too. He was surprised by her story. He said he didn't anticipate any difficulties, and the Treehouse application duly made its way through the normal channels.

In the end, English Heritage didn't raise any objections, though we'll never know whether that was due to the Duchess's powers of persuasion. When the planning application came before Alnwick District Council a few weeks later, a substantial number of councillors who were Friends of the Garden had to declare their interest and abstain. In the end, the fateful votes were cast by just a handful of local officers. From start to finish, the planning application went through without a hitch and I for one could hardly contain my surprise or delight.

PLAY AREA

In the trees around the Treehouse, the Duchess wanted to create an aerial play area. This is the kind of amazing, Alice-in-Wonderland thinking you get used to when you spend time with her. She wanted a state-of-the-art playground that would give children the same sense of excitement at visiting the Garden that she used to feel at the prospect of a trip to Alton Towers or Thorpe Park. John Harris came up with some suggestions that he estimated would cost around £175,000, but they didn't have the 'wow' factor the Duchess was after. So we started looking for play specialists. John Lovett, meanwhile, knowing the Duchess didn't do anything by halves, budgeted £400,000 for the proposals. 'Good,' said Jane. 'That should take us further.'

By chance, we soon found out that it was possible to get wheelchairs up in the trees on rope bridges and walkways, provided everything was massively reinforced, which of course pushed the price up exponentially. That budget of £400,000 would only pay for three reinforced aerial walkways, but the Duchess insisted, 'We've got to do this. It would be unforgivable not to provide the same facilities for wheelchair users as we do for the able-bodied. We need to find someone who can help us.' We had several depressing meetings with British play specialists, but nothing they came up with inspired us. They all used brightly coloured plastic and talked endlessly about health and safety, whereas the Duchess had in mind a wooden playground with rubber and steel that was 'safely dangerous' to challenge kids physically and mentally. Then someone mentioned the Peter Pan pirate ship in the Diana, Princess of Wales Memorial Garden in Kensington, which was created by Bavarian play specialist Günter Beltzig and Richter Spielgeräte GmbH, a German play company.

We were immediately inspired by their attitude: they used a different vocabulary, with a psychological and child-focused approach that concentrated on what kids get out of the play experience. They took the Duchess to see their designs at the Playmobil Funpark near Nuremberg, and she came back enthusing about the interesting areas they created for disabled people and wheelchair users, and the quality of their materials and standards of workmanship.

Originally the Duchess's instinct was to go for big challenges in a playground of superlatives: the highest this, the longest that. But over talks with Richter and Günter Beltzig, she modified her views. When play areas are very difficult – high zip wires or big climbing challenges – children can get egged on by older siblings or friends into doing things for which they're not ready. Timid children end up out of their depth, and as a result have a bad experience and a distressing day out. What was important, we came to understand, was to design the playground as a special world for children. Kids generally have to do what adults want, but here we could create everything from the child's height or perspective so it was easier for children to negotiate than adults, and they would be in charge for a change. It was fascinating to learn about the psychology of play from experts in the field.

Richter Spielgeräte could build the playground, but the Duchess still wanted someone to make them push boundaries, to create an innovative and original design. One day, she was picking up her youngest son Max, then twelve, from school, at Newcastle airport. I called her on her speaker phone in the car to discuss the design: I'd just read a depressing article saying how in Britain kids were more likely to vandalize playgrounds than actually play in them. 'What we want,' the Duchess said, 'is someone who's not necessarily into design but understands about adventure play – who will challenge the Bavarian design and who knows about aerial work.' All of a sudden Max's voice piped up in the background: 'I know who you need – this ex-SAS man, Brummie Stokes. He's just given a lecture at our school and he's brilliant. He runs an amazing adventure centre ...'

Brummie Stokes is indeed an incredible man: a rough diamond, SAS veteran and accomplished mountaineer who had his toes amputated after one trip to the summit of Everest. He runs Taste for Adventure, an activity centre in Herefordshire that aims to help under-privileged adults and children get a sense of achievement through physical challenges – just the sort of person to bring fresh thinking to our adventure playground design. He and his wife, Lynn, came up to meet us all.

The Duchess loves positive, committed people, and Brummie, who's full of ideas and energy, was immediately on her wavelength. He had an enormous input into the design of the elevated walkways around the Treehouse and is currently working on the extraordinary adventure play area we're planning for Phase 3.

As the concept of the Treehouse and adventure playground developed, John Harris worried that it was becoming too unmanageable for his small company, and decided to pull out. It was a shame, but I could understand his viewpoint: his business is building small, bespoke treehouses for people's gardens, not developing unwieldy commercial projects like this. Luckily, an excellent local firm, Napper Architects from Newcastle, took over. Although John Curtis and his team, including Dean Thody, the project architect, had never built anything similar before – in truth, not many architects have 'treehouse' written on their CVs – they moved into top gear and drew up the complicated technical specifications necessary to turn it into a working brief.

MCALPINES BACK

By November 2003, McAlpines were back on site to start building the Treehouse, the new car park, and the Labyrinth, Poison and Serpent gardens. In spring 2004, when the Pavilion and Visitor Centre build started, poor Aidan was overseeing four separate building contracts on site at the same time. It felt like a breath of fresh air to have Aidan back again: I'd missed his humour and optimism more than I realized. We'd kept in touch, and whenever I saw him, he'd say: 'Ian, I can't wait to be driving up to Alnwick again.' He was as glad to be back as we were to have him. Phase 2 was in motion, and it felt very rewarding to be on the go again.

The Labyrinth Garden, at least according to Aidan, was a straightforward build. McAlpines had to put lighting ducts below the surface, and build up the peat walls with subsoil, but how difficult could that be after creating something as ambitious as the Cascade? Soon we were ready to plant the 525 *Fargesia rufa* bamboos, only to find they had taken root on Richard Atkinson's tennis court in Bishop Auckland after being kept there for a few months. They looked rather anaemic after the transplantation but soon burst into rich, green life.

I had an adventure finding the right boulder for the Labyrinth entrance. The Duchess and I always liked the idea of the winding paths of the Labyrinth summing up the struggle we had to build the Garden. The maze reflects the journey we've been on: the dead ends, the straight clear runs, the trials and tribulations with design, planning and construction.

The idea was to inscribe two quotes in the Labyrinth: one on a big boulder at the entry point, the other at the exit. I went off to Hulne Park on Northumberland Estates, where I knew there was a hillside strewn with boulders. I was looking for a big boulder, flat enough on one side to carve the inscription 'Only dead fish swim with the stream' – our mantra about the battles with English Heritage and other nay-sayers. I clambered over the rocks on the hillside, and eventually came across a boulder that was perfect: it weighed about two tonnes, had one good face, and was in an accessible position. I sited it using a dead tree at the bottom of the hill.

Three months later, it was time to lift the boulder out. I went back to Hulne Park and found the whole hillside covered with a deep layer of bracken that obscured both my boulder and the dead tree. Boulders look pretty much alike from a distance, and it took me half a day to locate the chosen one again. When the contractors arrived with a crane, they decided to pull it up the hill, lifting it at the last minute on to a trailer. But when the crane operator started lifting, one of the straps holding the rock in place slipped and it started bouncing down the hill, gathering speed as it flattened huge swathes of bracken in its wake. There was an enormous crash as two tonnes of boulder hit the dead tree I'd used as a siting point. The tree vibrated like a giant tuning fork as silence fell over the mountainside.

'Did you get that, Jimmy?' I asked, deadpan, turning to Jimmy France, the camera operator who was filming the boulder's removal for the Garden archives.

'Of course,' he said, grinning at the thought of this health and safety nightmare being caught on film.

Luckily, the boulder and all nearby humans were undamaged, and this time we lifted it out without mishap. It was taken back to the Garden, where Classic Masonry's stonemasons inscribed our text.

A LATIN TAG

The other inscription in the Labyrinth is much more controversial – it's an old Latin farewell. At various stages in the Garden's development the Duchess and I have felt overcome by events and besieged by criticism and bad Press. Any project this size is bound to attract a lot of discussion and debate, not all of it reasonable or rational. The Duchess is fiercely anti-élitist: she wanted to show that you could write virtually whatever you wanted in Latin because 99 per cent of visitors wouldn't understand it. Jane asked an eminent Latin teacher (who wishes to remain nameless and *ergo* blameless!) if he could translate a phrase for her, and he came up with this valedictory:

> *Omnia, hospites, vidistis.*
> *Vobis gratias agimus.*
> *Nunc, fortuito mingite.*

We had this text inscribed around the perimeter of a circular stone feature near the exit of the Labyrinth, encircling a plan of the maze. It always astonishes me how few people ask what the Latin means and it's probably just as well, because it translates as:

Visitors, you have seen everything.
We thank you.
Now happily **** off.

I've only ever heard two people attempting to translate it and getting it 90 per cent right as: 'Visitor, you have seen it all, now happily on your way.' That's the polite version. 'Mingite' actually reads as 'piss off' – originally Jane had wanted to incorporate even stronger language, but I dissuaded her because I thought people might be offended.

The Poison Garden was the easiest and cheapest of the garden builds, but the Serpent Garden was more of a challenge for Aidan and the McAlpines team. To make Bill Pye's sculptures work, the water needed to be purer and cleaner than that in the Cascade and had to be processed through a special ozone filtration system. The McAlpines team had to drill a twelve-metre-long tunnel into the underground pump room from the Serpent Garden, wide enough to fit the sixty-centimetre diameter steel tube that supplied the filtrated water. They got within an inch of their aim: 'Not good,' Aidan joked, 'considering the guys drilling under the English Channel got to within half an inch!'

Once the services were in, the concrete groundworks were built up, the paths were laid and, finally, Bill Pye's stainless steel sculptures were dropped into place. Throughout construction, Bill Pye had been coming up once or twice a month to check on progress and he and Aidan clicked at once, sharing the same pleasure in the physics and engineering of the build.

McAlpines were also building a new car park across Denwick Lane. This was not just any old car park: it was designed and landscaped by the Wirtzes to fit into the 'Capability' Brown landscape. It had spaces for 850 cars and thirty coaches – on very busy days forty coachloads of visitors now arrived. It was also very expensive: the Duchess is fanatical about building the best, and as one of the nation's many dog lovers (every member of her family has a dog – hers is golden cocker spaniel called Derek), she wanted to create shady areas for dogs and put in canine drinking points that could be automatically pumped out and cleaned. The reasoning behind this was that many families and holidaymakers were travelling north–south on the A1 with dogs in their cars. There was no reason *not* to provide for dogs. I'd had a go at designing these drinking points for the old car park, working with Classic Masonry, but McAlpines now created slick new stainless steel versions.

Dogs have always been a point of contention in the Garden, and people regularly complain that they can't take them into the walled area. But as the Duchess says, 'Have you seen the effect of a strimmer on dog mess? Multiply that by 300 dogs a day, and it's not funny. It's a huge health risk.' People can give their dogs a good run in the Woodland Walk, but sometimes they still feel short-changed. Which is why the Duchess was so keen that dogs would get a great deal in this new and luxurious car park. Now, if necessary, our car park attendants will even look after people's dogs, provided they're on leads, while their owners enjoy looking around the Garden.

The car park development was progressing nicely, giving Aidan time to get to grips with the biggest technical challenge: the Treehouse. 'I thought the Cascade was bad,' he muttered to me one day, 'but imagine arranging a 300-tonne load the size of two Olympic swimming pools on to sixteen windswept trees. We must be mad.' What made it harder was that everything, even the scaffolding, had to be carefully placed to avoid damaging the trees' roots. It was vital to sustain the ecology of the site: if the trees died from damage, lack of rainwater or sunlight, the Treehouse was finished.

Napper Architects worked closely with McAlpines' structural engineering team and came up with the idea of a central platform supported by wooden struts in addition to the trees. The struts were in turn held in place by twelve-metre steel piles driven deep into the ground – a tricky job when you have to place them to within millimetres between the trees' roots.

The Treehouse acts like a sail in high winds, and the structural designers had to allow for it to sway and move with each gust of wind. But as the Duchess equally breezily said to Aidan about the practical difficulties: 'Think of it not as a problem,

Aidan, but as a challenge.' He probably wanted to hit her at that point.

The Treehouse build was fascinating because there was not a straight line in sight: all the elevations were broken up, the ridge lines were out of plumb and the wall lines jumped all over the place. This asymmetrical tour de force was made almost entirely of wood – Canadian cedar, Siberian larch, Scandinavian redwood and Scots pine – and Aidan had thirty joiners on site working flat out for over a year. They had to make snap decisions about how to create various quirky effects and irregularities, using over 280 tonnes of wood and 10,000 nails. Roughly hewn oak bark covers the towers, and irregular cedar roof tiles and distressed timbers give an olde worlde finish, as if the Treehouse had existed for centuries.

Throughout the build, the development of this other-worldly structure was filmed by producer and director Peri Langdale for a documentary called *The Treehouse*, commissioned by Tyne Tees Television.

THE ROOST

Set apart from the rest of the Treehouse village is the Roost, an education room with high-tech plasma screens that is completely supported by one tree, just like the kind of treehouse you'd build in your own garden. As the Roost was going to be full of children running in and out, McAlpines had to check that it was strong enough to support their weight by loading ten tonnes of sand on to its deck. It hardly wobbled.

The Treehouse has been designed at various levels – some up to twenty metres high – to allow the branches to enter and exit at various points through the turrets, balconies and rooms. One tree, number five, was trimmed off inside the restaurant, and now spreads throughout the room, giving a thick, living canopy of leaves and adding enormously to the atmosphere.

Napper found a brilliant prop designer called Paul Doran, of Doran's Design and Build, whom the Duchess worked with closely on the interior design of the Treehouse. Her strength has always been her imagination: she can picture in vivid detail the finished product she's after. She saw the restaurant as mysterious and

RIGHT: Fifteen metres above the forest floor the suspension bridges within the treehouse area were built to accommodate wheelchairs and buggies.

dark inside, a magical place with rich stained wood, a socking great open fire dominating the middle of the room, oversized wooden chairs and tables lit only by candlelight. The candles wouldn't pass health and safety, of course, so thin spotlights now penetrate the gloom. Everything in the Treehouse, from the clunky, primeval cutlery and rock-salt candleholders to the 2.5-metre high-backed, higgledy-piggledy chairs sourced from old ox carts in the Philippines, was created to the Duchess's script but with Paul Doran's inspiration. He used local materials wherever he could: Northumberland Estates' Douglas firs were cut to provide the stunning, 2.5-tonne fireplace, and other locally sourced wood was used for his fabulous root sculptures in the restaurant.

The suspended playground walkways, fifteen metres above the forest floor, needed turning circles big enough to accommodate wheelchairs and buggies, and had to be strong enough to allow tens of children to play on them at any one time. Richter Spielgeräte built them to look as if they float around the Treehouse, bringing reality to the Duchess's vision to expand children's play horizons and provide 'safely dangerous' play facilities. People often tell me their minds boggle at the thought of wheelchairs careering round an adventure playground up in the trees, but this is just the start – the Duchess wants to develop a multi-level area where disabled and able-bodied children can play together. As a result of the outstanding educational and play facilities and the provision for disabled users, we've called the Treehouse a 'unique transformational cultural project'. This £3.3 million fantasy tree village aims to take people out of their everyday lives to experience something spellbinding. The Garden's patron, HRH The Prince of Wales, wrote to Jane saying that, like the rest of the world, he had a passion for treehouses and couldn't wait to look round it.

The Treehouse build took much longer than planned and by January 2005, when we finally opened to the public, we were five months over schedule. The opening was a fantastic event at which schoolchildren from five local schools and nurseries came to run around the Treehouse village and walkways. However, the opening weekend turned into something of a private disaster for

Jane. The Duchess had booked two tables in the restaurant to entertain a big party of guests including Mark Getty, son of John Paul Getty, and the *Sunday Times*'s rebarbative restaurant critic, A. A. Gill, who were staying nearby. Unfortunately, everyone in the rest of Northumberland had the same idea and the Treehouse restaurant was packed. Jane's party wanted to look round the Garden before eating so turned up half an hour late, by which point the restaurant manager had given away one of their tables to people standing in the half-mile queue outside.

Jane had to squash twelve powerful bankers, businessmen and journalists on to one small round table, all the time thinking what a truly terrible idea this was. Then things got worse: the menus arrived – it was at that stage a fairly basic menu with pizzas, hamburgers and the like. Everybody wanted pizza. 'Sorry, there's only one pizza left,' said the waitress, but she did have a hamburger they could share. Oh, and one bowl of spaghetti! Jane was dying inside, but she turned to A. A. Gill, whom she hardly knew, and said, 'Please, whatever you do, don't write about this. This is a really horrific experience but it's a one-off. We didn't expect so many people to turn up.' He said no, no, of course he wouldn't write about it, and was true to his word. But for several weekends afterwards the Duchess anxiously scanned the papers, muttering that she'd kill him if she saw anything about that horrendous lunch.

MORE OPENINGS

Over the next two months, we had three more openings: of the Labyrinth, the Poison Garden, with Northumbria Police's Chief Constable, Crispian Strachan, in attendance, and the Serpent Garden. The Serpent Garden opening was delayed because three water features, weren't quite ready, and Bill Pye, Peter Wirtz and I were very concerned that the finish and planting weren't quite up to scratch.

Behind the scenes, John Lovett and the accountants were pressurizing us to compromise, but thankfully the Duchess agreed with the design team. She memoed me: 'Ian, you're right, please do not open the Serpent Garden unless and until it is perfect.' We both knew that if we opened without sorting out the snags, they'd come back to haunt us.

The Serpent Garden opening was full of fun. Bill Pye borrowed Aidan's jacket and he and sponsor Roy Leech got soaked standing in Torricelli with a group of excited local schoolchildren (who'd all been asked to bring towels and a spare set of clothes). All of a sudden ninety jets encircled them in a curtain of water and they got drenched to the skin. And not a single one of them without a big happy beam on their faces!

Apart from the Pavilion, which was proving to be the most complex and problematic build we'd ever faced, Phase 2 was up and running. It was with delight that the Duchess received a message from HRH the Prince of Wales wishing her a million congratulations for the unstoppable courage and determination she'd shown thus far in pursuit of her vision.

CHAPTER 12

ANNUS HORRIBILIS

Some years flash by; others are full of problems, pain and worry. The final year of
Phase 2 during 2004 to 2005 was the most difficult I remember in the whole of
my working life. We'd been coshed by five years of construction work and everyone
was exhausted. Yet still the Garden was a mud-filled building site with areas
roped off, and two monumental tower cranes reminding us things weren't going
to get easier any time soon. The Pavilion build was a nightmare of difficulties and
delays with everyone shooting blame at everyone else, which made morale drop
quicker than a stone in water. Meanwhile, the Garden team had grown so big so
fast that we had difficulties delivering many new functions – food and beverages,
retail, customer services. No wonder visitors were cross. The townspeople of
Alnwick were up in arms about the impact the Garden was having on their trade
and daily lives. The Garden had become so large and unwieldy a monster that the
Duchess no longer knew her role and was threatening to resign. This was indeed
our *annus horribilis*.

PAVILION

To get the Pavilion built, we'd had to take a calculated risk and start underground
structural works without having funding fully in place. This meant money was
tighter than usual: we were over budget, strapped for cash to pay our burgeoning
wage bills and penny-pinching in every area. My job was one of the first casualties
of the new cost-cutting regime. Siân Johnson and John Lovett asked the Duchess
to talk to me about cutting my hours to twenty a week. I can see why they did it: on
paper I looked like one of the most dispensable members of staff. I didn't have a
job title with a tangible area of responsibility such as 'marketing' or 'retail'. But the
decision came out of the blue, and it was painful.

I remember the conversation well: it took place in the Duchess's study and she was obviously as embarrassed as I was. She said she couldn't believe she was in a position where she had to do it, because she felt I was as much a part of the project as she was. In some ways the new hours suited me well – Ann wanted me to spend more time with her at home now I was nominally 'retired' – but what hurt was the fact that nobody had discussed it with me. I felt I was being slowly edged out of the project. One of the immediate effects was that I was no longer around to represent the Duchess at design meetings for the Pavilion and Visitor Centre, or 'PVC', as we came to call it. In retrospect, that was our first mistake. The Garden needed somebody to support the Duchess's wishes, and I felt I was falling out of the loop.

The PVC was a complex, innovative building using new materials in a very modern way, and everybody underestimated how hard it would be to build. The stakes were high: at £11 million and counting, it was the biggest single expense in the project and proved Elisabeth's toughest fundraising challenge. One morning – and Elisabeth says it was her J.F. Kennedy moment – the regional funder OneNorthEast announced that it was unable to offer the amount it had originally proposed, from which Elisabeth had constructed her delicate funding 3D house of cards. The whole edifice threatened to come toppling down. The Duchess wrote in her diary: 'We are short of money. £1.2 million shortfall ... surprise, surprise.' She never believed money would come in until she saw the cheque.

Of course, it was nobody's fault, least of all Elisabeth's, but the decision created panic: we might have to call a halt to the PVC build, leaving a gaping hole in the ground because we couldn't afford to pay McAlpines to continue work. But McAlpines rose to the challenge: they've always been committed to the Duchess and the project, and agreed to work on in good faith knowing we'd find the money to pay them as soon as we could. Meanwhile, Elisabeth and John Lovett did some fast footwork restructuring the project in consultation with the forward-thinking Northumberland Strategic Partnership, and came up with a solution. Unfortunately, and against all the Duchess's better instincts, it involved taking out a loan. But beggars can't be choosers and there was no alternative.

It was a shaky start to the build and soon things spiralled further downwards. From the beginning we'd found it difficult to adapt to Hopkins & Partners' working practices. I certainly hadn't appreciated the huge cultural difference between the way 'signature' and 'normal' architects operate. Companies like Hopkins are hired for their particular style and tend to be purist and independent in outlook, presenting clients with final solutions rather than involving them in developments *en route*. At The Alnwick Garden we'd always worked the opposite way, having extensive consultation and input at all stages of the design process. As the client, we expected Hopkins to pass ideas through us and when they didn't we weren't sure what to do.

Although the Duchess was confident and assertive about dealing with designers and contractors by this stage, she somehow felt Hopkins were so well-known and sure of their ideas that she wasn't able to question them as she might have done a smaller firm. For example, the roof was originally a wooden structure, but Michael Hopkins himself changed it to a construction of high-tech, air-filled membranes with a reflective sheen. Jane preferred the wood, but because her 'biggest failure', as she sees it, is that she can't visualize an architectural drawing in terms of bricks and mortar, she didn't feel she could jump in and say, 'I'm not sure that looks appropriate for the Garden …'

I was keener than her on the Pavilion roof and thought it would look impressive once Peter Wirtz's vertical plantings brought it into perspective. My major concerns were practical: was the roof – a complex wooden frame of diamond shapes each filled with pressurised air 'cushions' made of opaque PTFE (polytetrafluoroethylene) or clear ETFE (ethylene-tetrafluoroethylene) – workable in a visitor attraction open 364 days of the year? What about wear and tear: how would these pillows look in twenty-five years' time? I'd been alarmed when I was casually told one day that the pillows would start deflating if the generator stopped – though it would apparently take two to three days for the whole roof to collapse.

Neither Jane nor I was fully involved in design discussions, most of which took place in London, so none of these concerns were sorted out. 'As the project goes on,' Jane said in the office one day, 'I can see designers becoming more difficult. In Phase 1 it was easy to get the best out of everyone. But now there are more designers and contractors involved and they're all critical of each other's work.' It was true: we had little success persuading Hopkins to liaise with Wirtz International, for example. 'Dealing with great architects and great garden designers has not been a piece of cake,' wrote the Duchess to the Prince of Wales with some understatement, 'and occasionally egos get in the way.'

The lack of communication at the heart of the PVC build meant that the inspiring, hands-on, all-in-this-together approach we'd established in Phase 1 disappeared overnight. Hopkins's concept and our financial team's budgets became the driving forces, and many of the Duchess's original ideas to amuse and thrill visitors – such as the stunning wave-shaped glass washbasins in the toilets lit with multi-coloured lights, and the outside terrace underlit with twinkling white stars – were casualties that got left out along the way. It wasn't until two years down the line when the Duchess, who doesn't forget a thing, asked 'Where are the washbasins we talked about? What about the lighting under the terrace?' that they were finally added in, by then at considerable extra cost.

Then there was our innovative 'Rockstore', an ecologically sound heating and cooling system, which draws air through a layer of thermally efficient rocks under the Visitor Centre. It uses massive, Malteser-shaped stones that Aidan eventually sourced from a glacial river bed in the Lake District. I was in a design meeting with about fifteen designers and contractors when the conversation came round to how 'irrelevant' the Rockstore was in terms of heating or cooling the building. 'Wait a minute,' I said. 'Are you telling me we've gone through all the work, trouble and expense of designing and building this ecologically great concept, and now we're not even going to use it?' The answer was yes. It shocked me that we only found out at the eleventh hour, too late to sort out the problems if we wanted the Visitor Centre to open on time. We would have to fix it later.

At the start, Hopkins negotiated a traditional architect's contract to oversee the build and monitor standards of quality. We agreed, even though on all other areas we'd given McAlpines a 'design and build' contract, in which they took responsibility for developing services and engineering, and maintaining the quality of the build. This had worked excellently over the past five years and McAlpines had become a trusted part of the team. It must have been difficult for them, knowing the project so well, suddenly to find themselves working under the design coordination of the Hopkins team 300 miles away in London. Hopkins brought in other sub-contractors including Buro Happold, structural engineers, who designed the wooden roof structure, consulting and mechanical engineers Battle McCarthy, and the German firm B+O Hightex GmbH, who built the air-filled roof membranes in Poland.

The roof was always the biggest problem. The pressurized cushions were built to spec off site, but when McAlpines tried to put the wooden frames and pillows together, they didn't fit. This wasn't a simple matter of getting out a pair of scissors and trimming the edges: the pillows would have to be shipped back to Poland and reconfigured at great expense – but whose expense? Everyone was accusing everyone else: the spec was wrong, the diamond frames couldn't be properly anchored so were millimetres out, the PTFE was creasing more than expected ...

Tensions rose, stalemate set in, and everybody stopped talking to each other. In cases like this, the client gets pushed out of the picture as the blame game starts. All we wanted was for the roof to be finished: the building was already over schedule, with all the overrun cost implications of that, but everybody was sitting on their hands, one group in Germany, McAlpines here and Hopkins in London, all saying your fault, your fault, your fault.

There was talk of going to an independent body for mediation, and it looked as if the Pavilion might derail the whole Garden project, when the Duchess stepped in. She had been kept out of the loop just as I had, and was horrified when she was told what was happening. She immediately wrote to Klaus Michael Koch, the President of B+O Hightex, inviting him to Alnwick to talk about the pillow problem. One of the Duchess's greatest strengths is that she always sees the big picture. She was focused on finding solutions, and knew she needed to generate

goodwill to avoid a potential stand-off between the roofers and architects. So after the meeting, and despite Michael Hopkins's reservations, she took thirty roofers, Polish, Indian and German – they hadn't a fluent English-speaker among them – out to the pub for dinner and footed the bill herself. It was a great night and it did the trick: everyone got behind her and started saying 'Let's get this roof on' instead of walking off the project. Of course, we still had a £1 million overrun on the PVC build. 'Bad,' the Duchess said. 'But it could have been worse.' We could have had no roof at all.

RETHINKING

One day the Duchess and I were in a rare meeting with Aidan, trying to negotiate some technical problems, when Aidan looked at her and said wearily, 'The trouble is, Jane, I just don't know who the client is any more.' He felt there were so many steps and buffers between the Duchess's wishes and what he was asked to do that the right message never got through. Jane was appalled, all the more because she realized he wasn't just talking about Hopkins and the other contractors, but also about the level of interference from the rest of The Alnwick Garden team, who were trying to run the Garden first and foremost as a business. They, not we, were in the meetings with the contractors. They were having an impact on design and quality control. They were under big financial pressure, and the result was that they were pulling the Garden in a different direction from the Duchess's original vision.

This was a moment of epiphany for Jane. For the first time, she felt isolated and unsure of her role in the Garden. She felt she was being wheeled out whenever the team needed a 'Duchess', but wasn't being told about the things that really mattered to her, like the design and finishes. Aidan's comment triggered a period of serious reflection.

By now we were well past the PVC opening date of May 2005, and the roof still wasn't on. Our financial overrun was compounded by unpredictably high running costs in the Garden – for example, we weren't prepared for the incredible success of the Poison Garden. Every day there were queues round the block waiting for guided

PREVIOUS PAGES: The interior of the Pavilion during construction. The complex diamond shapes that make up the roof can be seen. These 'diamonds' were filled with pressurized air-filled membranes, *aka* 'cushions'.

tours to see the toxic plants and hear the gruesome stories about them. Originally we thought we'd be able to use our Volunteer force to do the tours, but the large number of visitors made that impossible, and we suddenly needed a big investment in manpower and training to provide the guides and level of policing that the Poison Garden required.

Money was so tight that poor Aidan couldn't get in his usual supply of chocolate biscuits. 'It's not the £4 a week it costs,' he told me ruefully, 'it's the principle. It can send out the wrong message.' For him, the chocolate biscuits were a litmus test: if there are biscuits in the tin, the money's okay, but if not ... The Duchess missed the biscuits too – in fact, those biscuits came to symbolize everything that was right with Phase 1 and wrong with Phase 2: the bonhomie, cooperation and sense of fun we felt we'd lost during this difficult time.

IT ALWAYS BOILS DOWN TO MONEY

The managers were worried by the Garden's financial problems, and because of our open-plan offices their anxiety permeated down to the rest of the staff. Everyone was on tenterhooks, worried about where and when the next crisis would erupt. John Lovett had to make the finances work, and he was trying to persuade the Duchess to put up entry prices to ease the Garden's financial pain. But the Duchess's first principle had always been to make the Garden affordable for people of all income levels, and she fought like a lioness to keep prices down.

I remember her once coming back from a day at Legoland and telling me how shocked she was that it had cost nearly £100 for an adult and three children to get in. At that time, the same day out in The Alnwick Garden would cost just £6 – children under sixteen get in free. The Duchess always resisted price increases and hated the thought of charging for children. She was insistent that we didn't price ourselves out of the market as she thought some other attractions had done: once you make a mistake over-charging, you lose visitor support and repeat visits, and the lack of goodwill is irreversible. Instead, she wanted to offer those who had the money a choice of ways to spend it – for example, on ice creams, a book or gift from the shop, or lunch in the Treehouse. The Duchess believed so much of our success was down to commonsense decision-making, not decisions made on finance, and that was what differentiated us from other profits-driven visitor attractions.

John lost the argument over entry pricing but he won another, about charging for the car park. Every day, our new 850-space car park was full and we couldn't understand why. After research, we discovered that the townsfolk and people from outlying villages were leaving their cars there all day while they went to work or into town, forcing *bona fide* Garden visitors to use overflow car parks. John instigated a daily fee of £1.50 for Garden visitors and £3 for others, which quashed the problem but of course annoyed the townspeople no end.

PROBLEMS CLOSER TO HOME

Our relationship with Alnwick was becoming strained, as the size of the Garden and influx of visitors were having a marked effect on local people's lives. Traffic jams were becoming endemic, and not just in the traditional bottlenecks within Alnwick itself: on busy days in Denwick Lane, cars were backed up waiting to get into the Garden car parks, making it difficult for people to access the housing estates in nearby Allerburn Lea. Townspeople started complaining non-stop: the town was too busy in summer so residents couldn't park their cars; the Garden was hogging visitors instead of encouraging them into town to spend their money there. We couldn't win. Jane took the town's temperature at her monthly visit to the local hairdresser's. 'Oh Jane,' the hairdresser would exclaim, 'you're not flavour of the month at the moment! You don't want to know what someone was saying about you today.'

The relationship between them is complex, but the reality is that the Garden has brought huge amounts of extra economic activity to the town. Over two million visitors have passed through the gates of The Alnwick Garden, only 19 per cent of whom are from Northumberland itself. Sixty per cent also go into Alnwick – we give visitors a map to encourage them to explore the town's excellent cafés, shops and pubs – and statistics show that the Garden helps create £45.5 million worth of extra spending in Alnwick and Northumberland each year. B&B providers have flourished as visitors stay for an average of three nights in the region. Everyone – trader, retailer or accommodation provider – has their own agenda, and it's down to each individual business to try to take advantage of the opportunities that come along.

That's where the problem lies. Alnwick is a traditional, old-fashioned town and many shopkeepers still shut on Sundays and have a half-day closing during the week. Their fathers closed, their grandfathers closed, so they close too. On Easter bank holiday Monday – one of the Garden's busiest days of the year, when over 5,000 visitors walked through the gates – John Lovett went to buy something in Alnwick town. He was struck by how few shops were open and called the Duchess on her mobile. Jane said, 'Would you mind walking round and telling me exactly what you see?' So he walked round the town saying, 'Open, closed, closed – oh, Woolworths is open ….' He found that more than 50 per cent of the shops were shut while the Garden was bulging at the seams.

A couple of weeks later, John Lovett and I invited business and townspeople to a breakfast in the Marquee to address their concerns. Their main worry was that they weren't benefiting enough from the success of the Garden, and that not enough people were coming into the town. Neither John nor I thought it opportune to point out that at peak times half the shops in Alnwick were shut and therefore unable to pick up any business at all! When we reported the events of the meeting back to the Duchess, she said 'Damn it!' at our faintheartedness and called Andrew Smith, then editor of the *Northumberland Gazette*, whom she knew would be doing an article about the meeting. She explained that there were two sides to the story, and that the complaints of traders seemed unfair when half of them hadn't even been open on Easter Monday, one of the busiest days of the year.

'Jane, what are you saying?' asked Andrew Smith.

'All I'm saying is that if I were a shopkeeper in Alnwick, I'd make sure I was open all week, at weekends and on bank holidays when visitors were around, and I'd shut for a couple of weeks in January or February when it's quiet instead,' she said.

'Are you prepared to be quoted on that?' asked Andrew Smith, sensing a hot story.

'Absolutely,' said the Duchess.

The uproar was immediate. 'Duchess slams town traders' seemed to be the general response. One shopkeeper said Jane's comments were like being hit in the teeth by a Rottweiler, another that they were open on Easter Monday and took just £5. We later found out that they were a specialist golfing shop, so perhaps that wasn't surprising!

Both sides have a point: Alnwick has to wake up to the realities of trading opportunities in the twenty-first century, but equally, the Garden has to be sympathetic to the problems traders face, one of which is the physical distance from the Garden to the town. Nobody recognizes this more than the Duchess, who I often think has the word 'fairness' carved into her soul. A few days later, she came over to my desk, sat down and looked at me seriously. 'Ian,' she said, 'it's really important we get on track with the town. People trust you. Everywhere I go, they say, "Oh, you've got a great man in Ian August, he's so respected in the town." I want you to start liaising properly with the townspeople again. I want us to get back to that Phase 1 footing when things went right.'

I've always enjoyed working with local people and am delighted that my job now means that I can help develop, improve and maintain positive links with the community, ensuring that social and economic benefits influenced by the success of The Alnwick Garden can provide opportunities for others. I hold regular meetings with Alnwick District Council, and invite representatives of local businesses, shops, pubs, hotels, B&Bs and guest houses to working breakfasts to debate town and Garden issues, finding ways to work together to our mutual benefit. I sit on many local committees and am organizing a Town Open Day, where the Garden is open free of charge to the local community so they can see exactly what's going on.

DOVES

Still, there are always unpredictable local matters to test one's diplomatic skills. Doves, for example. The Duchess loves white tumbler doves and, much to Peter Wirtz's horror, placed several big dovecots on the walls of the Ornamental Garden. The doves started roosting on the roof of nearby Bondgate House, a guest house that backs on to the Garden walls. The owner complained that guests were getting woken up by the cooing, and that his roof and gutters were becoming congested with pigeon muck. One day, he sent me an email picture of twenty or so doves roosting on his roof, saying the picture was taken at 11.00 that morning when the 'entire flock' was settled there. Something had to be done.

The trouble was that the Duchess and our visitors adore the doves and we wanted to keep them in the Garden. They bathe in the water rills and add to the Garden's beauty. Showing what initiative I could muster, I bought a decoy hawk and organized a steeplejack to put it on one side of Bondgate House's chimney stack – and clean the pigeon muck off the roof while he was up there. Right, I thought, problem solved!

That afternoon I went round to the hotel, sure that the doves would have been terrified into submission. The owner said he greatly appreciated the effort I was making, but would I like to step into the garden for a moment. We went out together and gazed open-mouthed at the doves enjoying the sunshine on the far side of the chimney stack away from the hawk. The damned birds had found a sunny spot they liked and a paltry plastic bird wasn't going to stop them enjoying it.

So the doves, unrepentant and untrainable, were shipped off to the Duke and Duchess's summer home at Burncastle, where they remain to this day. I bought in a new flock of six white tumbler doves and, following advice from a pigeon fancier friend of Chris Gough's, trained them to stay in the Garden by feeding them just once a day. It worked, and now our tumbler doves roost on the arbours in the Ornamental Garden and wander around the paths, ignoring the warm and tempting roofs of Bondgate House just a short flight away.

It was around this time that we also started getting complaints from visitors who were disappointed to find parts of the Garden a muddy building site. Every day, rather like a cabinet minister, the Duchess gets a red box of correspondence from people about the Garden, to which she always personally replies. She writes her notes by hand, and Sarah Darling, her marvellous, cheerful assistant, types the replies and sends them off. Normally this is a smooth and seamless operation, but occasionally a letter so aerates the Duchess that she calls for my help in dealing with it.

When people are very rude, in person or in writing, the Duchess gets hot under the collar and can make impulsive decisions. My role is to take a level-headed view and say: 'Let's think about this a bit so we can decide what's best.' By then she's usually cooled down and sorted it out for herself. In this case, though, tolerance was beyond her. She passed me a long, handwritten letter from a disappointed visitor, on which she had scrawled 'COW!' in huge capitals, surrounded by her trademark doodles. On a sticky note, she'd written:

> Ian,
> Using your great skills in diplomacy and tact would you please reply to this COW and tell her to get lost. She's obviously an embittered old bag and she needs to know that most people, fortunately, don't think like her.
> PS: This is going to test even you!

I read the letter, which was indeed very rude about the Garden, complaining that the Cascade was a 'great disappointment', the Treehouse was 'extremely tacky', the Garden was a 'theme park' full of 'ice-cream vendors and sausage cooking stalls', and that Chatsworth was much, much better.

I sympathize with visitors' disappointment: many people make the journey to visit the Garden after reading a glowing article in the Press and don't quite grasp that this is still a work in progress. My instinct is always to explain the situation and try to get them on our side, and in this case I spent hours composing what I hoped was a tactful and persuasive reply.

Often when the Duchess was on the verge of blowing a fuse, I'd quietly try to sort things out behind the scenes. I remember another unbelievably rude letter we got from a local visitor, but instead of writing back, this time I decided to ring her up. I didn't tell the Duchess until we were sitting having a quick lunch in the beautiful gardens of a country house hotel in Yorkshire, before giving one of our talks. Jane had just taken a bite of her ham sandwich when I said: 'Remember that lady who sent in that filthy letter criticising the Garden? You won't believe it but she's become a Friend now.'

Jane spluttered bits of ham into her cider: 'What happened? Did you write to her?'

'No,' I explained. 'I rang and talked to her.'

'Rang her? You must be mad. What on earth did you say to make her change her mind?'

'I said something like: "You've written this letter and we're obviously very concerned you feel this way and I'd just like to have a chat about it,"' I replied. 'She said, "I never expected anyone to call me – I thought you'd just bin the letter." So I said, "We don't work like that. We want to consider people's concerns and criticisms and the only way we're going to get this right is by listening to people like you."

'We then had a twenty-minute chat, and at the end she said, "I feel really bad about writing that letter now. I realize I've got it all wrong. I'd like to join the Garden – will you send me your Friends' membership?"'

'Ian,' said the Duchess, almost in hysterics as I recounted this story, 'only you could have pulled that off!'

WORKING TOGETHER

It's a small example, but I was always trying to make the Duchess see the value of working together with locals, Friends and Volunteers. The Duchess thought people would follow us once the Garden was built and ready, but I knew how people in Northumberland operated. It's a traditional place and it takes thirty years before you're accepted and no longer considered an outsider. I knew it was vital to get locals supporting the project as it developed and not expect them to accept a *fait accompli* at the end.

External pressures like these are difficult to deal with, but internal rifts cause more damage and pain. One of the biggest battles the Duchess faced at this time was with the horticultural team about the concept of the Wirtzes' layout. Most of our gardeners were used to working in traditional English gardens packed with wide colourful borders; gardens where the flowers are of prime importance. Visitors, too, expect a big colourful splash in a public garden like Alnwick, and people were always asking the gardening staff: 'It's March/April, why are there no flowers?' In Britain, we came to realize, a garden is not considered beautiful unless flowers are bursting forth from every border.

Green, it's sometimes forgotten, is a colour too, and the Duchess and I gave every new gardener an induction and tour to explain the Wirtzes' concept of 'green architecture', where structure is more important than colour, and flowers are the icing on the cake. The Wirtzes had just published a beautiful book on their work and the Duchess bought two copies, one of which she lent to the gardening team; she also offered to pay for the team to go over to Belgium to see the Wirtzes' gardens for themselves. As she said, 'This concept is going to be difficult for the visitor to understand until the Garden's finished, but you have to hope your gardening team understand and are on side.'

So she was horrified when Head Gardener Chris Gough plonked down hundreds of pink and orange geraniums in the empty borders in the top garden. When she told him they'd have to go, he replied that the public liked them.

'If the public like them, they can go and see them in the municipal gardens in Newcastle,' Jane retorted. 'But they're not coming to Alnwick to see 150 shocking-pink geraniums!'

Although the geraniums disappeared, the problem didn't go away. Just before I went on holiday in 2004, the Duchess and I heard through the grapevine that Chris Gough was threatening to resign – he'd wanted to make his mark on the Garden and perhaps felt thwarted by the Duchess's intransigence. Jane thought the problem wouldn't wait until I got back, and asked the eight members of the gardening team to come to see her at once. She was worried and angry, but I was just worried: I wanted to be there when she talked to the gardening team, not just to back her up, but also to get the situation resolved with as little damage as possible.

At the meeting, the gardening team explained their position, saying there were not enough flowers in the garden and visitors were complaining about it. Why couldn't they have some lovely bright geraniums? Why couldn't they fill some pots with colourful plants and dot them around the Garden?

The Duchess went ballistic. 'But that's like putting a daffodil in Van Gogh's sunflowers,' she said. 'He's famous for his sunflowers – you don't just go and stick a geranium in because you think it's what people want.'

'Why not?' they said. 'What's this Garden all about?'

After all the years of discussion and debate, after all the pep talks the Duchess and I had given the gardening team over the years, that felt like the final straw. Jane said, 'I'm really worried about your attitude. If you don't love this Garden and understand what we're doing here, how can you be selling it to the visitors? And if you really don't understand what we're doing, as you seem to be saying, and don't feel you're working towards a final plan – the very same plan we discussed from the very beginning – then you're in the wrong job and should consider moving to a garden that's more to your liking.'

Dead silence, then everyone trooped out. Jane immediately called me on the mobile in a panic. 'God, Ian,' she said. 'I think I've blown it – they're all going to walk out.'

Actually, only two of the gardening team resigned in the wake of this meeting and, hopefully, found places where they felt more in tune with the prevailing ethos. But for us, the canker lingered. Peter Wirtz had worked very closely with Chris Gough over the years and had enormous respect for him. But in January 2005 he wrote to John Lovett and me saying how worried he was about the Garden and especially about Chris Gough:

What puzzles me profoundly is that the offices are well filled with administrative staff, but the gardeners are undermanned and overstretched. What Chris Gough does with the hands he has is miraculous, but that will not last. Please trust my opinion, the passion and quality he delivers and the long hours he performs to cope with his job are unusual. We are all getting used to and are spoiled by gardeners that are in reality overstretched. If he gets demotivated and goes, we are in trouble!

How prescient he was, though at the time Chris promised us faithfully that the problem was solved and he was happy in his role.

LONELY AT THE TOP

This in-fighting was proving stressful for the Duchess at a time of great personal unhappiness. Her father had recently died, and I remember being staggered on her behalf by the insensitivity of many staff. Just a day after his death, she and I were giving a lecture about the Garden to Estates workers and heads of departments. She was standing talking and I remember thinking how pale and controlled she looked. She told me later it was as if a loop was running through her mind: 'My father died yesterday – do any of you know or care? Is anyone going to come up and say they're sorry to hear of his death?' Nobody did. Various people thanked her for the talk, but no one said anything about her father.

At the end she came up to me and said, 'I can't believe it. Has anyone mentioned my father to you?' I told her they hadn't, and her face fell. 'It's almost as if I don't exist as a person,' she said sadly. 'I don't have a life – I'm just wheeled out to do the Garden.'

When she told the Duke, he said she shouldn't blame anyone. People find it difficult to talk about a close death and say they're sorry – they're never sure whether the other person's going to burst into tears or break down.

This was all part of a toughening-up process for Jane that started when she was thrust into the limelight as Duchess. In her ducal role, she's like the head of a big corporation, distant and privileged, and people don't feel they can respond to her on a real, human level. There are few people who can see past her title to what she is, and that can make her position a very lonely one indeed. Even her friends find it hard to talk to her about the Garden, and Ralph has always made it clear it's her preserve, and stays well out of the way.

Tim Smit was the only external person who recognized Jane's sense of isolation at this time. After a visit, he sent her a note saying the Treehouse was gorgeous and if she put in a grand piano he'd happily live there. Then more seriously he added, 'It's lonely being a leader and I know I don't need to say it, but if ever you need to bounce an idea or have a moan – just get on the blower.'

Jane was becoming more drained and exhausted. She'd faced year upon year of planning problems, money crises, vitriolic personal criticism, building difficulties – and swung high over hurdle after hurdle. But now things started getting to her. It came to a head when she discovered that there had been two staff leaving parties and an annual staff Christmas party to which she was not invited. The organisers had simply forgotten to ask her and she in turn assumed that the staff had preferred her not to be present. She felt isolated and wasn't sure what her role was anymore. On top of this standards in the Garden had begun to slip.

TROUBLED WATERS

The operational side of the Garden was not running smoothly, despite our huge staff. Things were starting to look grubby and grey round the edges, the food quality wasn't high enough, some staff weren't treating visitors with enough friendliness or respect... the Duchess felt everything was getting out of control. 'Ian,' she said 'don't they realize we don't have an attraction unless it looks immaculate?'

Jane is fanatical about 'delivering'. She goes out and sells the Garden, which employs a team of seventeen managers and 200 staff, and expects them all to live up to her very high standards. She feels that any of us can talk about something, but what matters is the delivery. Standards were not up to scratch and she wanted to know why.

One day she rang me from the Garden on her mobile to say that one of the toy ride-on tractors that we provide for children to play on was sticking out of the bottom pool in the Grand Cascade with a wheel showing. Various managers had walked by and yet no one had bothered to remove it. Jane would have gone in to fish it out herself but the water was too deep. She moved on to the Serpent Garden where she noticed that a newly designed circular pool had been given a finishing coating of dark brown paint instead of the standard black used throughout all our designs. She would never have sanctioned this and suspected, correctly, that a cheaper finish had been selected and hadn't been run past her for approval because she would have instantly rejected it. Her insistence on top quality throughout the design and build, running down to the garden staff, seemed to be being ignored and this went against everything she'd fought to achieve. All this was depressing enough, but the final straw came when, one morning in a meeting, Elisabeth asked the Duchess a question. 'We've got a bit of difficulty,' she said, 'in that we never know how to refer to you and explain what you do in the Garden.' The Duchess, who'd headed the team and worked full-time for nine years without a penny's payment, was flabbergasted. 'Elisabeth,' she said as kindly as she could, 'everything you see in the Garden, down to the last teaspoon in the Treehouse, the candles, the lights, is a design I've chosen and worked on for the past nine years. I don't know what you call that and how you give it a job title but that's for you to think about.'

'Oh,' said Elisabeth, still missing the point, 'I suppose we could call you the artistic director, and explain we need your vision to get the funding.'

Then John Lovett said something similar. He was showing some people round the office when he casually commented, 'Jane, you're here what, one day a week?'

'I can't believe it, John,' she said. 'Three, four, five days – sometimes six!'

John, Elisabeth and the rest of the staff don't see the work the Duchess puts in behind the scenes, when she gets up at 6.30 a.m. to do a ten-hour round trip to Helensburgh or Essex to give a lecture, or spends hours every night replying to the letters in her red box. Jane is constantly thinking and planning the next stage, asking everyone she meets in every social situation to help the Garden, or giving hours of her time doing publicity to raise its profile. Not that the Duchess thinks she does any more work than anyone else in the Garden, but it's lowering when nobody seems to appreciate the effort you put in and she had reached breaking point.

The Duchess is a very black and white person. She called me and said: 'I've had it. I'm unhappy, I don't like the way things are going and if it can't be sorted out I'm going to resign and move on. There has to be more to life than this.'

I was deeply concerned – I knew this wasn't an idle threat: she could and would walk away – but also annoyed that many of the new people in the team couldn't see her leadership was the engine that drove the project. Without her, there was nothing.

I didn't try to reason with Jane; she'd made up her mind. The next day she told John Lovett she wasn't happy, and if he and the team felt it was better she resigned, she would happily do so. I think John was genuinely surprised by the Duchess's statement: he hadn't seen it coming. It had been a difficult balancing act for him and the team to know how much to include the Duchess in the running of the Garden. She felt they were using her in a rather self-serving way – wheeled out when she could impress someone, then shunted off and ignored the rest of the time.

After her conversation with John, the Duchess left the Garden for the day. She was going on a trip to Africa and went off to get her injections. When she came back the Castle was in uproar. Everyone had been calling Sarah Darling to try to get hold of the Duchess: Elisabeth was in tears, John Lovett was worried, I was upset. I finally got through to Jane who by contrast was icily calm. She asked me to get John, Elisabeth and the other managers together. 'I want you to go through this without me being there,' she said. 'Decide honestly whether or not you want me involved in the project, and if so, exactly what my role is to be.'

A couple of months earlier, a risk assessment had been carried out in which the worst-case scenario for the Garden's long-term survival was that the Duchess got run over by a bus and was out of the project. It looked as if this might come to pass without the intervention of any big red vehicle. At the meeting, I explained to John and Elisabeth why we needed the Duchess leading from the front. She was the key player – she might not be in the office all the time, but she was directly responsible for the vision, design and quality of the Garden. She was the concept designer and inspiration, and it was her leadership that brought us all together. Without her, we would be rudderless and drifting.

The meeting cleared the air enormously. John memoed the Duchess saying we were 100 per cent behind her, and outlining how the team saw her strengths and future role. The atmosphere changed immediately: people in the team started to realize she wasn't just a figure who floated around on the periphery, coming to the occasional meeting, but an integral member of the team whose guiding influence was the very reason we were there. Now she is plugged in at every level and widely consulted on every issue. We also hired a new customer services manager, David Bulman, to address concerns about standards and the quality of the visitor experience. All in all, it felt as if our *annus horribilis* was finally coming to an end.

LOSS OF A GOOD MAN

There was just one more blip: still troubled, Chris Gough, our head gardener, resigned. I was in the Garden office when the Duchess called to let me know. Chris had just rung her on her mobile, saying: 'I want to be the first to tell you I've got some bad news: I'm leaving.'

It was clear his mind was made up, but the Duchess wanted desperately for him to stay. She asked him if it was the money – he said no, and in fact one of the Garden's policies has always been to pay horticultural staff higher wages than usual in the sector. Was it the house? No. What was it then? Chris said he just wanted a change. He'd had enough. Peter Wirtz's premonition had indeed come to pass.

The Duchess took it as a terrible personal blow. Although rationally she knew no member of staff was indispensable, she thought Chris was so full of character, strong and larger than life, that he had almost become so. 'I'm so fond of him,' she cried. 'He's inspiring, he's great for the project.' He'd done a remarkable job, arriving in a half-developed Garden with no team and no money, dealing every day with hordes of questioning and at times angry visitors, handling TV crews and newspapers with aplomb, to say nothing of his superb horticultural skills...

Chris worked out his month's notice, and when he left the gardening team crumpled. The Duchess and Peter Wirtz spent three days interviewing candidates for the job. I remember getting a call from Jane as she was driving back to Burncastle one night. She was almost in tears, and told me about the depressing day she'd spent interviewing people who weren't a third as good as Chris. 'This is a terrible, awful time,' she said. 'Chris is gone and it's made me realize this Garden is only as good as the people working in it.'

Eventually, we hired an excellent candidate, Derek Horton, who'd worked for Andrew Lloyd Webber and at Leeds Castle. The Duchess wanted someone who wasn't just a great gardener and could work well with Peter Wirtz, but was also good fun, with whom she could pop down and have a cup of tea and talk about how things were going. Peter Wirtz gave Derek and the gardening team a long talk about his approach, and perhaps for the first time I have confidence that the gardening team fully understands the Wirtzes' vision.

Thankfully, my role was soon sorted out too. In the car going off to give a lecture one day, the Duchess asked if it ever annoyed me that I got paid for twenty hours a week and usually ended up doing double that. I'd always worked long hours, especially under previous Dukes, so I could put it into perspective. I told her that just as she did so much without payment, I was happy to put in my bit too. But once the Duchess gets hold of an idea, she doesn't let go, and from then on she became more and more annoyed and hurt on my behalf. She'd often say she thought the management team were wrong to be so wrapped up in their finances that they didn't understand how important I was to the project. She was ashamed to have been the messenger who'd had to ask me to cut back my hours. It was wrong for her to have been involved and she was going to set it right.

And so at the end of 2005 the Duchess got my job description rewritten to include what jokingly came to be called the 'succession clause'. I formally became her representative in matters relating to the Garden, interpreting her wishes to other directors and managers and supporting her in presentations, publicity and PR, as well, of course, in liaison with the town. Just in case she was run over by that bus, Jane wrote to all the team saying that she wanted it officially recorded that:

> In the event of my death (prematurely, I mean), Ian will be 'required' to take my place and ensure that the Garden is completed according to the vision. Ian knows that I want this officially recorded, as does John Lovett. I'd like the Trustees to sign it off and everyone to be aware of the huge esteem in which I hold Ian August and the importance I place in his role. I consider this to be vital and would die happy!

Perhaps we are committed to the Garden in a different way from other people because of our long history together. If anything happened to the Duchess – God forbid – I am probably the only person who's on her wavelength, who knows exactly what she wants and can follow her vision through. I've always felt secure in my role with her, but this seemed a great public acknowledgement and reward. It sounds corny to say it but it's true: I too will die happy.

That autumn was also the fiftieth anniversary of the day I started working for Northumberland Estates. I said to the Duchess, 'I've already had my retirement party, so I don't want any carry on. What I'd like best is a quiet drink with you and the Duke to say I've reached this point in my life with the Percy family.'

'Right,' said Jane. 'Definitely no carry on, then.'

The day arrived and I remember being in a long meeting with Aidan. As we were walking out of the door, I said to him, 'Do you know, I've been working for the Dukes of Northumberland for fifty years today.' 'That's incredible,' he said. 'I never knew that. Congratulations!'

I turned up a bit early that evening to the Treehouse, and in the car park bumped into an old contractor I used to work with. 'What are you doing here?' I asked. 'Oh, I've come for a function in the Treehouse,' he said. Then I recognized a tenant I used to know years ago, and saw Rory Wilson crossing the yard and thought, 'What on earth has Jane done?' Five minutes later the Duke and Duchess turned up in the car park, and I said: 'I've got a strange feeling about tonight. I saw quite a lot of people I know going in – you haven't organized anything, have you?'

'No,' said the Duchess firmly. 'They must all be coming for some other event.' I remembered how sincere Jane sounded when she was playing her trick on Flossie, and was still slightly suspicious. But then she said, 'Let's go and show Ralph the Serpent Garden now all the water features are working so well,' and my mind was set at rest.

Walking up to the Treehouse entrance twenty minutes later, there was Dowager Duchess Elizabeth. 'Do you mind, Ian?' asked Jane. 'Elizabeth wanted to join us and share this moment with you.' I was thrilled. I've always got on very well with Ralph's mother, and often show her round the Garden. Then the Duchess flung open the Treehouse door and a huge roar nearly knocked me sideways. My son and daughter, Simon and Philippa, came over to me but I still didn't understand what was going on. 'What on earth are you doing here?' I said. It's amazing how slow on the uptake a person can be!

When I walked in there was a huge, heaving party of 150 people, everyone I've enjoyed working with over the years. Friends, tenants, contractors, people who worked on the Estates and in the Garden team too. 'You bugger,' I said, when I saw Aidan. He just grinned.

The Duke and Duchess each gave a speech, then presented me with one of Alexander Creswell's watercolours of the Garden. He's been painting views of the Garden since before building started. As a keen watercolourist myself, I admire the freedom of his work, and this painting, looking down from the arches of the Ornamental Garden to the Pavilion, has a very special place in my heart.

It was a wonderful night, with more speeches and toasts, and lovely nibbles including my favourite, the chef's special mini fish and chips wrapped in tiny corners of newspaper. At the end the Duchess told me the planning had been going on for nine weeks – I couldn't believe I didn't pick up on it. It's been a roller-coaster fifty years, but I'm glad it didn't end quietly – what a way to celebrate!

BACK ON TRACK

Soon after, the problems with the Pavilion and Visitor Centre were sorted out. Worried about delays and cost overruns, McAlpines offered us a fixed-price contract to finish and fit out the build, with Summers & Partners, our quantity surveyors, acting as contract administrators. John Lovett and the Trustees evaluated the offer and thought it in the best interests of the Garden if we wanted to open the PVC at Easter 2006. Immediately, Jane and I started to get involved in weekly site inspection meetings to determine and approve the finishes. Everyone from McAlpines kept coming up to me saying, 'It's great to have you and the Duchess around again. It's fantastic to talk to you and get things sorted out on the spot.' It was a joy to be back in the thick of things, and I felt an instant resurgence of the team spirit and happy atmosphere we had during the Phase 1 build.

As a result, the PVC build started motoring along and was completed in March 2006. I like the finished building. It's a simple counterpoint to the complex drama of the Wirtzes' garden. But it has its detractors. Some people think the opaque plastic roof makes too definite a statement against the surrounding brick and stone surfaces of the rest of the Garden. My feeling is that great modern buildings always provoke controversy, and it will be interesting to see how people judge it in twenty years' time.

The Pavilion and Visitor Centre opened to the public at Easter 2006. The Duchess and I were jubilant. This was the end of an era. It had taken ten years, but finally Phases 1 and 2 were complete. From here, surely, it must be downhill all the way.

CHAPTER 13

THE LIGHT AT THE END OF A TOPIARY TUNNEL

The Duchess had proved she wasn't just another 'toff with a garden'. She and the Garden have won many prestigious awards, including the Outstanding Contribution to Tourism from the Enjoy England Excellence Awards 2005. Tim Smit wrote a lovely note complimenting the Duchess on her effort: 'You are a star and you've battled like a tigress to do the thing properly ... it's a funny thing to say but I'm really proud of you.'

Phase 2 is built, but the Garden is still a long way from being finished and nobody is sitting back enjoying the view. 'The moment for me, Ian,' said the Duchess as we walked round the new Pavilion, 'will be when it's all finished. I won't be happy until then. I hate all these phases and gaps between phases – you're selling something inaccurate. What I'm interested in is the human element; I want to sit here sipping coffee and watching 100 pensioners dancing and having fun. That's the bit that gives me the buzz.'

The Duchess doesn't switch off, she doesn't give up, she doesn't slow down. We're all in her wake trying to catch up. If she went on a hiking trip, she'd be the one stomping off, setting the pace ten miles ahead of the pack, and she wouldn't stop for a breather until the finish line was crossed. Mentally, she's already several years into the future, standing beside the Prince of Wales as he cuts the ribbon at the next huge celebration to open the completed Alnwick Garden. Now the rest of us have to get there too.

We know exactly what's to be done, and how much money we need to do it. So far, the Garden has cost £33 million, bringing in around 500,000 visitors a year and massively boosting the North-East's economy. But the Duchess's ambitions haven't stopped there: Phase 3 includes developing the Garden as a transformational cultural project of world-class standard, providing a stimulating, nurturing and beautiful environment where visitors can enjoy learning and skills development, healthy activity and play, and experience all kinds of art and culture. Her dream is to inspire and educate for 364 days a year.

I'm still not quite sure how we got from the Wirtzes' original plan to this vast, transforming project, but it can only be a good thing for the region. When Phase 3 is delivered, the Garden will generate up to 445 full-time jobs, offer £150 million in economic benefits to the local community over ten years, and transform the rural economy and social life of the North-East. But now, we're once again in the uncomfortable position of needing large amounts of funding before we can move forward. We've applied to the Big Lottery Fund for £25 million through their one-off Living Landmarks initiative, which we'll match with £9 million from private funding. The Duchess is optimistic that the money will come through – we're a rural regeneration project that hasn't received any Lottery benefits before and we're fully backed by the local community and major groups in the North-East. If we get this money, the project could be finished within two years. If not...

Undaunted, the Duchess and I are already planning the slalom down the final slope, advancing the designs as far as possible so that when the money comes in, we're ready to build. We're developing a new Cherry Orchard, using 350 *Prunus* 'Tai Haku' or Great White cherry trees. In spring, their blossom will look like snow, with dazzling white flowers over two inches wide set against copper-coloured foliage – and the Duchess of course has formulated a secret idea for making the Orchard compelling to young and old alike! There's a Quiet Garden, where a large jet-black pond creates a startling optical illusion; and a Garden of the Senses with raised beds, an educational area in which able-bodied people will come to understand what it means to be a wheelchair-user or without sight.

Gardens should be great in winter too, but in Britain they're usually shut. We want to change that ethos. I went to the States and Canada to research Longwood Gardens in Pennsylvania and Butchart Gardens on Vancouver Island. At Christmas, these gardens have queues waiting to see their fantastic light displays, shows and carol singing. Tourists have never come to Northumberland in winter before, but the Duchess is gambling that we can extend the season of interest by creating the same kind of stunning winter attractions at Alnwick. The lighting around the Garden – for which we incorporated the infrastructure during the Phase 1 build – will be hugely important for creating night-time and winter drama and will hopefully become an attraction in itself.

The Cascade was always built to be frozen, and in sub-zero temperatures it looks like a glacier moving down the hill, with dramatic shards of ice emerging from its surface. Jane's idea is to illuminate this with electric blue light along every step. There are plans for a frozen Crystal Grotto and a huge ice sculpture by renowned Norwegian sculptor Carl Nesjar, who worked for many years in collaboration with Picasso.

The Duchess and I first met Carl Nesjar in 1998 when he gave a lecture on Frozen Fountains at the Royal Society for British Sculptors in London. We asked him and his wife out for dinner afterwards and fired him up about the idea of designing a cascade of ice for The Alnwick Garden. Using controlled thermostats, the Cascade will be made to freeze at night and thaw slightly throughout the day so that it drips and refreezes to create a glittering, show-stopping mass of ice never seen in this country before.

In Peter Wirtz's Spiral Garden, pleached hornbeams will reach up to fourteen metres high to create an Alice in Wonderland area enclosing one of Wet Design's most dramatic water features. Jane's idea is that you walk out of the Pavilion to see a classic and beautiful garden, then hear noise and shouting and can't understand why. You walk towards the Spiral and realize it's the sound of excited children, running around on a big non-slip stainless steel plate from which erupt hollow marbles of water, colourfully lit with fibre-optics. The children career around trying to catch and smash the water marbles, getting soaked, laughing and having fun.

Then there's the Pavilion Garden, which the Duchess sees as a peaceful, private area where two lead sphinxes, donated to the Garden by Calder lead works in

Newcastle, will find a resting place. The sphinxes, gorgeous ladies affectionately known as Gert and Daisy, were thought to have graced the portals of Northumberland House, once the Duke of Northumberland's London home, but have been moved around the country for the past sixty years. Poor old Gert in particular has had a rough ride, getting hit by shrapnel in an air raid during the Second World War and surviving collisions with two London buses. She's being restored now, and I hope she and Daisy will be very happy in their distinguished new home and bring delight to many visitors.

The Duchess also wants to build a state-of-the-art facility for bus drivers, who have a boring time at most attractions. 'Think airport executive lounge, Ian,' she said to me out of the blue one day. 'With satellite TV, internet facilities, loos, showers, fresh coffee, pastries, newspapers and comfy seating.' She and I went down to give a talk about the Garden and the drivers' facility at a trade and tourism fair in Birmingham. We presented our plans in front of the many coach companies in attendance and they seemed thrilled with the idea. The Duchess wants the facility to be built to the same high standards of design and quality as the rest of the Garden, not a nasty pre-fabricated hut tucked away in a corner. In her opinion, bus drivers deserve the best treatment possible as they have played such a vital part in the success of the Garden and in the regeneration of north Northumberland. Hopefully, they'll have a good experience at The Alnwick Garden and will be keen to come our way again.

There are also plans to build a new bridge stretching from the car park over Denwick Lane to the Treehouse. Thousands of visitors cross this road every week, but pelican crossings and traffic lights don't ensure pedestrian safety. Of course, it can't be any grotty old footbridge: it has to be beautiful, designed by the same team and of the same quality as the rest of the Garden, so the whole experience reads as one.

But perhaps the most important development in Phase 3 will be the children's adventure playground. With four children of her own, the Duchess knows from personal experience the lure television and computer games have for kids and wants to forge a new and radical play opportunity where children can climb through the trees, get wet and dirty, open themselves up to imaginative challenges and have the freedom to take risks and enjoy excitement and adventure in a 'safely dangerous' aerial environment. Günter Beltzig and Brummie Stokes are designing a £4 million playground fifteen metres high in the trees where 1,000 disabled and able-bodied children and adults can play together. It will be a world first! There are plans for a scary glass walkway – the Duchess saw a picture of something similar being developed over the Grand Canyon, and thought that if they can do it there, we can do it at Alnwick. It'll lead to a healthy, fast-food café with a wonky roof and eating pods, where parents can sit and watch or play with their children. There will be a separate entrance fee so families can use the Treehouse playground without visiting the rest of the Garden – great for local kids on repeat visits. The Duchess plans to open a Young Friends of the Playground, so parents and grandparents can buy children a good healthy present of free entrance throughout the year.

The sheer ambition of these Phase 3 developments shows just how far the Duchess has come in the past ten years. Her role has changed enormously: in the beginning, she was shy and reserved, and found it hard to present her ideas. A decade on, she's invited to speak on a platform alongside Prime Minister Tony Blair and local government minister David Miliband at the pioneering North-East forum 'Raising Aspirations, Changing Culture'. She found herself eating dinner with chopsticks ('I made such a mess of my food,' she sighed) at the Chinese Ambassador's home in London discussing a deal in which Chinese visitors are encouraged to travel up the east coast of Britain, instead of travelling to Edinburgh via the West Coast and then flying south – missing out all the history of the North-East. As a result of that meeting, she's planning a lecture tour in four Chinese cities, to encourage Chinese tourists to visit the Garden and understand the historic importance of the North-East, scene of centuries of border warfare and the site of many great castles. At the invitation of Graham Meadows, the European Commission's Director-General of Regional Policy, she's also giving a lecture to the EU in Brussels about regional regeneration and the cultural, social and economic development of the North-East. The Duchess is so passionate and clearly very honest when she talks that, despite herself, she's becoming an ambassador for the Garden and the region.

We were recently chatting about what we'd both learned from the project and she joked, 'I've learned to say no! I used to be such a mouse, but even at the beginning I remember saying to you, "Although he or she is the expert in their field, I don't think their advice is right." Now I *know* if they're not right. And I'm prepared to let them know too. I also honestly don't worry any more about what people think of me. I just don't care.'

She used to get irate when she'd ask Tim Smit how to do this or that, and he'd say, 'You're on your own, kid.' He wouldn't give away trade secrets to a potential rival, and that's fair enough. The Duchess had to learn the hard way, all by herself. It's been fascinating watching her grow in confidence and aplomb; the downside is that she's become more guarded about people's motives. That's where we differ: temperamentally I still enjoy being everyone's friend (at least so says the Duchess!) whereas she thinks it's human nature that everyone has their own agenda and wants something from the project. 'I'm more cynical about people now,' she comments, 'which means I'll stick to my guns no matter what anyone says.'

Years ago, I remember reading the phrase 'all gardens are a form of autobiography'. I think The Alnwick Garden's transformation from a derelict, overgrown site to a public garden of elegance and quality is due almost entirely to Jane's courage, passion and sheer bloody-mindedness.

This Garden is her autobiography, as even her children agree. Last Christmas, the Duchess and I were chatting in the Castle kitchen with Katie, Melissa and Max, who were home for the holidays. Who knows you better than your children, I thought, and took the opportunity to ask them which of Jane's personal qualities and characteristics they thought were reflected in the Garden.

'Quirky', 'ambitious', 'adventurous', 'original', 'what you see is what you get', they shouted out quick as a flash, no thought needed.

'Tenacious,' I added.

'What about "perfectionist and control freak!"' asked the Duchess, tongue in cheek.

When you come to think about it, these qualities sum up The Alnwick Garden too. This is a place that defies conventional wisdom, that's beautiful, quirky and unusual, and has the ambition to provide tangible human benefits by instilling a sense of pride, motivation, confidence and aspiration in the people who visit. That's a tall order, and it taken all Jane's tenacity and, yes, perfectionism to get there.

The Duke has now renamed Jane 'Miss Marple' because she spends half her time snooping round the Garden watching visitors to see how they use the facilities, so she can better understand what works and what doesn't. She hides in the arbours, and is thrilled when she sees older folk heave the benches into a straight line on each side of the Cascade, so they can watch the kids running up and down between the two pools. She loves the pleasure they get, sitting with their handbags on their knees and laughing at the children getting wet.

Last summer, she told me she'd watched a father with his children at the Cascade. Three of them were running through the water jets, getting soaked and laughing uproariously. The other boy was in a wheelchair and the man – 'What a man!' exclaimed Jane – wanted to give the same experience to his severely disabled son. He ran up and down between the jets as fast as he could, pushing the child in his wheelchair. 'You should have seen his son's face,' said the Duchess. 'His head was twisted in laughter as they ran towards me. It was a moment to die for. It was the most wonderful sight!'

Her dream is to see 150 elderly people get together in the Pavilion on a dank winter afternoon. We thought genteel tea dances would be the thing but James Glover, the dreadlocked, forward-thinking and inspiring representative from Age Concern, put us right, saying the first event his elderly people wanted was speed dating. 'Right, speed dating it is,' said the Duchess. 'That's what the Garden's built for!' She wants to get elderly people out of their houses and socializing together, just as she wants to get children away from their televisions, and loves it in midweek when the rope bridges around the Treehouse are full of seventy- and eighty-year-olds, bouncing up and down, laughing at each other and having the time of their lives. The Alnwick Garden and Age Concern have formed a working partnership, as a result of the opportunities offered for older people by the Garden,

A few years ago, an elderly man stopped Jane in the Garden saying he wanted to thank her for building it. 'I'm unemployed and used to watch the cars go by on a bench in Alnwick,' he said. 'Now I can come here with a newspaper and it's a nice place to sit. But I want you to know one thing: this Garden's not yours any more. It's mine.' For Jane that was a great moment. It was exactly what she'd hoped would happen. One genuine comment of appreciation like that makes the whole journey worth while.

The Garden has started a conversation that looks set to go on for generations. The challenge is to make it relevant and sustainable for the next ninety-nine years, until the lease comes to an end and it's finally time to rethink. It's important to the Duchess that her children, who've grown up watching the Garden evolve, treasure it as much as she does. She's optimistic they will. I remember when she and I were showing George round the Garden when he was fifteen and he turned and said: 'You know, Mum, I think this Garden is going to be even better at night than in the daytime. People will love it once they see the lighting.' Jane was amazed, because that reflected her instincts exactly. 'It's the best thing he could have said,' she said laughing with delight. 'It shows he understands the Garden completely.'

Now she hopes that George, who will one day become the 13TH Duke of Northumberland, will instil in his own children and grandchildren the same love and regard so they nurture the Garden in the generations to come and it continues to be a successful public charity.

As for me, I'm not getting any younger – I could do with another ten years on the right side of sixty. I've enjoyed nothing so much as working with the Duchess. She's a daily inspiration, a lightning ball of energy and fun, and I want to go on supporting her for as long as I'm able. The priority is to get the Garden finished, and when that's done I'll step back from my day-to-day role and finally retire –

much to my wife Ann's delight, though in all honesty it saddens me that I can't go on for ever.

The Duchess is always kind enough to say my role in the Garden has been as important as hers. She's more than courteous, of course, but I've been the quiet man on the side, watching in awe and helping out as much as I can. When the Garden's finished, she's suggested I become a trustee of the charity, meeting four or five times a year to hear what's going on. To me that will be heaven. I couldn't ever cut myself off from the Garden or the Percy family: the connection and loyalty I feel goes back so long and has become such a profound part of me it would be like losing a limb.

I'll retire and walk my Norwich terrier on the wild and wonderful beaches of Northumberland, get out the watercolours and the golf clubs, and start tending to my own 1.5 acres of garden. And of course, my wife Ann and I will be visiting The Alnwick Garden as Friends at least twice a week. You couldn't keep us away.

Sometimes now I get up at the crack of dawn and walk round the deserted Garden. It's magical. I climb up the steps past the sparkling Cascade waters to the gates of the Ornamental Garden and look down as the sun rises higher and bounces thin slices of orange off the Pavilion roof. The Garden, bathed in sharp blue and orange iridescence, breathes a sign of anticipation. It's waiting, like the tumbler doves cooing round my ankles, for the drama of the day to begin. At that moment, I'm proud enough of my small part in this momentous achievement to burst.

Often now, I think about what the future holds for the Duchess. There's a paradox at the core of her being: her achievement at Alnwick is a sign of someone who loves and enjoys being with people, yet she is one of the most intensely private individuals I know. She's charming and friendly, but never lets people really know her. She's led a big and at times unwieldy team, though by temperament she's a loner who prefers to work on her own. There almost nothing she wouldn't do to get the Garden finished – and yet she could walk away from it all tomorrow.

Unusually for someone in her position, she's not defined by her role as Duchess. It's not who she is or what she is. I was knocked for six when she announced last year that if she had to move out of the Castle tomorrow, she would genuinely, honestly be thrilled. 'I'd want a little cottage by the sea, with a tiny greenhouse to grow things. I'd have a small garden and a dog. And I would be really happy,' she said.

I'm not so sure. I remember Tim Smit once joking that he and Jane were like brother and sister, and a genetic mix-up had separated them at birth. His point was that they think the same way. Just as he progressed from Heligan to the Eden Project, he thought the Duchess would move on to something bigger. At the time, Jane was astonished by his comments but I have an inkling he might be right. She's masterminded a £60 million project that has become the biggest attraction in the North-East and I can see her moving on to another venture. But it would have to be on her terms.

APPENDICES

Grand Cascade & Lower Basin

- Constructed in a series of 21 weirs with a total weir length of 323 metres
- 2,500 cubic metres of concrete used in the construction
- 600 tonnes of steel reinforcement
- 7,260 gallons per minute flow down the Cascade during a display
- 250,000 gallons of water stored under the Cascade in two reservoirs and continually recirculated to create displays
- 16 pumps located within the two plant rooms to serve the water displays
- Water displays comprising 120 side and central jets controlled by a computerized programme. A further 38 jets form the eruption in the Lower Basin
- Natural sandstone walls quarried from the Darney Quarry in West Woodburn, Northumberland
- 400 metres of natural stone copings all hand dressed
- 149,000 block paving stones have been used around the Grand Cascade and its pergolas

Pergolas

- 850 hornbeam *carpinus betulus* trees

Ornamental Garden

- 16,500 plants – one of the largest collections of European plants in the UK

Rose Garden

- 3,000 English shrub and climbing roses
- Over 180 varieties
- The Alnwick Rose launched at 2001 Chelsea Flower Show

•Fox Sculpture originally stood within the Courtyard at Syon House, the ducal residence in London. English leadwork c1750 originally made for Painshill Park in Surrey by John Cheere. The four figures represent the four seasons.

Serpent Garden
•8 original water sculptures by William Pye

Bamboo Labyrinth
•500 *Fargesia rufa* Chinese bamboo plants

Poison Garden
•Ornamental entrance gate pillars originally part of suspension footbridge within the private grounds over the River Aln, manufactured in the Regent Works at Brighton in 1815

Pavilion & Visitor Centre
•Pavilion is 60 metres long
•Floor area of Visitor Centre is 412 sq metres
•Timber barrel-vaulted roof structure
•Roof covered with pre-sealed inflated 'pillows' using ETFE/PTFE materials that were originally developed for space exploration. ETFE – Polyethylenetetrafluoroethylene – i.e. transparent and PTFE – Polytetrafluoroethylene –i.e. translucent
•'Pillows' shape maintained by air pressure continuously being pumped through system at a controlled pressure of 1 p.s.i.
•Structure formed in British larch from sustainable sources from Wales
•1,500 cubic metres of concrete used to form the foundations and basement structures
•Roof water collected in harvester tank below East Terrace and re-used to flush toilets

- 16,000 porcelain tiles used over a paved area of 3,000 sq metres
- Fibre optic lighting creating a starlight effect throughout Terraces and Courtyard
- 5 lifts within Pavilion – 2 passenger, 2 service and 1 dumb waiter
- Rockstore below Visitor Centre is 52 metres long and is the first of its kind in the UK. It is used as a 'thermal battery' storing surplus heat generated by the visitors and the build-up of solar energy within the building, which is subsequently cooled and returned to control air temperature within the building
- Rockstore filled with large rounded cobbles from glacial deposits in the Lake District
- 2 90 metre deep boreholes provide water for the underfloor heating/cooling system at a temperature of 110°c
- Boreholes supplement water requirements for toilets through harvester tank during dry periods

Treehouse

- 558 sq metre complex of timber buildings linked by suspended walkways
- 31 lime trees form the overall site with 16 lime trees built into the Treehouse design
- 372 sq metres of satellite walkways, all accessible for wheelchairs and buggies
- Treehouse built using natural materials from sustainable sources including Canadian Cedar, Scandinavian Redwood, English and Scots Pine, and Douglas Fir
- 300 tonnes of timber used to build Treehouse
- 10,000 nails
- A multi-function 186 sq metre catering facility
- Meets all building, insulation and fire regulations

General

- 12 acre walled garden
- 18th-century Grade 2 listed perimeter walls
- Archaeological survey revealed six gardens previously laid out on site, with the

first garden in 1750 being 2 metres below the present ground level

•Over 65,000 plants in Phase 1 contract sourced from Belgium and Holland, including 14,590 boxwood hedges, 10,000 perennials and 32,143 beech 'whips'

•Total area of Garden, Woodland Walk and Car Parks is 50 acres

•When completed The Alnwick Garden will have 2.5 miles of footpaths within the formal garden

•118 metres of Kilkenny Blue Irish Limestone copings and edgings used around eight pools and their connecting rills

•56,000 beech whips planted on main Car Park landscape plus 500 trees

THE WATER GARDEN SCULPTURES

Coanda

This sculpture shows the Coanda effect, which makes water cling to the underside of smooth overhanging surfaces, appearing to defy gravity. The Coanda effect was discovered by Henri Coanda, a famous aeronautical engineer who went on to develop a flying saucer. He studied sculpture with Rodin and engineering with Alexandre Eiffel.

Meniscus

This sculpture shows a meniscus, which is the convex surface of the water at the top of the sculpture. A meniscus is created because the water molecules on the surface stick together to make an invisible skin, as a result of surface tension. Some insects, like water striders, can walk on water because the surface tension is strong enough to hold their weight.

Vortex

This sculpture shows a vortex, which is the air core at the centre. Water creates a vortex as the forces of water pressure, air pressure and gravity make it move downwards in a spiral. There are many vortices in nature, such as tornadoes and the black holes of the universe.

Reflection

This sculpture shows a reflection. Reflection both extends and compresses space, and depths become unpredictable. Here it transforms a hemisphere into a sphere. The mirror-like hemisphere reflects the colours around it: the green of the hornbeams and the blues, whites and greys of the sky.

Canyon

This sculpture shows water creating rollwave patterning as the thin film flows down its smooth surfaces. Surface tension pulls the water into these rhythmical wave patterns (surface tension results when the water molecules on the surface stick to one another). A canyon is a narrow, steep-sided valley, like the space in the middle of this sculpture.

Torricelli

This sculpture shows water under hydrostatic pressure, which fascinated the 17th-century Italian physicist, philosopher and mathematician Evangelista Torricelli. This is the pressure that comes from the head, or the distance between the surface of the water and a point below, regardless of the volume of water.
A pool on high ground overlooking the Serpent Garden overflows to fill up the sculpture below through underground pipework.
The water rises in the transparent tubes until it is level with the surface of the nearby pool, representing the head of water that has been reached.
A pneumatically powered valve below the ground opens to release the hydrostatically charged water into a circular manifold that feeds 90 jets. They then leap vertically up and gradually subside in unison with the dropping levels visible in the transparent tubes. When these jets have all but died, the valve closes, allowing the system to fill up again and the cycle to continue.

Starburst

This sculpture shows droplets bursting and radiating, changing and transmuting, as they travel to the limits of their world, until they reach a moment at which they appear unable to hold on any longer, and reluctantly drop away into the the abyss below.

Waterglass

This sculpture shows a single curtain in the form of a transparent, clear, unbroken membrane of falling water wrapping around a circular enclosure that can be entered and experienced from within, the outer views seen through a thin film of water. When there is no wind, the film can be as clear as glass. The flutter effect at the foot of the water curtain is a cyclic phenomenon caused by a difference in pressure on each side of the water, which causes it to suck to and fro.

THE ROSE GARDEN

A selection of David Austin Roses from the Rose Garden

MIDDLE STRIP – FEBRUARY 2002

R. *Sweginzowii*
The Alnwick® Rose
Morning Mist
Sally Holmes
Felicia
Tuscany Superb
Pat Austin
Penelope
Buff Beauty
Crown Princess Margareta
Ambridge Rose
Winchester Cathedral
Snowdon
R. *X Richardii*
Smarty
Moonlight

Comtesse de Murinais
Boule de Neige
A Shropshire Lad
Mrs Doreen Pike
Mme Hardy
Glamis Castle
Barbara Austin
William Lobb
Ferdinand Pichard
Comte de Chambord
Sarah Van Fleet
Vanity
Chianti
Cordelia
Kathryn Morley
Anne Boleyn
William Morris

Evelyn
Zigeunerknabe
Penelope
Pat Austin
Belle Story
Ann
Windrush
Charles de Mills
La Belle Sultane
Ispahan
Portmeirion
Jacques Cartier
Redouté
Tour de Malakoff
Mme Isaac Perriere
Shailer's White Moss
R. Centifolia
Ferdinand Pichard
Charles Rennie Mackintosh
Mousseline
Fantin-Latour
George Arends
Hermosa
Noble Antony
Sally Holmes
De Meaux
Smarty
Agnes
Scepter'd Isle
Roseraie de l'Hay
Sharifa Asma
Raubritter
Indigo
Louise Odier
Gruss An Aachen
Tess of the d'Urbervilles
Barbara Austin
Peach Blossom
Snowdon

Cottage Rose
Teasing Georgia
Jacqueline Du Pré
Francine Austin
Reine des Violettes
Mary Magdalene
Charlotte
Grace
The Alnwick® Rose
Buff Beauty
Penelope
Blanchefleur
Jude the Obscure
Félicité Parmentier
Charity
Little White Pet
Alba Semi-Plena
Mme Legras de St. Germain

EASTERN STRIP – FEBRUARY 2002

The Alnwick® Rose
Ludlow Castle
William Lobb
Crocus Rose
Chianti
Margaret Hilling
Sally Holmes
Penelope
Shropshire Lass
Windrush
Comtesse de Murinias
Blush Noisette
Francine Austin
Alba Maxima
Nevada
Agnes
Mme Legras de St Germain
Boule de Neige
Zigeunerknabe

R. *Macrantha*
R. *Rugosa Alba*
Falstaff
Cerise Bouquet
Mme Alfred Carrière
Félicité Parmentier
Fantin-Latour
Francine Austin
Marinette
Tuscany
Tour de Malakoff
Charles de Mills
Maigold
Teasing Georgia
Thisbe
Golden Wings
Nevada
Autumn Delight
Buff Beauty
Penelope
Nymphenberg
Fritz Nobis
Cornelia
Snowdon
Anne Boleyn
Aloha
Ispahan
Jacques Cartier
Felicia

WESTERN STRIP – FEBRUARY 2002
Ballerina
Rosy Cushion
Nevada
Penelope
Little White Pet
Vanity
Buff Beauty
Snowdon

Mrs Doreen Pike
Agnes
Schneezwerg
R. *Rugosa Alba*
Crown Princess Margareta
Zigeunerknabe
Tuscany Superb
Alba Semi-Plena
Adam Messerich
La Belle Sultane
Rosa Mundi
Duchesse de Buccleugh
Petite de Hollande
Pink Prosperity
Buff Beauty
Cornelia
Mme Legras de Saint Germain
Vanity
Queen of Denmark
Bloomfield Abundance
Charles de Mills
Cerise Bouquet
Windrush
Penelope
Buttercup
Pegasus
Danae
Golden Wings
Pat Austin
Celsiana
Fantin-Latour
La Ville de Bruxelles

CENTRAL PATH – RIGHT 'B'
Molineux
Comtes De Champagne
Graham Thomas
Pegasus
The Pilgrim

Blythe Spirit

Winchester Cathedral

St Swithun

The Countryman

Eglantyne

The Dark Lady

Noble Antony

Marinette

L D Braithwaite

Charles Rennie Mackintosh

Kathryn Morley

Brother Cadfael

Sharifa Asma

Gertrude Jekyll

Geoff Hamilton

Ludlow Castle

Mayor of Casterbridge

Charlotte

Grace

A Shropshire Lad

Evelyn

Golden Celebration

Teasing Georgia

William Morris

Cottage Rose

Wenlock

L D Braithwaite

Tess of the d'Urbervilles

William Shakespeare 2000

John Clare

St Cecilia

Windflower

Sweet Juliet

Abraham Darby

The Alnwick® Rose

R. Californica 'Plena'

R. Officianalis

Sweet Juliet

A Shropshire Lad

Maigold

R. Pimp 'Harisonii'

Cardinal de Richelieu

Ipsilante

Frühlingsgold

Mistress Quickly

Camaieux

President de Sèze

Kathryn Morley

The Countryman

Celsiana

The Mayflower

Belle De Crécy

Heavenly Rosalind

Francine Austin

Crocus Rose

Wenlock

The Alnwick® Rose

Louise Odier

Shropshire Lass

Golden Celebration

Boule de Neige

Ludlow Castle

Grace

Fritz Nobis

Hugh Dickson

Ballerina

Queen of Denmark

Teasing Georgia

R. Rugosa Alba

Felicia

Jude the Obscure

Frühlingsanfang

William Lobb

Tuscany Superb

Ipsilante

Fantin-Latour

Duchesse de Buccleugh

Kathryn Morley

Eglantyne
Stanwell Perpetual
Nur Mahal
Blythe Spirit
The Mayflower
Buttercup
Golden Celebration
Celebration 2000
Jude the Obscure
Celsiana
Hebe's Lip
R. Pimp. Dunwick Rose
Agnes
Frühlingsgold
Golden Wings
Rushing Stream
Cornelia
Geoff Hamilton
R. Rugosa
Mrs Doreen Pike
Charles de Mills
Queen of Denmark
Châpeau de Napoléon
Lilian Austin
Penelope
Erfurt
Roseraie de l'Hay
Tour de Malakoff
Reine des Violettes
Marguerite Hilling
Dapple Dawn
Pink Grootendorst
R. Canina Hibernica
R. Complicata

CENTRAL PATH – RIGHT 'A'

The Alnwick® Rose
Crown Princess Margareta
Charity
Jude the Obscure
Ambridge Rose
Mary Rose
Sceptres Isle
Cottage Rose
Heritage
The Mayflower
The Prince
Noble Antony
Falstaff
Corvedale
Barbara Austin
Winchester Cathedral
Glamis Castle
Crocus Rose
Francine Austin
The Pilgrim
The Alexandra Rose
Graham Thomas
Buttercup
Blythe Spirit
Golden Celebration
Charlotte
Pat Austin
Eglantyne
Anne Boleyn
Cordelia
The Prince
James Galway
Wenlock
Sophy's Rose
L D Braithwaite
Redouté

THE POISON GARDEN

Aconitum lycoctonum (Wolfsbane)

Actaea spicata (Black Baneberry)

Aristolochia longa (Birthwort)

Arum italicum (Marmoratum)

Bulbocodium vernum (Spring Meadow Saffron)

Chelidonium majus (Greater Celandine)

Colchicum autumnale – mauve and white doubles

Convallaria majalis (Lily of the Valley)

Convallaria majalis (Hound's Tongue)

Daphne laureola (Spurge Laurel)

Daphne mezereum (Mezereon)

Brugmansia suaveolens (Angel's Trumpet)

Echium vulgare (Viper's Bugloss)

Fritillaria – imperialis and meleagris (Fritillary)

Galanthus nivalis (Snowdrop)

Helleborus foetidus (Stinking Hellebore)

Hyacinthoides non-scripta (Bluebell)

Leucojum aestivum (Snowflake)

Lithospermum officinale (Gromwell)

Mercuriali sperennis (Dog's Mercury)

Narcissus pseudonarciss, 'Tresamble', bulbocodium

Oenanthe crocata (Hemlock Water Dropwort)

Prunus laurocerasus (Laurel)

Rheum rhaponticum (Rhubarb)

Rumex obtusifolius (Broad-leaved dock)

Scutellaria lateriflora (Virginian Skullcap)

Senecio jacobaea (Ragwort)

Solanum dulcamara (Woody Nightshade)

Symphoricarpus albus (Snowberry)

Symphytum officinale (Comfrey)

Taxus baccata 'Fastigiata Aureomarginata' (Yew)

Viscum album (Mistletoe)

Digitalis purpurea (Foxglove)

Veratrum album (White False Mottlebare)

Helleborus niger (Christmas Rose)

Digitalis purpurea 'Alba'

Aconitum napellus (Monk's Hood)

Vinca major (Periwinkle)

Polygonatum odoratum (Solomon's Seal)

Cimicifuga racemosa (Bugbane)

Helleborus cyclophyllus

Veratrum nigrum

Digitalis ferruginea

Aquilegia atrata

Helleborus viridis

Helleborus purpurascens

Atropa belladonna (Deadly Nightshade)

Dracunculcus vulgaris

Helleborus niger

Bryonia dioica

Polygonatum odoratum

Papaver somniferum

Aconitum napellus

Artemisia absinthium

Ruta graveolens

Helleborus orientalis

Foeniculum vulgare

Pulsatilla vulgari

Lolium temulentum

Ranunculus acris 'Multiplex'

Lactuca serriola

Vinca Major

Helleborus 'Early Purple'

Atropa mandragora

Euphorbia x martini

Aquilegia alpina

Papaver somniferum

Pulmonaria angustifolia (Blue Ensign)

Ricinus communis

Foeniculum vulgare (Giant Bronze)

Nicotiana sylvestris

Artemesia absinthium

Conium maculatum

Rosmarinus officinalis

Papaver somniferum

Hyoscyamis niger

Nepeta faassenii 'Six Hills Giant'

Mentha pulegium

Digitalis ferruginea 'Gelber Herold'

Verbascum olympicum

PLANTS UNDER CLOCHES

Cannabis sativa

Catha edulis

Erythroxylum coca

Heracleum mantegazzianum

Psilocybe semilanceata

Strychnos nux-vomica

SOLITARY PLANTS

Euonymus Europaeus

Nerium oleander

Hippophae rhamnoides

Ilex aquifolium 'Alaska'

Juniperus anagyroides

Malus 'John Downie'

Mespilus germanica

Salix alba 'Liempde'

Vitex-Agnus – castus

HEDGES

Buxus sempervirens

Hedera helix 'Hibernica'

CLIMBERS/VINES

Clematis vitalba

INDEX

ACKNOWLEDGEMENTS

I would like to express my sincere gratitude and thanks to those who, through their support and contributions, have been influential factors in the writing of this book.

First and foremost I must thank my wife Ann and children Simon and Philippa for their support and understanding throughout the past ten years, during which time they have had to live with The Alnwick Garden as another member of our family. To them I give my grateful thanks and love for allowing me to make this memorable journey.

The Alnwick Garden Trust and its Trustees for their agreement to my writing this story and the use of information contained within their records.

To the Duke of Northumberland for his support, understanding and sense of humour in allowing me to use a particular image within the book, and to Northumberland Estates for their support and the use of archival information.

I am indebted to Jacques, Peter and Martin Wirtz who through their combined intellectual, cultural and horticultural imaginations have created a truly wonderful design, ably supported by Ronny Nulens.

Tim Smit, for his ability to see beyond the obvious and enable us to open our minds to new challenges.

I have developed many friendships through this journey, none more so than with Aidan Harrison and Iain Ramage, whose professional commitment and enthusiasm to the project has been a major factor in its success.

My grateful thanks go to John Lovett and Elisabeth Smith for their professional contribution, and to Sarah Darling for her unstinting support. Clare Ralph, Rachel Johnston and Leigh Stevenson for their assistance in producing information, images and marketing support.

Andy and Brenda Marks of Skyscan and Ron Bridle of Sky Eye Photography for their aerial photographs, Philip Deakin for the use of his image of the 1900 garden and to Christopher Sykes, Jane Coltman and Graeme Peacock for the use of their photographic images.

As a keen amateur watercolourist myself, the inclusion of Alexander Creswell's paintings of the Garden is a special pleasure, and working with the artistic talents of William Pye, Caroline Holmes and Adrian Fisher was an experience I would not have missed.

To the architects, Sir Michael Hopkins and Partners on the Pavilion and Visitor Centre and Nappers on the Treehouse, who in their individual ways have created two very special buildings on the site, not forgetting John Harris who produced the concept designs for the Treehouse.

A special thanks to Jane Phillimore for somehow translating all the memories, experiences, fact and figures into a very organized and readable storyline. To Kate Oldfield, Lizzy Gray and staff for all their efforts on my behalf in publishing this book, and to Borra Garson for her negotiating skills.

It is impossible to mention all the many people who have played their part in developing such a wonderful Garden to its present stage, but I would like to take this opportunity to thank all the teams of designers, contractors, management, staff and volunteers for the part they have played in the ongoing successful development of The Alnwick Garden. It has been and still is a team effort.

But no team is complete without a captain, the driving force, and in Jane, Duchess of Northumberland, we have a captain whose commitment and influence has enabled us to achieve the success the Garden now enjoys. She has been my guiding factor in writing this book; it couldn't have been written without her, and her passion and dedication to the vision have in turn inspired me. I am eternally grateful to her for the unswerving support she has given when considering my interests, together with her valued friendship, which has made this wonderful journey such a pleasure.

PICTURE ACKNOWLEDGEMENTS

The publishers would like to thank the following people for permission to reproduce their images in this book:

Page 7 © The Northumberland Gazette; **pp10-11** © Alexander Creswell; **p14** © Ian August; **pp16-17** © Ian August; **pp20-21** © Ian August; **p22** © Ian August; **p23** © The Alnwick Garden/Jacques and Peter Wirtz; **pp36-37** © Alexander Creswell; **p48** © The Garden Picture Library; **p55** top right, top left and bottom left © Ian August; **p55** bottom right © Tim Smit; **pp58-59** © Ian August; **pp62-63** © Ian August; **pp64-65** © The Alnwick Garden/Jacques and Peter Wirtz; **p72** top and middle © Ian August; **p72** bottom © The Alnwick Garden/Paul Robbrecht; **p76** © The Alnwick Garden/Christopher Simon Sykes; **p78** © Ian August; **p88** © Ian August; **pp102-103** © Ian August; **p106** © Ian August; **pp114-115** © Ian August; **p124** © Ian August; **p130** © Ian August; **p136** © The Alnwick Garden/Christopher Simon Sykes; **pp145-7** © Ian August; **p148** © Ian August; **pp156-7** © The Alnwick Garden/Christopher Simon Sykes; **p162** © Ian August; **pp169-170** © Ian August; **p174** © The Alnwick Garden; **p176** © The Alnwick Garden/ Christopher Simon Sykes; **p180** © Ian August; **pp182-183** © Ian August; **p184** © The Alnwick Garden/Christopher Simon Sykes; **p188** © Ian August; **p189** © The Alnwick Garden; **pp196-7** © Ian August; **p201** © The Alnwick Garden/Christopher Simon Sykes; **pp202-203** © The Alnwick Garden/Christopher Simon Sykes; **p206** © Ian August; **p212** top © The Alnwick Garden/Christopher Simon Sykes; **p212** bottom © Ian August; **p213** © SkyScan; **pp216-218** © The Alnwick Garden/Christopher Simon Sykes; **pp222-223** © The Alnwick Garden/Christopher Simon Sykes; **p239** © Ian August; **p246** © SkyScan; **p249** top, © Sir Michael Hopkins; **p249** bottom © Ian August; **p251** © Ian August; **p261** © Ian August; **pp270-271** © Ian August.